Praise for
Defining You

"Helps you travel on the journey of self-discovery in a simple, yet thorough fashion. [*Defining You*] will provide you with previous undiscovered insights and help you craft an action plan to pull it all together. It is a 'must read' for anyone who has that essential quality of exceptional leaders, curiosity."

David Sole OBE, former Scotland Rugby Captain,
co-founder of School for CEOs

"This is a MUST read—read it, and then get your loved ones to read it. You owe it to them and yourself."

Wing Commander Jonathan McMullan, Commanding Officer,
Royal Australian Air Force Officers' Training School

"Cuts right through the chaotic and provides authentic, useful, relevant, and actionable exercises at every turn."

Mel Carson, Microsoft

"Puts the spotlight on your own journey, helping you find your way to a happier, more successful life."

Kenny Wilson, CEO of Cath Kidston

"Fiona's warm and engaging style springs from the pages, providing guidance and helpful pragmatic examples which really make the experience come to life."

Sue Langley OBE, Non-Exec
Chairwoman of Arthur J. Gallagher UK

"Whoever you are, and at whatever point you find yourself, here's a bespoke map for what happens next."

Jon Hendry, CEO of Prezzo Ltd

"[Fiona] manages to get to the bottom of complex issues, and communicate them in a way you can action."

Rowan Gormley, CEO of Majestic Wine, Founder of Naked Wines

"A really compelling and rewarding read that is highly recommended for anyone serious about understanding themselves and becoming the very best they can be."

Jo Walmsley, HR Director of Waitrose

"Every reader will find a range of really helpful tools to understand their values, passions, and interests—and to identify development goals to live life with a purpose."

Professor Anthony Forster, University of Essex

Defining You

How to profile yourself and unlock your full potential

Fiona Murden

NICHOLAS BREALEY
PUBLISHING

London • Boston

First published in 2018 by Nicholas Brealey Publishing
An imprint of John Murray Press
An Hachette UK Company

1

© Fiona Murden 2018

Text design and illustration design by Craig Burgess

The Credo test and participant report featured in Chapter 5 is provided by Tests Direct
Limited, Walker House, Walker Street, Macclesfield, Cheshire, SK10 1BH. The Credo test
will be available until at least 1 May 2019, after which time Test Direct reserve the
right to withdraw the test from use. All queries regarding the performance of the test
or supply of the participant report should be sent direct to Tests Direct Ltd at
admin@tests-direct.co.uk.

A CIP catalogue record for this title is available from the British Library

Hardback ISBN 978-1-473-66838-6
Trade paperback ISBN 978-1-473-66840-9
Ebook ISBN UK 978-1-473-66841-6
Ebook ISBN US 978-1-473-66973-4

Typeset in 10/12.75pt Celeste by Palimpsest Book Production Limited,
Falkirk, Stirlingshire

Printed and bound by Clays Ltd, St Ives plc

Nicholas Brealey policy is to use papers that are natural, renewable
and recyclable products and made from wood grown in sustainable forests.
The logging and manufacturing processes are expected to conform to the environmental regulations of the country of origin.

Nicholas Brealey Publishing
John Murray Press
Carmelite House
50 Victoria Embankment
London, EC4Y 0DZ, UK
Tel: 020 3122 6000

Nicholas Brealey Publishing
Hachette Book Group
Market Place Center, 53 State Street
Boston, MA 02109, USA
Tel: (617) 263 1834

www.nicholasbrealey.com
www.aroka.co.uk

For my family—those who are here and those who are gone. You are my story.

Contents

Foreword

• • •

There is only one corner of the universe you can be certain of improving, and that's your own self.

—Aldous Huxley

I have always thought the most attractive people were those who were "comfortable in their own skin." It's something I have been working towards myself and something I aspire to for my children. Working through the exercises and taking time to embrace the concepts in Fiona's book go a long way towards helping to achieve some of that self-awareness and identify one's purpose.

I met Fiona in 2008, when she was asked by my employer at the time to profile me for a promotion. I remember being incredibly nervous about going for my assessment. I had no idea what it would be like, what kinds of questions I would be asked, and, above all, what sorts of conclusions this occupational psychologist would draw about me.

I'm happy to say that it was actually a very enjoyable experience. Fiona was warm and engaging, and although she asked probing questions, she instantly put me at ease. I did get the promotion, I received a very insightful profile report, which I still refer to from time to time, and I gained a friend as well. Fiona's observations about my strengths, potential risks and limitations, my motivation and drive, and the environment in which I would thrive were spot on. Those observations and insights provoked a lot of thought, really helped to raise my self-awareness, and gave me a good baseline for my ever-evolving development plan.

I read *Defining You* with great interest, as I am a naturally curious person on a continual self-improvement mission. I also really enjoy meeting new people and understanding what makes them tick. I found the exercises and tools in this book really helpful to me in planning the next phase of my life (having recently hit the milestone of 50), but also in understanding and engaging with others. I would strongly recommend the book as a means of self-discovery and ultimately of optimizing your performance and overall well-being.

Brenda Trenowden

Brenda Trenowden is a strong advocate for women's economic empowerment and has been recognized with several awards for her global campaigning for greater gender balance across organizations. She is currently Global Chair of the 30% Club, working closely with leading chairs and CEOs around the world to increase the representation of women in senior roles and more broadly. The 30% Club, which originally launched in the UK, now operates in 11 global areas with the aim of improving the gender balance at each stage of life's journey, from schoolroom to boardroom. Brenda is also an adviser to the UK government's Hampton-Alexander Review for increasing the representation of women at the executive level of the FTSE 350.

INTRODUCTION

In the Company of a Psychologist

• • •

Have you ever wondered what it would be like to delve into your own story, to understand the twists and turns of your life in a way that makes you not only more successful but happier? It's rare that any of us has time to truly reflect on what makes us who we are—and I don't mean the kind of naval gazing or introspection that leaves us feeling miserable and questioning what life is all about. Rather, I'm talking about a positive, pragmatic, even self-indulgent exploration of what makes you *you*. It doesn't matter how old you are, whether you are 20-something, looking at where you want your life to go, 40-something, working out how to create more meaning in the prime years of your career, or 60-something, about to retire and wanting to continue to live with a sense of purpose—all of us can gain from learning more about ourselves. This book will take you through your journey in a way that will positively propel you into the next days, weeks, years, and decades of your life with a greater sense of clarity about who you are and what you stand for, an understanding of your purpose, and the confidence to live and breathe what you have learnt.

Over the years I have been privileged enough to hear hundreds of people's stories, working to understand my clients' unique personae, their purposes in life, and how to unlock their potentials to fulfill them. As a psychologist, I build up insights into who people are and what makes them tick in order to help them live a more successful, satisfied life and to excel in whatever it is they do. This raised self-awareness is the first stepping stone to attainment in nearly all walks of life. My clients are people who are already functioning well and typically at the peak of their profession, but want to gain an edge, unlock even more of their capabilities, seek out excellence. Having now gained the experience that comes with age, I operate in the UK, USA, Europe, and Asia Pacific with some of the biggest companies and institutions in the world. Typically working with leaders and other prominent people in these international settings, I have seen that they, like the rest of us, can be irrational beings. While people who've reached the dizzy heights of top-level leadership tend to have greater self-insight than most, they still have room to grow when it comes to understanding why they and other people behave in a certain way, why they sometimes struggle with their emotions, why they misdiagnose what drains them, where their deepest passions lie, and sometimes even why they question their place in the world.

As far as I'm concerned, the fact that these "successful" people can still learn and improve reflects the need for all of us to be better equipped to understand ourselves, in order to make the most of our lives. I am passionate about increasing everyone's understanding of how their mind works, to empower us all to reach our true potential. That's why I wanted to write this book. I want to democratize the opportunities I'm able to offer to these senior leaders, athletes, and other prominent people, equipping *you* with some of the tools to explore and better understand your own story. I not only want to give you a greater sense of purpose and help you achieve success, but, and in my view more importantly, to enable you to live a happy and fulfilled life and to better understand how to maintain your mental well-being.

What Does Fulfilling
Your Potential Really Mean?

You are not meant for crawling, so don't. You have wings
Learn to use them, and fly.
—Mevlana Jelalu'ddin Rumi, thirteenth century

Fulfilling our potential is core to being human. It has been a constant for centuries and across our existence. It is what has allowed us to thrive as a race, curiously seeking out opportunities, learning more and more, continuing to push boundaries in our societies and our world.

Today, for you, fulfilling your potential is about possibility and growth: exploring your opportunities and place in the world, what makes you uniquely you, how you can soar and shine with your strengths and embrace your weaknesses. It's about defining your purpose or your dream and living in pursuit of it, whatever that may be: being the best friend and relation you can to those in your life, giving back to your local community, breaking a record, starting a successful business, becoming an Olympic athlete, or taking over as Managing Director of an international company. It's about unleashing your personal possibility, developing yourself in order to express your individuality, and living your life to the full extent of your capacity.

In order to fulfill your potential, you need to understand your behavior and your motivations, and you need to be aware of why you are the way you are, and the impact that has on other people. You not only need to "define you," but to define the path you want to take through life, to understand your purpose, and to feel confident in pushing the boundaries. At the same time, you must be willing to accept setbacks and learn from them. You need to know how to recognize your tipping points, both psychological and physiological, and to be aware of how best to respond in order to keep going. You have to understand the massive organ that is your brain, and learn to respect it in order for it to function optimally. To really fulfill your potential, you need to recognize that occasionally pausing, taking a breath, and stepping back from the fast-paced world is not a "nice to have," but a "have to have." Finally, you must understand your environment, to be curious and open to what's going on around you and tuned into the network in which you exist. All of this will allow you to join the dots on who you are, to create the narrative of your story, memories, and values that make up your identity now. You are valuable as you are, but with an understanding of what your potential is and how you want to fulfill it, you will be able to release more of yourself and ultimately will feel a greater sense of accomplishment and be more complete as a person.

That may sound like a lot to take on, but I'm here to help you. This book distills some of the knowledge I have gained as a Chartered Psychologist, a qualification process that takes 7 years, combined with 18 years' experience and hundreds of hours' worth of profiling and coaching with clients. I will share techniques and anecdotes in order to help you explore your own story. This book will offer you recommendations about the most robustly tested approaches and explain some of the science in simple, pragmatic, and accessible ways. You will benefit from research on the best methods and my own expertise and experience, as well as from the knowledge of a range of different academics and professionals. And although I can't meet you face to face, I can walk you through the process I would take a client through so you can better understand who you are, what you are all about, and how you can best fulfill your potential.

When I profile someone, over three to four hours I explore all the elements that make them unique. Many people then go on to have coaching: support to raise their self-insight and put what they have learnt into action, as well as counsel on their physiological well-being (it takes a brain and body that are firing on all cylinders to make behavioral change possible). Although many clients are reticent about the profiling session—after all, it's pretty daunting to think that someone is going to try to unlock the essence of who you are—they generally leave saying that they really enjoyed it and found it incredibly helpful. I then get e-mails to say they are still thinking and reflecting on things several days or weeks later. Bear this in mind when you're working through the book: it takes time to digest it all.

As you read this book, you will have the opportunity to explore yourself in the same way as I would analyze you and your life if you were in the room with me. I'm going to help you piece together your experiences, strengths, and behaviors so you can better understand yourself and grow as a person, in the direction you want to go. Using this book you will be able to:

- Be totally in control of what you explore, when, and in how much depth.

- Have time to reflect and digest information before moving on to the next area.

- Have the opportunity to go back and add in reflections, insights, thoughts, and memories as they come to you.

- Choose to keep the output purely to yourself, if you want.

- Create a guide to who you are through insights into your potential, your purpose, and your personal development.

I have divided the book into three parts, which mirror the stages of profiling and development: reflection, insights, and action. Each chapter contains sessions that explore the areas you'll be looking at, before offering the tools, tips, and activities to guide you through gathering the insights you need. As you move through the book you will build your own story, gaining greater clarity over who you are, your place in the world, where your untapped potential lies, and where you want to go. You'll be able to apply the skills you develop to different aspects of your life as you go along. Toward the end of the book we'll look at the best ways of "optimizing you" both mentally and physically, given all you've learnt about yourself and the realities of the environment in which you live and work.

Reflection

In this section you'll reflect on who you are, stepping through your life story from your childhood to where you are today. This will help you to:

- Explore what makes you *you* in a helpful and constructive way.

- Build your personal story line by understanding how your experiences have shaped you, your core personality, strengths, passions, and interests.

- Begin piecing together the path you want to take in life based on your personal preferences and values.

The tools and tips in this section will show you:

- How curious you are and how open to the world around you, as well as the impact this has on numerous areas of your life, from unlocking creativity and building better relationships to building your intellect and improving your overall well-being. This session gives pragmatic suggestions on how to improve your curiosity.

- How self-aware you are, and how this underpins success in life and your overall mental health, with guidelines on becoming more self-aware.

- How changing your brain can change your life course, however old you are.

- How emotionally wise you are, and how this underlies effective communication, meaningful relationships, influencing skills, your ability to manage stress and anxiety, your ability to make effective judgments, and even your ability to build profits in a commercial setting. The session offers guidance, too, on how to grow your emotional wisdom.

• How to overcome obstacles, looking specifically at psychological blockers and reframing your thinking.

• How to find meaning in life through building more effective connections with others and understanding your core values.

Insights

Once you've reflected on your story, you'll have the opportunity to collect information from other sources, first by using a psychometric tool and second by gathering feedback. The sessions in this section will provide you with:

• A comprehensive report on your core personality.

• An understanding of how other people in your life view you, your unique strengths, and other tendancies of which you may be less aware.

The tools and tips in his section will show you:

• How to explore your personality in more depth and review the output through self-reflection and input from someone you trust.

• How to ask for feedback in a way that gives constructive output and yet is comfortable for both you and the person you're asking.

• How to incorporate other people's view of you into your personal narrative, making your view of yourself more accurately aligned with the world around you.

• How to take action on your feedback, turning it into pragmatic outputs.

Action

In the final section, we'll look at how to pull together everything you have explored in a coherent way, providing clarity about who you are, what you want, and what you need to do in order to fulfill your potential. The sessions in this section will:

- Allow you to capture what you've explored about your core personality, your values, passions, and interests, and your strengths all in one place—defining you.

- Help you to be clear about your purpose in life and guide everything you do with a greater sense of meaning.

- Provide you with an understanding of how to build your confidence and self-esteem, enabling you to carry out the goals you've defined and present yourself to the world with impact.

- Help you to understand what a toxic work environment looks like, how to deal with one, and what the best work environment is for you.

- Explain how to fuel your brain positively through optimizing your sleep, exercising, and reducing stress.

- Cover the benefits of networking and finding a mentor to help you to achieve your goals.

The tools and tips in his section will show you:

- How to uncover your purpose and pursue it in everything you do, creating a plan of action underpinned by psychologically effective strategies for achieving success.

- How to identify your optimal sleep pattern and whether you are naturally more of a morning or evening person.

- How to fit more exercise into your daily life, overcoming mental and physical barriers to your fitness schedule.

- How to better understand your personal stressors and address them.

- How to define and build your network in a way that feels authentic and provides you with the support you need to bring your purpose to life.

- How to find and approach a potential mentor to help you succeed.

> You may want to invest in a notepad specifically to capture your thoughts and ideas as you move through the sessions in this book. This will provide you with something you can revisit and add to over time. Alternatively, you may want to start a document on your computer or print off the sheets I provide online so you can fill them in. Do whatever works best for you.

Defining You includes a range of exercises, tips, and advice, but a large part of this process is finding out the techniques that feel right for you. So, take note of what does and doesn't work, and use that information to give you ready access to tools and techniques that will help you to flourish. This book is like a window into what makes you who you are. By the end you will have far greater self-insight, which in itself will have a massively positive effect on a range of areas in your life, from personal to professional. But although you may be keen to crack on and find out as much as you can as quickly as you can, I would suggest that to get the most out of it, you work through it slowly, step by step. Our brain takes time to assimilate new information and properly integrate it into our narrative and identity. Take the time to try things out and reflect on them in order to give you a really full understanding of who you are and what suits you best.

If you're ready to begin, it's time to start defining you.

PART I

Reflecting

CHAPTER 1

Observe, Don't React

● ● ●

To step into the company of a psychologist is to enter a world of observation and hypothesis. To do my job effectively, I need to move away from my normal everyday way of seeing the world. As humans our view is unintentionally and unconsciously riddled with biases and preconceptions. Before I meet someone in a professional capacity, the first and most critical thing I do is to get into the correct mindset. I step away from my "normal" way of seeing the world so that I am ready to explore my client's story open-mindedly, carefully, and constructively. To do my job effectively I need to observe, not react to what I hear. One of my key objectives is to meet the client with a clean slate, testing information from the standpoint of not believing it to be true. This requires a curious-minded approach, one that looks at things from different angles and perpetually explores alternative options.

In this chapter, we will look at "perpetual curiosity" and how it can benefit you in exploring who you are. You'll discover how curious you are and be given guidance on developing this crucial life skill. I'll then outline how you can step back from your emotions and biases in order to observe rather than react. This is useful on many levels, since an understanding of how your emotions are influencing your judgments can help you:

- improve your personal relationships and influencing ability;

- observe other people's reactions and respond calmly, rather than getting into the position where you think "I wish I hadn't said that";

- improve your decision-making skills;

- understand organizational politics and navigate them more effectively;

- and, most importantly, maintain a healthier brain.

The Delight of Curiosity

*Curiosity is the essence of human existence. "Who are we?
Where are we? Where do we come from? Where are we
going?" I don't know. I don't have any answers to those questions. I don't know what's over there and around that corner.
But I want to find out.*

—Eugene Cernan, American astronaut

Curiosity is a fascinating, even magical behavior that's relevant to each
and every one of us. It defines our natural inquisitiveness as humans,
since without curiosity we wouldn't have moved beyond being cave
dwellers. Exploiting our curiosity has enabled us to reach the advanced
scientific and technological world of the twenty-first century. Over the
past couple of decades, neuroscience, the study of how our brain works,
has taken massive leaps forward and has given us insight into how and
why we do things, at a level we've never experienced before.

You have already proven yourself more curious than the average
adult: a recent study revealed that only around 10% of the EU population aged 25–64 participated in "lifelong learning."[1] Picking up a book
on personal development puts you in a minority of proactive learners
who have a sense of curiosity.

We most commonly associate curiosity with children and their raw,
hungry desire to understand the world around them and their place in
it. While research suggests that as we age our inquisitiveness tends to
fade,[2] curiosity is just as relevant in adulthood, not only helping you
discover more about who you are, but providing a basis on which to
build better relationships, unlock creativity and innovation, grow your
intellect, and boost your general health and well-being.

In his book *Curious*, Ian Leslie describes the process of curiosity in
childhood.[3] This is a useful framework from which to see the psychological investigation carried out in a profiling session. Psychologists
have to be curious, persistently exploring meaning to get beneath the
surface of the complex layers of human behavior and intention and
really understand what makes someone tick. In a sense, I consider my
job to be very like that of a detective. Whether I'm watching Sherlock
Holmes, Hercule Poirot, Colombo, Inspector Morse, or Maigret, I always
feel connections and parallels between their work and mine: their
resolute approach and insistent need never to take anything at face

value. These masters of curiosity see things from every angle until they find the clues that unlock the mystery.

Leslie describes the three steps of curiosity as follows:

1 KNOWING WHAT YOU DON'T KNOW

You approach a situation accepting your own inexperience. You're not presuming you know the answer, but rather asking questions with an open mind and really considering the answers. This is known as empathic curiosity: an interest in the thoughts and feelings of other people, and remaining ready to encounter the unexpected.[4]

I meet every client from a position of naivety: no expectations and no presumptions. This way I can really connect with them, putting my own presuppositions aside in order to understand their personal experiences and how those have affected who they are.

I encourage you to use this approach when working through the book. Rather than answering questions with your habitual response, think about what you really think, feel, and want. Don't assume you know the answers until you've looked at things from every angle, dig beneath the surface, and ask yourself why you feel the way you do about certain things, how the beliefs you have formed came about, what led you to take certain decisions. Doing this will provide far richer insights to work with in defining you.

2 IMAGINING DIFFERENT, COMPETING POSSIBILITIES

You hold more than one possibility in mind at any given time, and explore which one is right. For example, when meeting someone shy, consider "Is this person shy when they meet new people?" or "Are they quiet in this situation because they're nervous?" This element of curiosity is essential when it comes to the line of questioning I take in profiles, drawing inferences about a client's mental state, judgments, and actions while recognizing that nothing is a foregone conclusion. Any thought or idea needs to be explored and tested.

When you're working through this book, try to remember that the first decision you come to about yourself may not be the right one. It's essential always to consider more than one inference and thoroughly explore it before jumping to a conclusion. Try to suspend judgment until you have explored all the options. It may help you find out something about yourself you'd never considered before.

3 UNDERSTAND THAT YOU CAN LEARN FROM OTHER PEOPLE

Keep an open mind to others' thoughts, attitudes, and experiences. In social situations, we have a natural tendency to show other people what we know about a familiar subject, rather than listening to what they can tell us. Yet pausing to learn about them and asking questions inevitably provide information that we can reapply to ourselves. For example, you may find a different way of seeing things, a means of overcoming an issue that you hadn't thought of, an opportunity that you didn't know about.

When profiling, I employ these three steps on a perpetual loop, testing and retesting hypotheses. In the same way, a detective doesn't close down an investigation before every avenue has been explored.

The positives about being curious extend beyond the role of exploring your own makeup. Here are some examples.

CURIOSITY MAKES PEOPLE FEEL VALUED

When we show genuine interest in others, wanting to know them and not to judge them, it builds trust and allows a deeper connection to form, ultimately fueling positive relationships.

Matthew Lieberman, a social psychologist and neuroscientist who wrote the book *Social: Why Our Brains Are Wired to Connect*,[5] explains why it's an evolutionary necessity for us to connect with others. Social connections are as important to our survival as the need for food, safety, and shelter, and are essential to our mental well-being. As a result, the brain rewards us by releasing neurotransmitters that lead to feelings of pleasure when we build meaningful relationships, and curiosity helps us do this.

CURIOSITY ENABLES INNOVATION AND CREATIVITY

Todd Kashdan, who's carried out extensive research on the topic, says: "When curiosity is supported in the workplace, employees feel energized, engaged and committed, and this helps drive innovation."[6]

Being given the freedom to think divergently, to investigate and follow different streams of thinking, and to hold different possibilities in mind, allows people to "think outside of the box." I've seen numerous examples of cultures that close down creativity by preventing this form of curiosity. On the other hand, I've worked with organizations where innovation thrives as a result of employees being allowed to make mistakes and being encouraged to explore, learn, discover, and create.

CURIOSITY UNDERPINS INTELLECT

Sophie von Stumm from the University of Edinburgh worked with colleagues to look at curiosity within an academic setting. She found that intellectual curiosity influenced academic performance to the same extent as IQ.[7]

When I profile leaders, I sometimes quantify their intellect using ability tests. People automatically expect these successful individuals to have a high IQ, and hiring organizations tend to panic if they see a low score for their preferred candidate. Yet a high IQ does not denote success in business, career, or life. Intellectual curiosity is often as important or in some cases more important in indicating an individual's ability to succeed.

CURIOSITY KEEPS YOU YOUNG

A study following over 1,000 older men and women over time found that those who were more curious were actually more likely to survive the five-year study than those who were not. Curiosity literally kept them alive longer.[8]

CURIOSITY IMPROVES YOUR GENERAL WELL-BEING

A paper by Matthew Gallagher in the *Journal of Positive Psychology* showed that the "exploration" component of curiosity is positively associated with well-being.[9] Further to this, a German study found that curiosity has a more positive impact on well-being than gratitude, hope, or even humor.[10]

In short, it's not only important for you to remain curious throughout this book in order to fully understand your own story, it's also an incredibly helpful life skill.

TOOLS OF THE SESSION

Measuring Your Curiosity

How curious are you? Do you follow up leads and explore beneath the surface? Do you persistently investigate different angles and solutions? Do you want to know more about people and places? Complete the Curiosity and Exploration Inventory to find out how you fare against the general population.

Try to be as honest as you can when answering the questions. Don't worry if you're not as curious currently as you may want to be—it's an exciting opportunity to develop.

CURIOSITY AND EXPLORATION INVENTORY

Instructions: Rate the statements below for how accurately they reflect the way you generally feel and behave. Do not rate what you think you should do, or wish you do, or things you no longer do. Please be as honest as possible.

1—Very slightly or not at all
2—A little
3—Moderately
4—Quite a bit
5—Extremely

1. I actively seek as much information as I can in new situations

1 2 3 4 5

2. I am the type of person who really enjoys the uncertainty of everyday life

1 2 3 4 5

3. I am at my best when doing something that is complex or challenging

1 2 3 4 5

4. Everywhere I go, I am out looking for new things or experiences

1 2 3 4 5

5. I view challenging situations as an opportunity to grow and learn

1 2 3 4 5

6. I like to do things that are a little frightening

1 2 3 4 5

7. I am always looking for experiences that challenge how I think about myself and the world

1 2 3 4 5

8. I prefer jobs that are excitingly unpredictable   1 2 3 4 5

9. I frequently seek out opportunities to challenge myself and grow as a person   1 2 3 4 5

10. I am the kind of person who embraces unfamiliar people, events, and places   1 2 3 4 5

Source: T.B. Kashdan, M.W. Gallagher, P.J. Silvia, et al. (2009) The Curiosity and Exploration Inventory-II: Development, factor structure, and psychometrics, *Journal of Research in Personality* 43(6): 987–98. Reproduced with permission.

WHAT THE RESULTS SAY

Kashdan believes that there are two key elements to curiosity:

• Being motivated to discover new knowledge and experiences.

• Having an inclination to embrace novel and unpredictable situations.

Looking at your responses, you may find that you are more curious in one area than another, which tells you what you need to focus on if you want to develop. For example, if you aren't someone who embraces uncertainty, if it makes you anxious, then there are tools throughout the book that will help you overcome that feeling. For now, total your ratings and use Table 1.1 below to see which level your overall score corresponds to.

If you didn't score highly, don't worry—this is a skill you can develop and we'll have a look at some easy ways to do that later in the chapter. For now, let me tell you about someone I worked with.

TABLE 1.1 FIVE LEVELS OF CURIOSITY

Total	Levels	Definition
10–16	1—Very slightly or not at all	Focused on own task and indifferent to broader world. Fear and avoid uncertainty of any kind.
17–23	2—A little	Prefer comfort of what is currently known. Uncomfortable pushing beyond predictable elements of everyday life.
24–32	3—Moderately	Relatively interested in learning new things. Approach novelty with a degree of caution.
33–41	4—Quite a bit	Open-minded with a receptive attitude toward new and novel information and situations.
42–50	5—Extremely	Persist with tasks until goals are met. Willing to embrace the novel, uncertain, and unpredictable nature of everyday life. Desire to continually accumulate new abilities and experiences.

How Curiosity Can Change a Life

A few years ago, I coached a man, let's call him Antonio, who was on the board of a large organization. He was very good at his job and I was coaching him simply to take his communication skills to the "next level."

To improve any behavior more than superficially, it's critical to understand the whole person, so my conversations with Antonio extended to his life in general. What transpired was that he was struggling to find meaning in his job and was frustrated by the politics that surrounded the role. As a result, he felt trapped and was miserable.

Antonio was an inquisitive person, but that curiosity didn't span the whole remit I've described above. Although he was continually searching out facts and information, he wasn't experiencing new situations, places, and people. Most significantly, he wasn't coming across experiences that challenged how he thought about himself and the world, didn't feel he was growing as a person, and was definitely not doing things that were a little frightening.

When I encouraged him to be more curious, Antonio began to explore a business idea, one that had nothing to do with his current role. He started to embrace the opportunity to try something different, contacting new people, putting himself out into the world in a big way. Most important of all was that he did this in spite of the anxiety he felt. Antonio is now not only in a role that is far more meaningful, positively challenging, and offers continued learning opportunities, but because he pursued his business idea he's also a very successful entrepreneur.

Antonio is an example of how you can nurture curiosity. If you have the desire to develop you can, and sometimes all you need is a conscious awareness of how to do it. Even if you scored highly on the inventory, there's still an opportunity to grow, to think of different ways to extend and stretch your abilities. For example, if you scored 5 on "Everywhere I go I am looking for new things or experiences," then find even more new experiences. If you've explored 10 different cities in your country, then aim for 20; or if you've traveled to 7 different countries in the world, then aim for 15. The pointers below should help you to define your personal aims. When you've done so, write them down on your notepad or in the document you're creating—somewhere you can check back on to see your progress.

SEARCHING OUT NEW KNOWLEDGE
If you scored lower on questions 1, 3, 5, and 7 in the inventory, these points will be particularly helpful.

Feed your brain
- **Read, read, and read some more**. Reading broad and varied material not only helps to develop curiosity, but has been shown to improve emotional intelligence and understanding of social nuances.

- **Learn from people with experience and expertise**. Watch documentaries, view TED talks, attend talks on different topics.

- **Listen to other people's stories**. I learn so much about different industries, cultures, careers, and so on from hearing people's stories. There's nothing stopping you from asking people about themselves, what they do, what their challenges are. Reading biographies and watching biopics are also helpful.

- **Take a course**. This can be in whatever appeals to you—it doesn't have to have anything to do with your job or what you've done in life so far. Try not to classify or restrict yourself, just give something different a try.

> Tip: Feed your brain in a way that works for you. If you like reading magazines, buy different magazines on topics you wouldn't normally consider. But remember, it's persistence that's key: you need to keep going, stay following a thread to see where it will take you.

Speak to people

- **Ask questions**. In the leadership environment, people who ask the most questions tend to be the most impactful, knowledgeable, and insightful leaders. For a leader of a retail organization, for example, listening to what someone on the shop floor thinks tells them more about what's going on than only looking at company data and analytics, and as a bonus it makes the person feel valued. It doesn't matter who you are, there is *always* something you can learn from another person.

- **Consult others on their expertise**. Even if you know something about what a person is telling you, don't be tempted to jump in straight away and share what you know. Instead, listen and look for things that add to or give you a different angle on your own knowledge.

> Tip: When asking questions it's easy to begin
> overenthusiastically. Without meaning to, this can risk
> appearing intrusive, nosy, or at worst belligerent. It's worth
> taking a moment to "check in" on what you're going to ask
> and how you're going to frame it before you start.

- **Be interested in everything**. Even things that don't appear on the surface to have much significance for you can be fascinating. Sometimes I get calls from industries that don't appeal to any of my natural interests, but I have to be attentive in order to understand fully how things work so that I can do my job effectively. Without exception, every single company that may have seemed a little boring had much to explore beneath the surface. If you make the effort to look beyond the obvious, I guarantee you will be surprised at what you find.

- **Just watch**. Be an observer. For instance, sit in a restaurant with your back against the wall so you can watch people and be aware of what you see and hear. Watching rather than interacting with people prevents us from changing what is going on between people. This makes it easier to see and learn from what's going on (I will discuss this more in the following section).

- **Pursue your own personal growth**. Follow the pointers in this book to see where they take you and what more you can learn about yourself.

EMBRACING UNCERTAINTY

If you scored lower on questions 2, 4, 6, 8, and 10 in the inventory, these points will be particularly helpful.

- **Speak to strangers**. I talk to strangers wherever I am: service staff in restaurants, drivers on buses, cashiers in shops. Everyone has something interesting to say if you're prepared to ask and then listen. The added benefits are that every interaction is a learning experience, it will leave the other person feeling good, and it will give your brain a boost (this kind of connection positively stimulates the brain). It may feel a bit scary, but give it a go.

- **Embrace opportunities to go to new places**. Rather than always going to the same bar, restaurant, café, holiday location, or taking the same route to work, try going somewhere new or taking a different route.

- **Push yourself beyond your comfort zone**. This requires you to accept your fears and anxieties. That's easier said than done, but is something that can be developed through mindfulness and an approach called acceptance and commitment, both of which we'll be exploring in this book. Using these tools, you can try to embrace some of the things that scare you, attempt things you always wished you could but never had the guts to, and throw in some completely new things too. Kashdan, the psychologist who designed the curiosity inventory, explains how we are "socialized" to believe that certainty is better for us than ambiguity. Yet research consistently shows that the negative anxiety we feel when approaching new situations is greatly outweighed by the more intense, longer-lasting, meaningful experiences we create.

Make a note of your personal objectives and how you're going to develop your curiosity. Keep this realistic, otherwise you won't manage to do it, but allow enough of a stretch to take you beyond your comfort zone.

Your Observing Brain

Psychologists need to combine curiosity with observation to get beneath the surface of what makes up behaviors, intentions, and beliefs and really understand people. However, observation in the psychological sense doesn't just mean watching something or someone; it's a state of mind that requires a basic understanding of the brain. Let me explain:

A physician called Paul MacLean originally presented the triune or three-layer theory of the brain.[11] He explained how our brain evolved to its current size and capability while preserving features of two much more basic formations, developing one stage at a time, literally one layer on top of another. The three parts of the brain have dramatically distinctive structures and chemistry, and react quite differently to stimuli even though they are interconnected.

The first layer, known as the **brain stem**, resembles the brain of a reptile, the first creatures to evolve about 310 million years ago. This part of our brain monitors basic functions such as heart rate, breathing, and body temperature.

The second layer, known broadly as the **limbic system**, developed as reptiles evolved into early mammals about 160 million years ago. This takes care of our basic drivers, and can be crudely described as the emotional part of our brain.

The third layer, known as the **neocortex**, was the final layer of the brain to evolve. This part is responsible for more complex thinking, including intellectual reasoning, language, and the running dialogue we know as conscious thought.

The neocortex is the part of our brain that makes us most distinctively human and comes least "pre-programmed" when we are born. It rapidly fills with information specific to our society and culture in the early years of our life. This is one of the reasons why a psychologist will look into "where your story started" during a profile: the experiences you have and what you are exposed to at this time form the foundations of who you are.

The main aims of the first two layers are the same for humans as they are for other animals: they drive reproduction and self-survival. For the purposes of this book, I'll refer to these two parts of the brain as the "reacting brain." This part of the brain is not conscious and responds quickly to environmental cues. It is surprisingly dominant in our everyday lives, influencing things as varied as eating, sleeping, behaving in an agreeable way with others (which helped our ancestors' chances of survival), and belonging to a group.

The more complex areas of life are the responsibility of the slower but more deliberate neocortex. For the purposes of this book, I will call it the "observing brain." The areas it looks after include more evolved behaviors such as finding a purpose in life, our broader social agenda, and contributing to a society where we can all live agreeably. The neocortex also interprets messages coming from the reacting brain and allows us to search for reasons, answer questions, and live a meaningful life.

Although it's far more useful to think with our observing brain, which takes carefully considered action, our reacting brain is biologically dominant. As it's faster than our observing brain, it frequently overrides rational thought and even ethical behavior when it comes to matters that relate to survival. While we may think of these situations as infrequent, they're actually intertwined with just about everything we do. That's why it's so important to understand the interaction between the observing and the reacting brain.

A large part of being a good psychologist—and, indeed, of being a good leader, building positive relationships, and maintaining good mental health—is learning to manage the reacting brain, to step back from emotions to prevent the biases and misjudgments that are kicked up by more primitive responses to situations. This helps to minimize the opportunities for the reacting brain in effect to hijack our observing brain. That doesn't mean ignoring the reacting brain or the messages it provides, which are invaluable. However, you do need to know how to decode them.

To look at how this works in practice, let me tell you about a situation that involved consciously thinking with my observing brain while making use of messages from my reacting brain.

Decoding the Reacting Brain to Make Helpful Judgments

A few years ago, I profiled a woman for a leadership role in the Asia Pacific region of a global organization; we'll call her Felicia. I'd worked with the company for a number of years, so they knew me well and trusted my judgments, having seen how they played out over time. The CEO, a board member, and the HR Director all thought this candidate was "brilliant," but as a standard process I still profiled her before they offered the role.

As with any other profile, I put myself into a nonjudgmental and unbiased mindset, or in other words observing not reacting. However, I quickly felt belittled and insignificant. There didn't appear to be anything specific Felicia said or did that was causing this, so I carried on while working hard to remain in my observing mode. Still the feeling didn't go away.

I excused myself for five minutes to give me space to think (with my observing brain) and try to work out what was going on—what my reacting brain was up to. I was especially tired that day, so didn't trust that I was thinking clearly. Nevertheless, I decided to use the feeling as evidence that something may not be entirely as it had appeared to the company members Felicia had met.

I went back into the profile with a clear intention to explore specific areas that would help me gather the evidence to make accurate judgments, rather than simply going with what my gut appeared to be telling me.

> Tip: Our judgments about people can never be proven true: we don't know for definite that someone is a particular way. From a scientific viewpoint, we can only disprove a hypothesis, not prove it. Therefore, you should arrive at a judgment via a working hypothesis, which guides your search for further data.

Table 1.2 gives some simplified insights into how the process of data collection and hypothesis testing works, looking at four of the steps in this situation.

TABLE 1.2 INSIGHT INTO FOUR STEPS OF HYPOTHESIS TESTING

1. Data (gathered from reacting brain):	Hypothesis:	Judgment:
She made me feel uncomfortable even though I was in "observe don't react" mode.	She may make other people feel uncomfortable. **OR** She may make other people feel uncomfortable when she is in an unnerving situation (i.e. a profile).	There is something about her interpersonal style which is received negatively in certain situations.

This is not enough data to make a robust judgment or to consider which hypothesis is correct, so there's a need to look for more data.

2. Data (from information shared by client):	Hypothesis:	Judgment:
She didn't make the other people she spoke to in the process, i.e. very senior males, feel uncomfortable.	She may make other people feel uncomfortable when she is in an unnerving situation (i.e. a profile). **OR** She only makes females or people who she's not so concerned about impressing feel uncomfortable.	There is something about her interpersonal style which is received negatively in certain situations. **OR** There is something about her interpersonal style which is received negatively but focused on a specific population of people.

This is not enough data to make a robust judgment or to consider which hypothesis is correct, so there's a need to look for more data.

3. Data (gathered through questioning):	Hypothesis:	Judgment:
She doesn't speak positively or encouragingly about people who have worked for her. →	She is not supportive of her team or direct reports. →	There is something about her interpersonal style which is received negatively and focused on a specific population of people including her team and direct reports.

As we collect more data we shift our hypothesis in the light of that new information – it is either disproved or the likelihood of it being true increases.

4. Data (gathered via psychometrics and tested with participant):	Hypothesis:	Judgment:
She has a high need for control and is not open to direction or input from others. →	She does not have a high level of respect for the opinions of others. →	There is something about her interpersonal style which is received negatively and focused on a specific population of people including her team and direct reports.

And so on and so forth. We stop collecting data when we have enough to justify the probable truth of the hypothesis. When making judgments about other people, this is when we confirm to ourselves that our hypothesis is true of their typical behavior or thinking. It cannot however be proved to be true, it is still a hypothesis; but it is now backed up with different data points.

When I reported back to the hiring organization, I gave them my professional observations from a data perspective, but I also explained how Felicia had made me feel (pointing out the potential biases) and what I thought the possible consequences of this could be within the workplace, given the additional information gathered.

They had put a great deal of time and effort into finding and putting this woman through the recruitment process, including flying her in from overseas, and were ready to offer her the position. Nevertheless, they didn't hire her. Although I believed this was for the best, I am always concerned in such a situation, and so I was greatly reassured when the HR Director later got feedback from an ex-colleague of the candidate who described her as "toxic."

In this example I had stepped back from my emotion to try to understand what it was telling me, using my observing brain to look at what my reacting brain was saying. I didn't take the message as correct; rather I tested it, coming at it from a number of different angles until I'd collected as much data as I could. This is the mindset you should try to get into as you're working through this book. It isn't a normal state to be in, it takes effort because your brain doesn't naturally operate like this, but given certain situations it is well worth the effort.

TOOLS OF THE SESSION

How Reactive Are You?

How aware are you of your reacting brain's messages? Do you just automatically respond, or do you question and test what it tells you? The ability to step away from your reacting brain is not only essential to making effective judgments in a professional setting; research has repeatedly demonstrated that this self-awareness is a critical component of successful leadership[12] and success in any walk of life. Most importantly of all, it also positively influences overall mental health.[13] This awareness enables you to understand your own emotions, and also to appreciate how other people perceive you, allowing you to adapt your responses in the moment. This skill is critical in being able to engage and influence other people, as well as to manage the impact that your emotions have on others. The good news is that self-awareness is something you can develop.[14]

The first step in improving your self-awareness is to work out where you're at currently. Greg Ashley and Roni Reiter-Palmon have developed a questionnaire for doing just that, which examines three key areas of awareness: insight, reflection, and performance.[15] I'm including the short form of this here; if you want to gain further insight, the full questionnaire is available online (see point 15 in the Notes section). These questions explore the typical ways in which you respond to situations. There are no right or wrong answers. Don't be tempted to answer in terms of what you think you should do, as this won't provide you with true insight.

SELF-AWARENESS MEASURE (SHORT FORM)
For statements 1–12 in the Self-Awareness Questionnaire, decide which of the answers best applies to you:

1—Never
2—Rarely
3—Sometimes
4—Frequently
5—Always

Write the number corresponding to your answer in the box to the left of the statement. Remember, you will find out more about yourself if you are as honest as you can be.

SELF-AWARENESS QUESTIONNAIRE

1. How often do you reflect on your performance standards after a failure? 1 2 3 4 5

2. How often has an emotional or difficult situation caused you to reassess your strengths and weaknesses? 1 2 3 4 5

3. How often do you modify your standards in order to improve performance? 1 2 3 4 5

4. When working on a project, how often
can you tell in advance what part would   1 2 3 4 5
be the easiest for you?

5. How often do you ponder over how to
improve yourself from knowledge of   1 2 3 4 5
previous experiences?

6. How often do you find yourself
searching internally for explanations   1 2 3 4 5
for your behavior and emotions?

7. How frequently have the outcomes of
your behavior in a given situation
caused you to reach an "a-ha" moment   1 2 3 4 5
about yourself?

8. How often do you check with someone
(adviser, teacher, boss) to see if you're on   1 2 3 4 5
the right track?

9. How often do you set personal goals?   1 2 3 4 5

10. How often do you write down your
goals and track your progress toward   1 2 3 4 5
them?

11. How often have you used others' level of
interest in a given activity to help you   1 2 3 4 5
decide the level of your own interest?

12. How often have you been surprised by
requests for help from friends?   1 2 3 4 5

Source: Greg Ashley & Roni Reiter-Palmon (2012). Self-awareness and the evolution
of leaders: The need for a better measure of self-awareness, *Journal of Behavioral
and Applied Management* 14(1): 2–17. Reproduced with permission.

Total your scores and use Table 1.3 to see which level they correspond to.

TABLE 1.3 FOUR LEVELS OF CONSCIOUSNESS

Total	Levels	Definition
12–24	1—Unconsciousness	You are less responsive to yourself and your environment than most, but the act of completing this exercise shows you have the potential to grow your self-awareness.
25–37	2—Consciousness	You tend to focus your attention on the external environment rather than on your own thoughts and feelings.
38–49	3—Self-awareness	You focus attention on yourself, processing private and public information that relates to you.
50–60	4—Meta-self-awareness	You are very self-aware, and aware of your self-awareness.

INTERPRETING THE RESULTS

Alain Morin[16] explains that self-awareness comes in degrees and relates to the recall of past personal events from memory, together with the use of cognitive processes such as imagery to allow the "self" to communicate with "itself." For example, when I was profiling the woman described above, I was using the "self" (my reacting brain) to communicate with "itself" (my observing brain).

Most people lie somewhere between level 2 and level 3. If you are at level 1 don't worry, that's the point of this book—to help you develop. Even if you fall at level 4, there's still room for improvement and refinement. Have a look at the next activity for some indicators on how you can improve.

TOOLS OF THE SESSION

Self-awareness

There's no quick fix to raising your self-awareness, but it is something you can improve regardless of where you are at the moment. There are three steps involved:

1. WORK THROUGH YOUR STORY

Research into what is known as "narrative identity" demonstrates that the stories you tell yourself about your life create the basis of your personality.[17] How you understand your own story informs not only your current actions, but also the goals you focus on in the future. As you work through this book you will be able to capture your narrative, reflecting on the major events such as leaving school, going on to further education, or getting your first job, and on how you felt and how these things shaped you. This is your personal narrative. At the same time as helping to improve your self-awareness, this will help you to define who you are more clearly.

2. PRACTICE MINDFULNESS

Mindfulness is the practice of turning our attention away from our thoughts and the "chatter in our head," and toward sensations, concentrating on what we can hear, smell, see, taste, and feel in the present moment. This puts us in the "here and now" rather than fretting over the past (e.g., why did I eat that?) or worrying about the future (e.g., will I ever lose weight?). Mindfulness has been scientifically linked to many successful outcomes in leadership and life in general, especially self-awareness. A paper in the journal *Emotion*[18] found that long-term meditation (which includes mindfulness) changes how the brain responds to emotion, providing mental regulation and the ability to process information more effectively. This is because it makes you more aware of your body, your mind and your intentions. It helps to train your mind to observe your emotions rather than engage with them. It gives you the space to pause and reflect.

Practice mindfulness as regularly as you can—it's one of the most useful tools for enabling you to reach your potential and for mental well-being. It may be useful to track your practice like you would physical exercise, so you can see your progress. An app like Headspace is an easy and effective method of practicing mindfulness and of keeping track (see Bioliography for other tools and apps). Write down in your notes whether you observe mindfulness having any impact on how you see yourself and how you react to the world around you. But be patient and persistent—you won't see results after only one or two sessions.

3. ASK FRIENDS FOR THEIR INPUT

Explain to trusted friends that you would like to understand how you come across to others and ask them to give you frank feedback. Questions could include:

- How do I come across when I'm really happy about something?

- How can you tell when I'm sad?

- Is it easy to tell if I'm angry or frustrated? What do I do?

Coming to the End of the Session

Keep all of the reflections from this chapter so that you can come back to them throughout your personal development journey. Ideally maintain your notes as a "live" document, adding information that you piece together as you go along, throughout this book and throughout your life. You may also want to reflect on these headline concepts:

- What have you learnt about yourself from this chapter?

- What do you want to work on and how?

- What do you want to bear in mind and watch for as you move through the book?

CHAPTER 2

The Story of You

● ● ●

To begin defining you, we're going to return to your early years and explore where your story started. Stories help us to create order and meaning and make sense of our lives. How you construct your personal narrative plays a massive role in the way you see yourself: the memories that you share, what you consider important, and how you connect experiences together. This "story of you" is your narrative identity; you internalize and continually evolve it. In this session, we're going to begin piecing together that narrative to help you be more aware of the journey you have been on through life so far and the route you want to take moving forward.

Your early years are particularly important to your personal narrative. Many of your experiences get laid down at the back of your mind, and it's only through intentionally exploring them that you can understand the core of who you are. The early years provide the underpinnings to who you have become as an adult, like the foundations to a house: although few people ever see them, without its footings the house would fall down. Reflecting on this time of life will bring useful, even powerful insights into the way you behave today, and as a result help you to understand what to focus on in order to really fulfill your potential. And if you approach this session with an open mind, curious about what you may find, you'll see things from a totally different viewpoint and understand yourself in more depth than ever before. Looking at your life with your "observing brain" engaged, you'll be able to identify patterns and understand what has held you back or compelled you forward, unblocking the negative and building on the positive.

In this session, we will be looking specifically at the environment and people that shaped you from childhood through to 18 years of age. We won't be digging up nasty memories or placing blame—that's not helpful, and it isn't an approach we'll be using at any point in this book.* We'll be taking a scientific approach to exploring and reflecting on the factors from childhood that are known to have an impact on adulthood. We'll also look at what made you "light up" or "get lost in time" as a youngster: the passions and interests that you may have let fall by the wayside. This will provide you with a basis from which to re-engage with the things that you naturally enjoy and that make you thrive. You'll have the opportunity to separate out which of your choices you made yourself, and which were driven by other people or the environment you lived in. Knowing this will provide you with more control over the decisions you make in the future. Furthermore, while much of what you have brought with you into adulthood is influenced by your childhood experiences, some of it is more biologically determined. So we will look at how much of your personality you share with your parents, and the ways in which you differ from them. This will help you to understand what is core to your makeup and what may be more malleable—because the good news is, it's never too late to change. In the final part of this session we'll consider how and why this is the case, unpicking what it means to have a "plastic brain."

Tip: Remember that it will be helpful to note down your responses to questions and thoughts as you work through this session in your notepad or document. Keeping it all in one place means you can add to it when thoughts pop up, and refer back to it as you move through the book.

Your Upbringing

Your childhood experiences, the environments you were exposed to, and the way your parents and other people related to you have all shaped your path through life. In the first part of this session we're going to look specifically at how your self-esteem, self-control, and social skills as a child have contributed to who you are today.

SELF-ESTEEM

Self-esteem is the belief that you can achieve whatever it is you set out to do. If you have high self-esteem, you think that nothing will derail

---

*   If at any point you feel that you are unable to cope with the memories that are emerging, then please seek professional help through your local counseling service.

you; if your self-esteem is low, you will be riddled with anxiety about your capabilities. Self-esteem is relatively fragile in childhood, meaning that it can be built or undermined quite significantly by people or events, and the effect can remain with you into adulthood.

Research shows that if you were lucky enough to have high self-esteem as a child, it will have had a positive impact on your income as an adult.[1] It will also have helped build better mental health,[2] which is the foundation not only to living a happy life, but also to fulfilling your potential. However, if you reflect on your early life and see a child riddled with self-doubt, that doesn't mean you can't succeed or become more confident in your abilities as an adult. It's never too late to bolster your self-esteem and have more optimism in your ability to achieve your goals, whatever they may be. Simply being able to pinpoint events or people that knocked or built your self-esteem as a child will help you overcome obstacles that had a negative effect, and reap further benefits from things that had a positive impact on you.

Think about the following questions, and if it helps take some notes (you'll be using these to help you create your storyline later in the session). Don't worry if you can't answer them right now, just move on to the next section and come back if anything springs to mind:

- How much self-esteem did you have as a child? Were you self-confident? For instance, did you throw yourself headlong into activities or hold back?

- Why was that?

- How do you think this relates to your self-confidence now? Is there anything that really helped build your self-esteem as a child that you could build on? Was there anything that held you back that still affects the way you see the world today?

SELF-MANAGEMENT

How much self-control, or as I prefer to call it self-management, you had as a child is also a strong predictor of how things turn out for you as an adult.[3] Being able to manage your emotions and overcome short-term wants and needs is a critical life skill that you begin to develop as a child. If you look back at yourself and see a child who was able to exert some level of management over their emotions, that ability will have positively influenced your overall life satisfaction, well-being, income, and even job prospects.[4]

Studies have shown that being given responsibilities as a child or a young adolescent—for example, being expected to assist with household chores or having a part-time job—helps to build self-discipline.[5] Although it's by no means a prerequisite, many of the successful people I see did contribute to family duties or had a part-time job as a youngster.

Perhaps you feel like you are self-disciplined in spite of not having had responsibility as a child? It's worth exploring where that came from. One possibility is your mother's parenting style. If your mother was more hands off and relaxed in her approach, research suggests that you will have a better level of self-control as an adult.

We all have a degree of self-management, but understanding your own level and how it developed is a useful starting point to build from. However much self-control you have, it needs constant practice and refinement to maintain your skills in this area.

Tip: Mindfulness is a helpful tool in building self-management. Look in the Bibliography for some resources.

Think about the following questions, and if it helps take some notes. Don't worry if you can't answer them right now, just move on to the next section and come back if anything springs to mind:

- What was your self-management like as a child? Did you stomp about or lash out when you were angry or upset, or were you able to manage your emotions?

- Did your parents help you to understand your emotions and how to deal with them, or have you come to this understanding later in life? How do you think that has affected you?

- Did you have responsibilities as a child? Do you think that helped you understand how to manage your emotions and prioritize your time?

- If you didn't have responsibilities as a child, do you feel like you are self-disciplined now? Do you think your parents influenced that or something else in your environment, like a teacher or the school routine?

- How can you build on any of these observations to help you as an adult?

SOCIAL SKILLS

Your environment when you were growing up also influenced the development of your social skills. These include a wide range of characteristics (e.g., empathy, kindness, and cooperativeness), but in a broader sense they refer to your interpersonal effectiveness and ability to forge friendships. Research shows that the social skills you developed as a child have an effect on your satisfaction with life, well-being, and mental health.[6] Social skills are a critical foundation to being able to fulfill your potential and be successful.[7] They are at the heart of all daily interactions, from deal making and engaging stakeholders to getting people to buy in to whatever it is you set out to achieve.

When it comes to family influences on your social skills, research shows that if you had a close relationship with your father, you're more likely to develop better relationships as an adult. If your mother left you to your own devices, you're likely to be more effective at dealing with other people, whereas if you had a more demanding or critical mother, it may have had a negative impact on your ability to relate to others.[8] The research has been carried out on these particular relationships, but most likely can be extrapolated to other situations too.

It's important to point out that this is *not* about blaming your parents: most parents want the best for their child and that's more likely than not to have been the case for you. Exploring how your parents influenced you is more about understanding yourself and the major influences on you than it is about pointing the finger at anyone. Just like everyone else, parents have their own complex life situations to deal with.

Although interpersonal skills are in part genetically influenced, they are modified by who we interact with and the situations we are exposed to, and this modification continues to happen throughout life. While profiling, I've heard many stories of social skills altering as people grow up, such as those who were incredibly shy as children becoming outgoing as adults. If your interpersonal skills are not as fine-tuned as you'd like, don't worry, this is something you can work on. It is worth investing time to think through when and how you developed your skills in order to build on what has worked, and to overcome or accept and move on from what hasn't worked for you. We'll be looking at this in more detail again later in the book.

Think about the following questions, and if it helps take some notes. Don't worry if you can't answer them right now, just move on to the next section and come back if anything comes to mind:

- What was your relationship with each of your parents (i.e., mother, father) or significant figures in your childhood?

- Was there anything that helped you become more sociable as a child that you could build on now?

PASSIONS AND INTERESTS

Although being passionate about something isn't in itself enough to guarantee success, without a real interest in what you do it's very difficult to stay motivated and be sufficiently driven to push through the highs and lows. Your childhood offers insight into what really drives and engages you and what you are deeply passionate about. Exploring your early years may remind you of interests you've long forgotten about and could usefully reignite. It may also help you to understand where you've taken the wrong path and how you could correct that.

One of the most helpful ways of looking at your passions and interests is through the lens of motivation. There are two basic types of motivation, one that is external to us and one that is internal.

Extrinsic motivation means being driven by something from the outside, for instance working toward a goal, or avoiding failure through fear of disappointing others. What led to your choices about the classes you took at school, whether you pursued higher education, or your first job? How much were you influenced by not wanting to let your parents down or living up to family expectations rather than following your own interests? There's nothing wrong or right about how this came about, it's just helpful to understand what might be driving you now.

Intrinsic motivation, or being internally motivated, is about loving an activity for its own sake, finding it exciting and engaging. It relates to the things that you have the energy for and want to pursue without any external rewards (e.g., money or recognition) and also to punishments or things you feel a need to move away from because they are less pleasant.

The people I meet as a psychologist often have a good deal of intrinsic motivation. They have a passion for what they do and see the meaning in it. Without this it becomes very hard to keep going over a sustained period of time. For example, some of the people I work with are motivated by external rewards: the potential to earn a lot of money, social recognition, status. They don't love what they do, or have a burning interest in the industry itself. This makes their work really draining and can lead to burnout. Constantly being driven by extrinsic goals alone is not healthy. Ideally, you need both internal and external motivation to keep following your true passions while remaining connected to the world around you.

Research shows that our parents' expectations have a huge influence on the career path we take and what we achieve, regardless of their own upbringing or income.[9] Studies also reveal that teenagers often set out to follow in their parents' footsteps, whether as an entrepreneur, shop assistant, council worker, small business owner, or doctor,[10] and those whose parents are in "top jobs" are more likely find themselves in such a job.[11] What parents think their child is interested in and capable of also strongly influences a young person's choices and the actions they take toward pursuing a specific career.[12] What is critical here is that parents' best intentions can lead children astray. For example, if they think their child is passionate about numbers so encourage them toward a career in accounting, but the child actually always adored drama, then the child may miss out on pursuing their real dream. If you look over your early life and conclude that you were led mainly by your parents' wishes rather than your own, that realization may be enough for you to take ownership and control of how you move forward.

School can also have a strong influence. For example, a highly academic, high-achieving school can put strong pressure on its pupils to continue to the best universities and pursue what society deems to be the top jobs. Conversely, a large school struggling for resources may not support children's individual passions, meaning they never have the opportunity to explore and fulfill their potential.

Think about the following questions, and if it helps take some notes. Don't worry if you can't answer them right now, just move on to the next section and come back if anything comes to mind:

- What were you really enthusiastic about as a child? Are they the same things that you get joy from now?

- How many of your own career or life choices were influenced by your parents and/or your environment? Do you think what your family wanted took you off on a certain path?

- How much of your time at work or in life is spent doing things because you have to and how much because you want to? Do you think you need to address this?

Your Biology

Although your environment has a strong influence on your development, it intertwines with genetic factors to form your overall identity. For instance, do you sometimes catch yourself doing something or saying something in exactly the same way as your parents? Those are aspects that are likely to be genetically influenced. It's impossible to know exactly how much of your personality is nature and how much nurture, or how far your genes would influence you regardless of what you've been exposed to. It is worth exploring, however, because the elements that are strongly genetic are core to your identity. If you understand these genetic factors better, you can work on optimizing the positive aspects and learn how to "turn down the volume" on the more negative ones.

Nature or Nurture? We Just Don't Know

I profile people from all social strata. One leader I met came from a working-class background, and while this wasn't unusual, his overall narrative was. This man, we'll call him Joseph, had grown up in a family who weren't that bothered about achieving in life; they weren't lazy, they just had no interest in engaging in anything that took them out of their comfort zone. In contrast, Joseph was deeply ambitious from an early age, finding himself a part-time job delivering newspapers aged 10 and working in a local business as soon as he was old enough. He knuckled down at school and had a thirst for knowledge, from academic to experiential, fueling his wide-ranging curiosity. He also took part in a vast array of activities. Meanwhile his family watched from the sidelines, slightly perplexed. He was nurtured and loved, but he was completely different from both of his parents and his siblings.

During his profile I was intrigued: although there is no set pattern to anyone's life, this extreme mismatch with his family didn't make much sense. Once he'd told me about his early life, I commented on this. He told me that in his 30s he found out he'd been adopted. Being the curious man he was, he'd traced his natural father and discovered that he was a very successful and highly driven business owner. It seems that it was in fact biology that had so strongly influenced Joseph's behavior.

Without a doubt, our genes influence our personality, and Joseph is a classic example of this. He was driven in spite of his environment and his family, not because of them. However, as scientists are learning more about genetics, they're also learning that there is no clear-cut line between nature and nurture. Current estimates of how much of our personality is inherited from our parents range between 33% and 65%.[13] For Joseph, the likelihood is that the biological influences were at the higher end of the scale, which in turn will have influenced the environment he put himself in, leading to a further strengthening effect.

TOOLS OF THE SESSION

Biological Influences

While you can't be certain how much of your personality is genetic, you can become more aware of what is likely to be biological and what is not by looking at your parents. (If you were adopted and don't know your biological family, this exercise is just as useful in helping to determine which factors may be biologically influenced because of how you are different from your adoptive parents.)

Think about your parents, or talk to your partner, a friend, or a sibling about them. How would you describe them, what adjectives do you use? How do other people describe them? Use this information to fill in the points below (you may find it easier to write this on a separate piece of paper, your notepad, or add to your live document).

I would describe my mother as being:

1.

2.

3.

4.

I would describe my father as being:

1.

2.

3.

4.

How I am like my mother:

1.

2.

3.

4.

How I am different from my mother:

1.

2.

3.

4.

How I am like my father:

1.

2.

3.

4.

How I am different from my father:

1.

2.

3.

4.

What does completing this exercise tell you about your personality? Which parts of your personality do you think may be more genetic and which are influenced by the experiences you have had and the people you have interacted with?

Keep hold of these notes, as we'll revisit them later. Meanwhile, spend some time contemplating what this exercise tells you about yourself.

Your Brain is Plastic

What if you don't like what you've seen so far or who you've become as a result of your experiences? You can't go back and change the past and you certainly can't change the genes you've inherited. Nevertheless, although your early years have a significant impact on who you are, it doesn't mean that you can't change.

Until quite recently, it was believed that who we are, whether genetic or environmentally influenced, became "hardwired" once we passed a certain age. However, scientists have now discovered that our brain is far more plastic than we previously believed, plastic meaning malleable. As eminent psychiatrist Norman Doidge explains in *The Brain That Changes Itself*,[14] neuroplasticity challenges a host of long-held beliefs about how much we are able to change and adapt. For example, he explains that children who don't do so well at school are not necessarily

THE STORY OF YOU

"stuck" with the mental abilities they are born with. He also explains how someone can rewire their brain to overcome seemingly incurable obsessions and traumas, and that it's even possible for a person in their 80s to sharpen their memory to function as they did when they were in their 50s.

It's still fundamentally true that you can't change your core personality, but you can change the habits of a lifetime, alter your outlook, change your behavior and attitudes, even, to an extent, modify your intellectual capability, because you can rewire your brain. Given the estimate that 33–65% of your personality is genetically determined, that leaves a lot open to influence by your environment, and consequently to the decisions you make about your development.

This is particularly important to know if you've ever been told you're "not good enough." Being told you're not clever or bad at something as a child will damage your self-esteem, and you will most likely carry it as an underlying belief for the rest of your life, influencing a range of behaviors. Yet as an adult it's up to you whether you incorporate the less positive aspects of your past into your personal narrative. Your brain really is plastic.

You Can Change the Course of Your Life

A number of years ago I was asked to assess someone for a director role in a global company. The candidate, we'll call her Ava, emailed before the session asking to talk over the phone. I'm open to people contacting me with questions, but it's unusual when the profile is part of a formal corporate process, as was the case here. So it was with a certain level of interest that I spoke to her. For a number of reasons, she was extremely concerned about completing the reasoning tests. Her anxiety risked undermining the whole process: it's very difficult to gather accurate information if the person you're profiling is anxious and on edge. At the time I was working for a company that placed a great deal of value on reasoning tests, as did the client organization, but I made the decision not to do them on this occasion.

When Ava talked through her life story, I began to

understand why she didn't want to do the tests. She had had a difficult and complicated upbringing, growing up with a single parent in an immigrant family, and attending a big state school. Because of dyslexia which hadn't been diagnosed at the time, her teachers told her she was "stupid." She left school and home at 16 and life went from bad to worse, but one thing she retained was her spirited determination. She took herself off to London, got a job in retail, and was quickly identified as having capability and promoted to manage a small team. From that point on her opportunities began to open up. She found a mentor who took the time to understand and guide her, enabling her to go from strength to strength, completing a college diploma and accomplishing a whole string of other significant achievements. I recommended her for the role and can happily report that she not only excelled in the job, but has continued to flourish, succeeding in her subsequent career.

Although when I met Ava she still had the ghost of being told she was "stupid," she had overcome that as well as all of the other obstacles. What she demonstrates is that you can change the course of your life, it is within your control, you just need to adopt the right attitude, find the right people and tools to support you, and work hard.

TOOLS OF THE SESSION

Working Through Your Story

You may find it helpful to write your experiences onto a storyline. This will allow you to take an overview, seeing how the events in your life may have influenced each other, identifying patterns in your behavior, and recognizing where there may have been obstacles. You may prefer to do this in a freely written piece that you then organize to suit your thought processes. It's totally up to you—whatever works best.

Plot your early story on the blank storyline I've provided. You may equally want to create a storyline on an A3 sheet of paper so you can capture everything in enough detail, or on a piece of A4 with notes written separately.

I've given the example of my own storyline on page 51 to demonstrate the sort of things you may want to include, but it's personal to you. An event that had an impact on me may have no significance to someone else. You may feel that nothing much happened to you before the age of 15, and that's OK, just take it from there; alternatively, a major event may have occurred when you were 3 that really shaped you. It's your story, so it's up to you what you incorporate. These prompts should help:

- **Mark on the line two or three significant events (or more if they come to mind) that shaped you or changed your direction**—e.g., going to a different school, taking exams, your first boyfriend or girlfriend, parents divorcing.

- **Mark with + or – how you responded to these events**—Explain in separate notes how you felt and what lessons you learnt.

- **Think about who influenced your behavior positively or negatively**—Was there anyone who inspired you? Who was supportive? Were there friends who led you astray? Did anyone undermine your confidence? Put their initials on your storyline by when they influenced you.

- **Consider how you made the big decisions**—Who and what influenced you? If you don't know, then explore this further by discussing it with someone you trust.

- **Notice any key themes and patterns that are emerging**—Does this give you any insights?

- **Decide any parts of your life you want to emphasize**—e.g., are there elements of your personality or experiences that you're particularly proud of or feel really define you?

A word of warning: although you want enough information to be able to make some inferences, be careful not to "over reason." Your aim is to look at your story in a way that enables growth and builds on meaning. If you spend too much time dissecting the information, it can become counterproductive.

BLANK STORYLINE

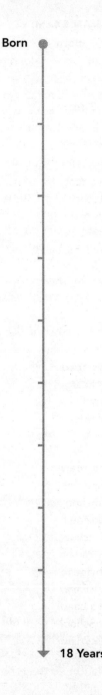

Born

18 Years

MY OWN STORYLINE AS AN EXAMPLE

Born

7 Years
Parents divorced—mother remarried
Lived with mother
First ski trip

8 Years
Moved house
Changed schools

10 Years
Father remarried

11 Years
Changed schools
In sports teams
Known as "chatter box"
Bullied for 1 year until bully
left school

13 Years
Moved house
Stopped dancing
Changed schools
Singled out as a swot so
  rebelled against working
  hard to fit in
Good friends in and outside
  of school
Maintained friendships
  from old school
Part-time job

15 Years
Decided on psychology
Convinced by physics teacher
to do medicine
Stepfather doctor

16 Years
GCSE exams—good grades
Changed schools—my choice
Stopped clarinet

16–18 Years
Chose A-levels needed for medicine
2 part time jobs
Bunking school when could
Good friends in & outside of school
Parties
Boyfriend
Piano
In a band
Music Captain at School
Lots of cycling

17 Years
Decided against medicine
Applied last minute to do
  psychology degree
Chose uni that had good reputation
  and felt good

18 Years

Another helpful and free resource for doing this activity is The History Project (now Enwoven): https://www.enwoven.com/individual. This site allows you to annotate your storyline, importing photos, videos, documents, and social media posts to add depth, and to edit as you remember events or change the reflections you have about something.

Coming to the End of the Session

You've now looked at some of the core aspects of your early story and how they inform who you are today. You'll have more of a chance to consider how to take action on any growth or development plans as you work through the book. For now, keep reflecting on your narrative and jot down things that come to mind while you're going about daily tasks.

In the next session, we'll be looking at what is technically known as "emerging adulthood." This is the stage of life when your brain develops to become more self-aware and emotionally mature, but also a time you start to experience more knocks and begin to understand how to overcome obstacles.

CHAPTER 3

Growing Up

● ● ●

In this session we are going to look into your early adult experiences. This will allow you to build on the data you collected in the previous session, drawing up a more comprehensive picture of your story. You will learn that from a neurological perspective, you develop self-awareness and self-management during early adulthood, improving your ability to manage and direct your emotions. You'll get the opportunity to explore your current level of emotional intelligence, to look at why that's important to leadership, reaching your potential, and life in general, and how to enhance it. You'll see why it's good to experience emotions rather than shut them down, how to "live with" negative emotions in a more helpful way, and how to overcome obstacles that may have been taking you in the wrong direction for some time.

Emerging Adulthood

The years between the ages of 18 and 29 have been termed "emerging adulthood," a stage that is currently being studied more intensely across various disciplines (e.g., psychology, anthropology, law, philosophy) as a unique developmental phase. Professor of psychology Jeffrey Arnett first referred to this paradigm in the journal *American Psychologist* in 2000. Having carried out analysis of 300 18–29-year-olds over a five-year period, he was able to define this as a time that's significantly different to either childhood or later adulthood.[1]

You were still highly impressionable and vulnerable at this stage of life, with influences from your social and cultural environment shaping your core identity quite simply because the very basic structure of your brain was still being formed. Like childhood, this part of your story will have shaped who you are today, perhaps more than you've ever realized. If you are still in this period of life it's worth understanding the impact various activities could be having on you.

Emerging Adulthood and the Brain

Neuroscientific research backs Arnett's findings. It was previously thought that, although the brain was in flux during adolescence, its development had largely settled by the time we reached our late teens. However, more recent studies have shown that critical areas of the brain continue to change well into our mid and even late 20s.

Unlike the multifaceted areas that shaped the younger years, brain development in emerging adulthood principally relates to the strengthening connection between the prefrontal lobe and the emotional centers of the brain. The prefrontal lobe is the "executive" region (the "observing brain") that manages emotion, and the stronger connections in effect enable better impulse control (of the "reacting brain"). We also start growing our ability to read other people and our environment at this time, which are critical facets of emotional capability.[2]

Unfortunately, society doesn't overtly promote such emotional development and consequently these brain linkages. People are encouraged to achieve goals and outcomes, but a focus on tangible measures such as good academic grades doesn't nurture these brain connections. Those society categorizes as the most "successful" at this stage of life can often be lacking in fundamental self-insight, which has a negative impact at later stages of their career. Having spent all of their time and energy focused on studies and work, they haven't fully developed their emotional awareness and understanding of where they fit into the world. And these emotional management skills are as vital to leadership success, reaching potential, and life satisfaction as more tangible results.

Engaging Head but Not Heart

I assessed Omar for a senior role in a multinational organization. He had an exceptionally strong track record both academically and in the workplace, having gained a first-class honours degree from Cambridge, and then worked at one of the world's premier strategy consultancies where he was supported in completing his MBA. Omar had climbed the ranks in his organization, carrying out some impressive roles with major blue-chip clients and leading teams of other consultants, before being headhunted for a new role.

During his 20s Omar had worked incredibly hard, which had been reflected in his career success. Unlike some of his school friends, he hadn't spent his college years socializing—his course took up too much time—and in fact he had lost contact with many of those friends. At work, he put in long hours to excel at what he did. The result was that while Omar was more than capable of doing the job in terms of his knowledge, experience, and intellectual capability, he was lacking when it came to emotional wisdom.

This insufficiency made it more difficult for him to connect with people from operational backgrounds, followers who needed to be led from the heart not just the head, and peers who had worked their way up through the ranks via hard graft. Nevertheless, this type of connection is critical to leading diverse teams of people effectively.

Omar was offered the role because, although he was lacking in this area, he had the fundamentals for building his skills. He was naturally warm, receptive to feedback, recognized the gap in his capability, and wanted to improve. I worked with him following the assessment with a focus on him being more attentive to interpersonal interactions, how people responded to him, how that made him feel, how he thought the person he was talking to was feeling, and how he adjusted his behavior accordingly. With time and persistence, this dramatically improved his emotional capabilities, enabling him to become a much more effective people manager.

Don't worry if you feel that you missed out on developing your emotional skills in your 20s. Omar is an example of how you can develop them whatever age you are. The brain is plastic, so with an awareness of your skill levels and considered effort it's possible to grow your capabilities.

Emotional Wisdom

The emotional capability that Omar lacked is what is commonly termed emotional intelligence. There are various academic perspectives on what emotional intelligence is, all of which have pros and cons. The concept was introduced by John D. Mayer and Peter Salovey of Yale University in 1990,[3] and was popularized by psychologist Daniel Goleman in his book *Emotional Intelligence*.[4]

Emotional Intelligence or Emotional Wisdom?

I refer to the concept as emotional wisdom, because intelligence commonly denotes something that is concrete, which we are born either with or without. However, our ability to interpret and manage our emotions is something we can and do develop. The better we are, the wiser we become.

Goleman's approach is the most useful to explore here, as it takes emotional wisdom into the context of the social and work environment. He categorizes the concept in four domains:

- **Self-awareness**—the ability to recognize your emotions and understand how they affect your thoughts and behavior. This involves having an understanding of your strengths and weaknesses, knowing where and when you need help, learning from your mistakes, and identifying what you need to improve.

- **Self-management**—the ability to manage impulsive feelings and behaviors in a way that's helpful to you. It also means being able to take the initiative, prioritize, follow through on commitments, and effectively manage emotional reactions.

- **Social awareness or empathy**—the ability to observe and not react impulsively or negatively to the emotional needs of other people, to notice and appropriately respond to emotional cues.

- **Social skills**—the ability to communicate and interact with people effectively, forge friendships, and maintain them over time.

Self-awareness is the critical foundation on which the other three skills are built. We'll be revisiting emotional wisdom and its component skills throughout this book, because they form a core part of your identity, how you interpret yourself, and how the world perceives you.

With more advanced levels of emotional wisdom come the abilities to communicate more effectively, connect with people more meaningfully, persuade others of your perspective, influence, network, and, particularly for leaders, navigate political situations and mitigate conflict.[5] A good level of emotional wisdom also allows you to manage stress and anxiety more effectively,[6] freeing up your observing brain to make clearer judgments and work more productively toward your goals.

It's not just the softer, less tangible aspects of success that emotional wisdom has an effect on; studies have also shown the positive impact on financial outcomes. For example, Richard Boyatzis, a professor of organizational behavior in the US, looked at the profits produced by partners in a number of financial services companies, measuring the four areas defined by Goleman. He found that three of the facets had a massively significant effect on bottom-line results, with good self-awareness adding 78% to incremental profits, social skills 110%, and self-management a whopping 390%.[7] Another study carried out by psychologist David McClelland[8] looked at leadership positions in more than 30 organizations from across sectors, and found that emotional wisdom repeatedly distinguished top performers from those considered to be average.

Having emotional wisdom also has an incredibly powerful impact on those being led. Researcher Hay McBer, for example, carried out a study looking at the heads of 42 schools in the UK.[9] This found that headteachers with a higher level of emotional wisdom enhanced the school's climate to the extent that it actually improved pupils' academic performance. This translates to any environment, whether that's school, home, work, or the community. In short, emotional wisdom is well worth having, and although emerging adulthood is the time at which we typically start to refine these skills, it's possible to develop them at any age.

TOOLS OF THE SESSION

Increasing Your Emotional Wisdom

How emotionally wise are you? The first step to improving your
emotional wisdom is to work out where you are currently. Take a look
at the following set of items to get an overview.

EMOTIONAL WISDOM SCALE

Instructions: Rate the statements below for how accurately they reflect
the way you generally feel and behave. Do not rate what you think you
should do, or wish you do, or things you no longer do. Please be as
honest as possible. Read each statement carefully and then circle the
appropriate answer.

1—Very inaccurate
2—Moderately inaccurate
3—Neither inaccurate nor accurate
4—Moderately accurate
5—Very accurate

1. I have the ability to make others feel interesting.   1 2 3 4 5

2. I am good at sensing what others are feeling.   1 2 3 4 5

3. I don't know how to handle myself in a
new social situation.   1 2 3 4 5

4. I know what to say to make people feel good.   1 2 3 4 5

5. I get along well with people I have just met.   1 2 3 4 5

6. I know what makes others tick.   1 2 3 4 5

7. I am able to fit into any situation.   1 2 3 4 5

Total your scores from each row, making sure you swap the score for statement 3, so that if you have put a 1 it becomes a 5 and a 2 becomes a 4.

Total your overall scores in this box.

Source: L.R. Goldberg, J.A. Johnson, H.W. Eber, et al. (2006) The International Personality Item Pool and the future of public-domain personality measures, *Journal of Research in Personality* 40: 84–96. Public domain.

Tip: It's difficult to rate your own emotional wisdom, so it would be helpful to get someone you trust and feel comfortable sharing this exercise with to go through and rate where they think you lie on each of the statements. This will bolster the accuracy of the outcomes.

INTERPRETING THE RESULTS

Use your totalled score to see where you lie on the three levels outlined in Table 3.1.

TABLE 3.1 THREE LEVELS OF EMOTIONAL WISDOM

Total	Level	Definition
7–15	Lower	You are able to identify emotion in how you feel physically, e.g., anxiety as a knot in your stomach.
		You can identify emotions in your thoughts, e.g., you know if you're feeling happy, sad, or angry and can articulate the thoughts you have about those feelings.
		You are able to identify whether someone's emotions are honest or dishonest, or if they are an accurate representation of what they're actually feeling.

16–26	Typical	You are able to vividly recall emotional responses you've had to previous events.
		When you encounter distressing or optimistic events, it has an impact on your viewpoint.
		When you're in different moods it affects the output of your work, e.g., when you are happy you are more creative, or when sad you are more poetic.
27–35	High	You are able to stay open to your feelings, regardless of whether they are pleasant or unpleasant.
		You can engage with or detach yourself from an emotion depending on how informative it is (i.e., "observe, don't react," see Chapter 1).
		You are able to observe your emotions in relation to yourself and other people, recognizing how influential or reasonable they are (i.e., "observe, don't react," see Chapter 1).
		You are able to manage your emotions and those of other people by moderating negative emotions and enhancing pleasant ones, without exaggerating the information they convey.

N.B. The results assume a normal distribution.

Source: Based on J.D. Mayer & P. Salovey (1997) What is emotional intelligence?, in D.J. Sluyter (ed.), *Emotional Development and Emotional Intelligence: Educational Implications*, New York: Basic Books, 3–34. Reproduced by permission.

Emotional wisdom comes in degrees and is relatively complex, involving intricate interconnections between different areas in the brain. Most people lie somewhere between levels 2 and 3. If you are at level 1 don't be concerned: the point of this book is to help you develop. Even if you have a very high score, there is always room to improve. We'll discuss how in the next section.

Accepting Emotions

How willing are you to grow your emotional wisdom? There is no quick fix, but you can improve, regardless of your current level or age. For now we will focus specifically on working with self-management.

We are taught that we can (and should) control our emotions. But in fact we can't, they are kicked up by our reacting brain too quickly for us to be able to stop them. We can, however, learn to be more skilled at stepping back from them and deciding whether or not we will act on the message they are giving us.

Do you avoid your emotions or are you able to accept them? Avoiding emotions, those such as failure in particular, can prevent you from trying new things. At the same time, being unable to experience emotions will stop you from fully flourishing. This doesn't mean you should suddenly start crying and telling everyone how you feel. It's a private thing—it's about how you experience your own emotions internally. But if you are able to experience your emotions in a productive way, you will respond much more effectively and get much more from people, which is not only healthier but also especially important as a leader or to achieve your potential whatever path you choose.

So, if you currently avoid your emotions, what can you do to become better at experiencing them? There is a very effective, evidence-based technique to help with this. It takes conscious effort and practice, but if you put in the time it will allow you not only to take action in situations you may have been avoiding, but also to accept negative emotions without letting them get in the way of your performance. The technique is known as **emotion surfing**, and it is a form of mindfulness. It involves accepting the emotion and then committing to take action or not take action depending on the situation (e.g., if it's a fear of failure stopping you from doing something, you will want to take action; if it's a bad habit, you won't).

TOOLS OF THE SESSION

Emotion Surfing

Read the paragraph below through once and then carry out the exercise.

Sit still for a moment, with your eyes closed, and think about a negative emotion you have recently felt. Bring the situation in which you experienced that emotion to mind. Try to relive the sensations you encountered, and to pinpoint where in your body you felt them. Stepping through the experience, see if you notice how the sensations shifted as time passed. Breathing deeply, sit with the emotion, don't fight it or engage with it, just let it be. Take deep breaths in and out to ride out the waves of the emotion, as if you're surfing, experiencing each wave as it comes along without reacting to it or trying to suppress or avoid it, simply riding it until it passes.

This is only one technique based on mindfulness, but practicing mindfulness more broadly really enhances your ability to observe your emotions and not engage with them.[10] It does take persistence, though, which is why even the Dali Lama does it every day. Mastering the ability to accept negative emotions rather than avoid or engage with them is hugely beneficial in terms of your general life satisfaction and potential to succeed. Leaders and people across all walks of life who are able to express positive emotions and actively manage negative ones are far more effective at persuading, influencing, motivating, and engaging others. They're also far better equipped to pass over negative events as if they were bumps in the road, as opposed to road blocks preventing them from reaching their destination. We'll look at another tool to help with this later in this session.

Successful people who are thought to practice mindfulness include talk show host Oprah Winfrey; comedian Jerry Seinfeld; Bill Ford, chairman of Ford Motor Co.; Arianna Huffington, co-founder of The Huffington Post; actor Emma Watson; billionaire investment banker Ray Dalio; tennis player Novak Djokovic; and Jeff Weiner, CEO of LinkedIn.

Obstacles, Uncertainty, and Emotional Instability

Dealing with setbacks is particularly relevant to emerging adulthood. It is a stage of life that presents you with a complex array of environmental transitions, punctuated by constant changes. While your brain is learning to understand and manage your emotions in your 20s, you inevitably experience events that don't turn out as you hoped. These situations offer up opportunity and possibility on the one hand, while presenting uncertainty, insecurity, and instability on the other. Arnett describes this as a period of "profound change, during which individuals typically explore the variety of options available to them" and "begin to make important first adult choices about career, lifestyle, love, leisure, morals, values, politics and religion. Patterns established at this time of life often persist long into adulthood."[11]

At this age you are less dependent on social norms and expectations for how you "should" behave and what you "should" be than at any other time of life, leaving you open to explore the world around you and how you fit into it (you may find it useful to plot these on your storyline). At the same time, in your late teens and early 20s you are exposed to more risks, as you move away from the safety net of your home and the security, both material and emotional, of your family. While this exploration of the unknown provides the possibility for growth, it also leads to a degree of emotional instability, obstacles, and, inevitably, also to failure of some kind. On the one hand this can build emotional wisdom and resilience, but on the other it can create and ingrain more negative responses and emotions, such as avoidance.

Learning from Life's Obstacles

Sofia experienced an exceptionally traumatic event in her early 20s when her brother was killed in a fatal accident. Shortly afterwards her father committed suicide, blaming himself for what had happened. This was followed by difficult working circumstances for Sofia, with a senior member of staff taking credit for her work and blocking her promotion. Simultaneously, there was an ongoing investigation into her brother's death and a great deal of unwanted media attention. She managed to see her way through this stage of life to create a career as a leader within her field.

When I met Sofia, it was simply to facilitate and accelerate her development to the very top. We began with a profiling session, and it became evident that there were barriers she needed to tackle in order to be the very best she could be. These were not to do with her capability, but emotional obstructions that weren't immediately obvious, even to her, as a result of her response to the extreme pressures she had experienced during her emerging adulthood. These factors were subtly undermining her leadership and, although not apparent at her current level, could well have become a major issue as she moved into more senior roles, where you are more prone to exposing and being undermined by your vulnerabilities.

Essentially, Sofia had been locking away certain emotions and preventing herself from being hurt by keeping people at arm's length. This meant she had developed a protective stance in her leadership style, which was already stopping her from engaging her followers at the level she was really capable of. By understanding and unpacking these psychological barriers, she was ultimately able to overcome them. We worked on this over a period of about 12 months. Initially, it involved identifying that there was an issue, then her accepting that she needed to do something about it, and, lastly, her having the drive to overcome it. Once she recognized the emotions she had locked away, we worked on how she could experience them without them becoming an issue or without her feeling like she had lost control. Achieving this allowed for people to get closer to her as she really was, for her to understand how to experience emotion without it becoming uncontrollable, and for her to more freely express her positive emotions rather than suppressing every reaction. Ultimately, she was able to lead with a much greater level of emotional connection, making her style more inspirational and enabling her to bring even the most stubborn opposition around to her way of thinking.

Hopefully you will not have experienced anything as traumatic as Sofia did in your emerging adulthood, but you will inevitably have been exposed to unwanted events, since the chances of encountering disruptive and unsettling situations become more frequent as we enter this phase of life. For example, Meg Jay, a clinical psychologist specializing in adult development, states that 80% of life's most significant events take place by the age of 35.[12] It's also at this time that you will have defined (or will be defining) your response to those events, whether, and how, you experience the related emotions, or if you suppress or avoid those emotions altogether. While avoiding emotions can, to some extent, help you get through and keep going like Sofia did, at some point they will inevitably trip you up or prevent you from becoming truly successful in whatever you do, whether that's fulfilling your potential or just feeling satisfied with life. It's important to realize that there are no quick fixes, but the tools and approaches that follow will, with persistence, help you to overcome your own barriers.

TOOLS OF THE SESSION

Overcoming Obstacles

Emotion surfing is a helpful technique for responding to the immediate emotions you encounter, but when dealing with more long-standing issues it's useful to use a strategy known as **cognitive reframing**. Reframing creates a more enduring change of attitude toward memories and events, altering them from something that potentially holds you back to releasing you to get on and achieve your goals. Research suggests that "framing" your life so that things have meaning and outcomes you are in control of is so powerful that it positively changes brain functioning.[13]

Go back over your storyline and think of any obstacles or events that have led you to a negative belief system. Then work out how to think about them from a different angle. For example:

- Thought: "I failed my exams because I am not very bright."
  Outcome: out of control and negative meaning.

- Thought: "I failed my exams because I didn't work hard enough."
  Outcome: within your control—"It was a good life lesson, because

of it I have worked harder at things that matter to me ever since"—and positive meaning.

If you think you are not good enough in any way, if you were led to believe that as a child or young adult and have held on to it ever since, it will lead you to avoid a whole host of opportunities. So it's worth taking a look at revisiting your storyline as a prompt to the areas that you may want to reframe.

Plot Your Story from 18 to Today

Your storyline can now be extended to where you are currently. Add answers to the same kinds of questions as before, but from the age of 18 onward.

- **Plot 2–4 events in your life that have shaped you or changed your direction since you were 18**—try to include 1–2 negatives, e.g., death of a relative, car crash, failing exams, as well as 1–2 positives, e.g., getting married, buying your first home.

- **How did you respond to these life events**—how did each of the events make you feel? What lessons did you learn from each? How has it changed the way you think about things? Capture these as notes to the life events.

- **Plot 2–4 people who have influenced you since you were 18**—try to include 1–2 who were a positive influence (someone who inspired you or was very supportive) and 1–2 who had a negative impact (e.g., a boss who undermined your confidence, a friend who led you astray). Don't worry if you can't think of anyone, you can always leave this and come back to it at a later point.

If thoughts come up from your earlier life—for instance, you remember something significant from when you were 16 that has altered the way you think—jot these down. Feel free to write down more events, influences, and so on. But also remember that while you want enough information to be able to make some inferences, you should also be careful not to "overreason."

BLANK STORYLINE

18 Years

Present day

Reframing

Now you have added to your storyline from 18 years old to where you are today, you can start to reframe any obstacles:

1. Look at your storyline and identify the negative events that you felt were out of your control or without meaning, things that may have held you back to this day.

2. Once you have identified those events, think about the consequences of the thought pattern or belief you hold around that event. What impact does that belief have on your personal narrative and your identity? Do you want this, or do you want to change it?

3. If you want to change it, then you need to consciously reframe the event. Our thoughts are like a continuous running dialogue that we rarely question, so it's important to stop and challenge them. This prevents the same record running over and over again, influencing how you feel and how you behave.

REFRAMING NEGATIVE EVENTS
Choose an event or a thought that is acting as a barrier and answer the following questions (there is an example under each heading, but also space for you to work through your own experience). The first statement should be purely factual, with no emotional judgments.

- **Event:**
  First public speaking engagement that didn't go as planned.

- **How I have always thought about the event:**
  I'm awful at presenting, I get scared and mess it up every time.

- **Does this way of thinking about it put the event within my control?**

  No, I am bad at public speaking and the only way I can control it is not to do it again.

- **Does this way of thinking about it give the event meaning?**

  No, it just means that I'm not very good at public speaking.

Reframing the event

I have listed some questions you may find useful in helping you to reframe the event, which remains the same as before. Think about these in detail and really unpick your thoughts, questioning why or why not in each of your responses. Write down the statements/questions and your responses on a separate piece of paper so that you're not tempted to rush over this exercise.

- **Event (insert your own example)**

  First public speaking engagement that didn't go as planned.

- **How can I think of the event so that it's within my control?**
  - What is the evidence for my original thought and what is the evidence against it?
  - Am I looking at all the evidence or just focusing on evidence that backs up my existing belief?
  - How might other people interpret the same situation and what might their interpretation be?
  - Is this thought black and white, when the reality is gray?
  - Am I misinterpreting the evidence? Am I making any assumptions?
  - Could my thought be an exaggeration of the truth? Could I have blown it out of proportion?
  - Am I having this thought out of habit, or do the facts support it?
  - Did someone pass this thought/belief to me? If so, are they a reliable source?

- **Reframed thought**
  I didn't speak as well I'd like because I didn't spend enough time preparing and didn't know the set-up of the room, so I was thrown by the situation. Other people said that I presented well, it just wasn't up to the standard I was aiming for.

- **How can I think of the event so that it has meaning?**
  Because of the event, I learnt that I really must spend longer preparing for public speaking and should also get as much information about the venue, other speakers, audience etc. as I can beforehand, so that I'm not thrown by the situation.

4. Once you have worked through the reframing for your own thoughts or events, consider what will look different for you by changing the way you frame this event. How will it change the way you see yourself and how will it alter your personal narrative? What are the positive impacts this could have on you moving forward? Thinking this through will help motivate you to make changes and to start moving in the right direction. Make sure you take notes as a reminder and reference.

5. Keep reminding yourself of the new way of thinking. You may want to write the reframed thought down on an index card or note in your phone so you look at it a few times a day. The pathways in your brain are currently strongly wired toward the old belief, and you need to build up stronger pathways toward the new belief to get it to stick. This takes persistence. It shouldn't be a struggle, though—just be tenacious. Gently pull your thoughts away from the old belief, because being harsh with yourself will cause your mind to go in the other direction.

6. When it comes to development planning later in the book, be sure to include actions that challenge the beliefs you once held, to prove to yourself that those things are no longer holding you back.

This is the first step toward reframing your narrative as a whole in a way that allows you to let go of things you don't want to carry through life. Take your time with this, and only focus on one event at a time, revisiting any others once you've managed to get a handle on the first.

N.B. Later in the book we'll also be focusing on the positives and strengths you captured on your storyline, thinking through the impact they have on who you are and how you go about living your life to the full.

Coming to the End of the Session

We have looked at some of the core areas relating to emerging adulthood, but while they are most common to this stage of life, they are not unique to it. They can be experienced and most certainly revisited at any time of life. There are consistent patterns across people's lifespans, but our adult development is not experienced in a linear progression. We have highs and lows that have impacts on us and influence our journeys and personal narratives at different times in our lives. Keep reflecting on your timeline, looking for any patterns that may emerge and capturing any thoughts you have. It's important that you don't feel pressured to rush on to the next chapter. Take some time to think through what you've learnt and put it into practice. We've covered a lot of ground and you will need time to assimilate. Alternatively, you may want to move on and come back to this section once you've had time to reflect.

In the next session, we'll be looking at how you can start putting some of the skills into practice: your emotional wisdom, empathic curiosity, and engaging your observing brain. We'll also be revisiting your passions and interests, looking at your values, and starting to get beneath what creates real meaning for you—what defines you.

CHAPTER 4

Meaning in Life

● ● ●

You have explored your life story up to the present, but that is not the destination. You are at a point where you are looking to grow and develop, to understand yourself and what you want from life in more depth—that's why you're taking the time to read this book. Maybe you feel like you want more than a tick-box exercise of doing a good job at work, buying an expensive new outfit, or upgrading to the latest iPhone. You've most likely realized that although this feels good in the short term, it doesn't bring any depth of happiness or satisfaction that lasts. That comes from not only defining who you are, but finding your meaning in life, which is what we're going to start exploring in this session. Finding what meaning means to you is quite an audacious goal, but to make it doable we're going to break it down into its component parts and build it back up again as we progress through the book.

Although meaning is unique to each one of us, it's built on some common foundations, which you can discover through self-exploration. Meaning is:

- made up of your values and passions;

- reached by making use of your strengths and preferences;

- found through connecting with others, giving back to others, and continually learning.

To open the session, we will explore why meaning is important, in terms of both your brain and life in general. Then we will begin building what meaning means to you by clarifying your values and your passions. This will not only give you a sharper understanding of this critical aspect of who you are, but also help you to realize the part it could play in your life from now on. Once defined, your values and passions will also act as a foundation from which to build your vision and purpose; we'll return to this later in the book.

In the second part of this session, we'll look at connecting with others, how and why that's important to meaning, and we'll explore some ways in which you can do so more deeply with the people you come into contact with on a daily basis. You will have the chance to try out different methods for connecting more effectively and, in line with defining you, find which one works best for you personally. This will provide ways to start to live with a greater sense of meaning immediately, while working to establish the bigger goal of uncovering your overall purpose in life. We'll continue to explore your meaning in the following chapters, focusing on different aspects as we progress.

Defining you in this way will be well worth the effort: it will allow you to take your life forward in a way that makes sense, as well as helping to clarify your goals and fit them within a bigger picture and, most importantly, *your* bigger picture. You'll be able to pursue what makes your heart sing in making use of what you're good at, really and truly fulfilling your potential. Best of all, this will provide a satisfaction in life that is more sustainable, allowing you to weather the lows and fully enjoy the highs. Your meaning, once defined, becomes a guiding light, remains constant, and keeps you going whatever life throws at you.

Why is Meaning Important?

As we have time to reflect, we inevitably search for "more" and, in pursuit of happiness, we are unconsciously encouraged by society to chase short-term and material gains. Unfortunately, that never really gives us what we need at a deeper level. Many of the leaders I see have big houses, expensive cars, and the prestige that comes with the job, but have found that those things don't bring lasting fulfillment. True satisfaction comes not from hedonic reward, but from finding our personal sense of meaning. In fact, research shows that only 10% of our happiness is linked to life circumstances such as income and social status.[1]

Your Brain and Meaning

The part of the human brain that ensures our survival (i.e., our reacting brain) doesn't know we live in a world that has moved on 50,000 years from the one it evolved to fit. As a result, at a subconscious level we are continually striving for "more," literally in order to survive. As a simple illustration, wanting a piece of chocolate cake or another drink comes about because our brain has evolved to want to eat and drink whenever possible (in order to survive), since our ancient ancestors never knew when their next meal would arrive. Our reacting brain is also driven to help us survive through reproducing (passing on our genes) and belonging to a group (for shelter and safety). In today's world these primitive impulses emerge as wanting to

- have more—a bigger house, a better car, a more talented child, nicer clothes;
- strive for more—a better job, a bigger position, more influence;
- be more—thinner, prettier, younger, cooler, brighter.

There's nothing wrong with this, it's fun and fun is an important part of life, but in and of itself it doesn't bring lasting happiness. On the contrary, it tends to breed dissatisfaction—there will always be someone who has more, has achieved more, or is more. It's like chasing the pot of gold at the end of the rainbow.

When our ancient ancestors were at rest and safe, their brain would switch to using what eminent psychologist Daniel Kahneman[2] calls slow thinking, using the observing brain. This is the part of the brain that searches for significance and purpose.

The problem is that our fast-paced world doesn't leave much room for slow thinking—our brain is still continually responding to threats. But now these threats come in the form of seemingly innocuous things such as messages to respond to, news to catch up on, deadlines to meet, appointments to make—and they don't go away. This leaves very little "safe time" to engage our slow-thinking brain.

We don't want to shut down our survival-driven impulses: they keep us safe (e.g., they stop us from getting run over) and they enable us to have fun. We can't switch off the environment we live in—emails, traffic, crowds of people, artificial light stretching our days into nights—but we can understand how to limit the impact of the mismatch between our brain and our environment. Doing this, using some of the techniques you've learnt in this book, will help you really get under the skin of what meaning means to you.

One way of going about this is to create space for your slow-thinking brain, by using one of the following, in a way that works for you:

- Being outside in nature[3]
- Walking, running, cycling, being active (preferably outside)
- Meditating (e.g., using Headspace)
- Reading
- Doing yoga
- Chatting to friends (steer clear of the overly competitive ones when you're wanting to unwind)
- Spending time alone

Then engage your observing brain in slow thinking, to pursue what it evolved for: finding your meaning and purpose, connecting with others at a deeper level, giving back, and continually learning.

Having a sense of meaning in your life literally gives you a reason to get up in the morning. It's so powerful that it has positive benefits via a wide range of physical and mental health outcomes: protecting against heart disease,[4] diminishing the impacts of Alzheimer's,[5] improving our ability to handle pain,[6] mitigating depression,[7] curbing anxiety,[8] and also lengthening our lives.[9] Alongside this, meaning is a major component of well-being and life satisfaction.

Viktor Frankl, a neurologist, psychiatrist, and Holocaust survivor, gives a powerful example of how critical purpose is in his book *The*

Search for Meaning.[10] He recounts his experiences in a concentration camp and how finding meaning, in even the most brutal of experiences, kept him going and gave him a reason to live. He also interviewed hundreds of fellow prisoners, and found that those who survived the mistreatment and were able to fight back from illness had a deeper meaning or purpose keeping them going. Frankl famously argued that within the context of normal life, people who lack meaning fill what he called the "resultant void" with hedonistic pleasures: power, materialism, obsessions, and compulsions—in other words, those things that the reacting brain chases after but gains no lasting satisfaction from.

In the past, people relied on religion and culture to define their meaning. These provided a framework from which to operate, the bigger picture from which to see life. However, as the world changes a lot of people are moving away from identifying so closely with religion and traditional cultures, and consequently purpose is no longer given to us on a plate—we have to define it for ourselves. This isn't easy to do, but this book and this particular session will begin to help you with that, not only in order to lead toward the physical and mental health outcomes listed above, but also to allow you to make the most of your life and the most of you, whatever you want to do.

We Aim for Success, but It's Meaning That Delivers

Recently I was discussing happiness with Alwin, the CEO of a company I work with. We both know some very "successful" people, and were exploring how the happiest individuals were not those who had earnt the most money or achieved the highest status, but those who had found meaning in their lives. Alwin gave the example of a friend who, despite having striven his whole career to make lots of money and now being worth £180 million, was still miserable. And another of a woman who had stopped working in her high-paid job to start a charity focused on a cause she was passionate about, which had transformed her life. I also know two CEOs who have voluntarily given away their own salary, not as a grand gesture but as a genuine indication that money really isn't what creates meaning for them. One distributed her bonus among her employees; the other took a dramatic pay cut because he didn't feel he needed that much money once the intensity of turning the company around was over. You may be thinking "well, that's easy for a CEO to do, they have quite a bit of cash to spare," and you would be correct: without a certain base level of financial security it's hard to behave like this. But once we have enough money to comfortably survive on, it frees up the opportunity to explore.

What is more, some people find this without ever having had financial abundance, for example Mother Teresa or Gandhi. Filmmaker Roko Belic traveled the world making the award-winning documentary *Happy*, which investigates what gives life satisfaction. The common theme was that from the slums of Kolkata to islands off Japan, to Bhutan and Denmark, those who were happy did not have money or status, but they did have meaning. All these populations had some sort of close community, intimate connections with others, and the opportunity for personal growth (which aligned with their values, passions, or interests).

What Does Meaning Mean to You?

In this section, I'm going to help you look at your values and then carry out an activity to explore your passions and interests, which underpin what meaning means to you.

VALUES

Our values form a core foundation of our life, supporting many of the choices we make and the direction our life goes in. Russ Harris, author of the *Happiness Trap* whose approach rests heavily on values, describes them as:

> *your heart's deepest desires for how you want to behave as a human being. Values are not about what you want to get or achieve; they are about how you want to behave or act on an ongoing basis.*[11]

We tend to adopt the values of the people we interact with as a child, so our values are largely informed by our parents and family, but also the culture and environment we grew up in. These factors have a major impact on our identity or "self-labeling," and consequently on our behaviors and the choices we make.

The following exercise is a chance for you to re-examine your values. Although they are heavily influenced by external factors such as your upbringing, this is your opportunity to reflect on what's true to you. There are no rights or wrongs; try to put aside what you feel your values "should" be, and really connect with your deepest desires by being honest with yourself.

TOOLS OF THE SESSION

Identify Your Top Five Values

STEP 1

Go through the list on the following two pages, putting a tick next to the words that mean something to you in the context of your values. Feel free to add any values that aren't covered here; these words are simply a prompt or starting point for your thinking.

Next, look through the values that you've ticked (and added) and put them into groups that share a common thread, giving them a short title that explains them in your own words. For example:

- **Having a sense of fun and adventure:** enjoyment, joy, fun, excitement, adventure, exploration

- **Being an ideas person and having a point of difference:** creativity, curiosity, imagination, innovation, uniqueness

- **Looking after my health and well-being:** acceptance, balance, calm, mindfulness, serenity, self-awareness, vitality, growth, fitness

These words may have another meaning to you and may be grouped completely differently, and that's fine. You may find that you have just one or two words or many words grouped together. Some words may not even sit within a group, so keep them as a category on their own. This is all about defining *your* values in *your* way.

Acceptance	Courage	Focus	Logic
Accountability	Courtesy	Foresight	Love
Accuracy	Creation	Forgiveness	Loyalty
Achievement	Creativity	Freedom	Mastery
Adaptability	Credibility	Friendship	Maturity
Adventure	Curiosity	Fun	Mindfulness
Altruism	Decisiveness	Generosity	Moderation
Ambition	Dedication	Genius	Open-mindedness
Amusement	Dependability	Giving	Openness
Assertiveness	Determination	Grace	Optimism
Attentive	Devotion	Gratitude	Order
Authenticity	Dignity	Growth	Organization
Balance	Discipline	Happiness	Originality
Boldness	Discovery	Hard work	Passion
Bravery	Drive	Harmony	Patience
Calm	Effectiveness	Health	Peace
Candor	Efficiency	Honesty	Persistence
Capablity	Empathy	Hope	Playfulness
Caring	Empowerment	Humility	Potential
Celebrity	Encouragement	Humor	Productivity
Certainty	Energy	Imagination	Professionalism
Challenge	Enjoyment	Independence	Prosperity
Charity	Enthusiasm	Individuality	Quality
Clarity	Equality	Innovation	Realism
Comfort	Ethics	Inquisitiveness	Reason
Commitment	Excellence	Insight	Recognition
Common sense	Excitement	Inspiration	Recreation
Communication	Experience	Integrity	Reflectiveness
Community	Exploration	Intelligence	Respect
Compassion	Expressive	Intimacy	Responsibility
Competence	Fairness	Intuitiveness	Restraint
Conformity	Family	Joy	Results orientation
Connection	Fearlessness	Justice	Reverence
Consistency	Feelings	Kindness	Rigor
Contentment	Ferociousness	Knowledge	Risk
Contribution	Fidelity	Lawfulness	Romance
Conviction	Fitness	Leadership	Satisfaction
Cooperation	Flexibility	Learning	Security

Self-awareness	Sincerity	Teamwork	Trust
Self-care	Skillfulness	Temperance	Truth
Self-development	Solitude	Thankfulness	Understanding
Selflessness	Spirituality	Thoroughness	Uniqueness
Self-reliance	Spontaneity	Thoughtfulness	Unity
Sensitivity	Stability	Timeliness	Vigor
Sensuality	Status	Tolerance	Vision
Serenity	Strength	Toughness	Vitality
Sexuality	Structure	Traditional	Winning
Silence	Support	Tranquillity	Wisdom
Simplicity	Sustainability	Transparency	

STEP 2

Prioritize your groups of words. You may find it helpful to think through the following questions:

- Recall a time when you got really angry or upset because someone violated one of your core values. What was that and what values does it relate to?

- When have you felt most proud and what values does that relate to?

- When have you felt most fulfilled and what values does that relate to?

Try to reduce your list to 5–6 themes or fewer.

STEP 3

If you still have more than 5–6 themes, then whittle your list down a little more.

Sleep on it, come back to the list, check the themes, and reorder them if you need to. It's important to get this right, because it's central to your life and will act as a guide to the decisions you make moving forward.

Ask yourself: Do these values make me feel good about myself? Am I proud of them? Do they represent who I am? Would I stand by these values even if my opinion wasn't supported or if it was in opposition to other people?

Your Passions, Interests and Story So Far

Next, look at your passions and interests, which also form a central component in understanding what meaning means to you. Reflecting on your passions and interests through the lens of your story so far will help you to understand their context within the highs and lows of your life, and to really get underneath what fires you up.

STEP 1
Plot the following points onto your storyline, capturing your detailed responses on another sheet of paper (which you can file, put in the notepad you have been using, or record online):

- Plot the 2–4 activities you have most loved and those you have most hated.

- Plot the 2–4 jobs and responsibilities you have most loved and most hated.

- Plot when you started the hobbies and interests you have got the most pleasure from and when you have done them most intensively in your life.

Look back at your passions and interests as a child and your responses to the questions in Chapter 2. In the context of that, think about the following:

- Do you still love doing the same things that you got lost for hours in as a child? Maybe you haven't engaged with them for years, or you use them in different ways now.

- What is working well for you in your current life and career? What do you find fulfilling, meaningful, enjoyable, and important? What drains you, makes you stressed and anxious, or wastes your time?

- What would you do if you didn't need to get paid?

Look for any themes and patterns in your responses, both in terms of what you love and what you loathe. Both tell you about the motivations that are truly intrinsic to you. Make a list of your 5–10 core passions and interests.

Over time, to pursue these things you need to consider two further steps.

STEP 2

Investigate how you can use these passions and get involved with your interests. Look for local clubs or obtain the things that mean you can follow your interests at home (e.g., if you like cooking and haven't done it for a while, buy the ingredients to make a special meal). Set time aside every weekend or whenever you can and try different things that involve your passions.

STEP 3

Think through how you could include these passions in your life, either as a hobby or maybe as a volunteering exercise, or how you could incorporate an element of them in your career over a longer period. You may even want to explore changing careers to make your true interests more central to your life.

Keep all of this information, because we'll be returning to it later in the book.

Connection

Connecting with others is a fundamental part of what makes us human, and is core to finding a sense of meaning and purpose. We have a need to connect at a very primitive level stemming from our reacting brain, driving a whole host of behaviors such as wanting to impress, to assert our social status, and to align our thinking with those around us. Yet our higher need, the one that our observing brain seeks out, is a much deeper level of person-to-person connection.

Connection creates what Emma Seppala, a researcher at Stanford University, calls a positive feedback loop of social well-being. Seppala explains how people who have more meaningful social connections have higher self-esteem, greater empathy for others, and are more trusting and cooperative.[12] As a consequence, people are more open to trusting and cooperating in return, creating an ongoing positive loop. Such connections also naturally create networks, which are shown to grow career and life opportunities, giving access to helpful guidance and advice, and raising people's profile. It's not hard to understand how these factors have positive impacts on leadership or the chance to get ahead in any walk of life. Added to this, connections have been shown time and again to have helpful psychological and health-related benefits,[13] such as strengthening our immune system, lowering blood pressure, reducing our risk of getting sick,[14] decreasing levels of anxiety and depression,[15] and even lengthening our lives.[16] The support of any social network, whether career related or personal, therefore enhances our opportunities to fulfill our potential and live a more rewarding life.

When we've developed through the emerging adulthood phase or "grown up," the nature of our relationships begins to change. Paradoxically, we learn to value relationships more, to understand through life experience that meaningful connections are fundamentally important, but at the same time we often de-prioritize investing time in workplace relationships, life-long friendships, and even family ties. This is quite simply because of the pressures of life that we face as we take on more responsibilities, at work and at home (e.g., a more senior role, starting a business, travel, finding a life partner, having a young family, coping with aging parents). It is particularly the case in an increasingly complex world (e.g., our personal to-do list, the "noise" of social media) that we are pulled in what feels like a thousand different directions. As a result, even our most intimate relationships take a battering: if we're busy we don't have time to connect properly with our spouse or children, or to speak to our best friend. When we have little energy to invest in our most important relationships, it can feel like an unrealistic task to connect more deeply with everyone we come into contact with. But the fact is that we have almost forgotten how to connect properly, we're so caught up in the busyness of life.

When it comes to meaningfully connecting with people, it's not about how many but how much, giving to others in the form of time, thought, respect, trust, attention, consideration, and mental space. As Adam Grant, professor of management at Wharton, explores in his book *Give and Take*,[17] people who give are far more likely to succeed in life.* In short, our brain is wired to connect given the right environment and it pays dividends. Unfortunately, many of the environments we find ourselves in today don't support this.

---

* Note that this does not mean blindly trusting anyone and everyone—there's an element of savvy involved to avoid being "walked on." See Grant's chapter "Chump change—Overcoming the doormat effect" for more on this.

So, although our brain is wired to connect, we have to give it the right platform to be able to do so. This involves removing ourselves from environments where we feel too overwhelmed to engage our observing brain, and giving that part of our brain the time and space to operate at its best. We will explore some tools to help with this "time and space" element in this session, and will consider how to find your optimal environment later in the book.

Making Tough Calls with Respect

I profiled Noam for a CEO role. He was aware that the job would involve taking some difficult decisions and making dramatic changes in the makeup of his top team. However, he was by no means a "hatchet man" or someone who could make these decisions coldly. One thing that really stood out about him was his deeply held value that you can and should treat everyone with consideration, respect, and understanding, even if you have to take a tough call about them. Many leaders understandably try not to get close to people they may have to fire, and often end up more emotionally removed as a result. Noam was not like this.

Nevertheless, the chairman and the hiring board were worried by the report I wrote on him, which clearly stated that he always really got to know people and carefully, emotionally even, considered people decisions. Would this mean he couldn't make the changes required? I explained how getting rid of people could be done much more effectively by someone who has the best interests of the employees at heart and really makes the effort to understand them, as long as certain conditions were met.

Noam was offered and accepted the role. I kept in touch with him, so was able to see how he performed. The board were astounded by how quickly he managed to make changes in his top team given all of the other equally pressing issues. Not only that, but he did so without negative fallout. Quite simply, this was because he took the time to connect with people, to listen to and understand them as individuals, to work with them in a respectful way. As such, he was able to move people out of the business by working with them, not undermining their self-belief. The result was they didn't become angry or upset, file a complaint, fight the decision, or cause issues that are typically expected in such circumstances. Noam went on to create a leadership team more quickly and effectively than I'd ever seen before.

TOOLS OF THE SESSION

How to Connect Better

In what follows I describe five different "connection characteristics." They all explain ways to connect better with people in your day-to-day life. Read them through and then try each one for a week, using the "how to do it" pointers to guide you. At the end of the week, give the characteristic a rating out of 10. Once you've tried all five, go back to the one that you scored the highest and commit to incorporating it into your life. If a week feels too long, then try a day. If you don't have the time or motivation to try all of them, read through the whole section and see which one looks or feels like it's most likely to work for you, and commit to trying that, finding ways to make it a habit. Doing this will help you to connect better with the people around you and bring the many psychological, physiological, and career-related benefits of connection.

CONNECTION CHARACTERISTIC 1: MAKE TIME
The most effective leaders I have met, the most senior, time-pressed people, seem like they have all the time in the world when they're speaking to you. That doesn't mean they let you talk forever or overrun on a meeting, but when they are there, they are with you, focused on you, with no interruptions from phones or anything else. The message here is that we should try to shed the belief that being busy makes us appear important, valuable, or more worthwhile. It's not true—so whatever else there is, it can wait.

How to do it:

- Block out time when you are with someone. Don't look at your watch, phone, or any other device. If you're time-pressed, then be clear at the start how much time you have and stick to that, but when you're with someone, be with them.

- Try letting pauses and moments of quiet just happen. This shows respect, not wanting to rush on with the conversation, and also allows the other person to open up more fully.

- Do this in at least three of the conversations you have over the next three days, and write down what you observed and felt.

Week tried (date): Score: /10

Observations:

> Tip: Neuroscientist Tania Singer found that the part of our brain involved in empathy is located in the more advanced, observing brain.[18] This region has an autocorrect mechanism, preventing us from looking only at our own feelings in a situation and ensuring that we are able to see things from others' perspectives. However, when we have to make very quick, reactionary decisions, we lose this capability—in effect, our reacting brain overrides our empathy. This is one example of why it's critical to take time to allow your brain to operate optimally.

CONNECTION CHARACTERISTIC 2: OBSERVE, DON'T REACT
In the context of connecting with others, this is about trying to quieten your reacting brain, allowing yourself to be in the moment with the

person you are talking to, being present. During a conversation your reacting brain will kick up all sorts of thoughts and emotions, such as deciding what you're going to say next, needing to interrupt so you don't forget what you've just thought of, jumping to conclusions about what the other person's leading up to, forming opinions over what type of person they are, deciding what you're going to have for dinner, wondering where they got their shoes from. Try really hard to observe those thoughts without responding to or engaging with them, stop your reacting brain from racing ahead with its own agenda, and give the person you are with time to express themselves properly.

How to do it:

- Observe the person you are talking to, not just what they say but how they are saying it, their intonation, the speed at which they're speaking, their body language, even when and how they pause. Think about what this tells you. Really be present in the moment with them, listening to what they are saying without judgment.

- Keep gently pulling your mind back to the conversation when it wanders off. Bear in mind the objective of being a detective and learning something new (see the next characteristic).

- Do this in at least three of the conversations you have over the next three days and write down what you observed and felt.

  Week Tried (date): Score: /10

  Observations:

CONNECTION CHARACTERISTIC 3: BE A DETECTIVE AND LEARN
Be open-minded and curious, no stereotypes, no simple definitions, no preconceptions, no jumping to conclusions. Go into all conversations with the objective of learning something, whether you're talking to a

child, someone you've known for years, someone you see every day, or someone you don't really think you have much in common with (or even so much in common with that there's nothing new). Ask questions from the standpoint of not presuming you know the answer. People are complex and individual, meaning that every moment they have lived offers something different to a moment you have lived. So, listen and learn.

How to do it:

- Focus on exploratory questions: Do they seem relaxed and then appear more anxious when the topic changes? What does this tell you about their experiences around this topic? Do they become really animated about particular subjects? What does this tell you about their passions and interests? Has anything you've said altered the way they act, or the mood they seem to be in? What does this tell you about your interaction?

- Have the objective of learning a new piece of information in every conversation you have with anyone, from a shop assistant to a best friend.

- Engage with more people to create a network of knowledge and piece together information from different angles.

- Write down who you've spoken to and what you've learnt over the course of a week, and look back at it at the end of the seven days. Take note of your observations.

Week Tried (date): Score: /10

Observations:

Tip: This connection characteristic can be a useful approach with someone you don't get on well with, find frustrating, or think you have nothing in common with. Try learning and understanding more about them and their situation. It will help you to connect more effectively with them, and the results may surprise you.

CONNECTION CHARACTERISTIC 4: SEE IT THROUGH THEIR EYES

Try to truly understand the experience the other person has lived through, asking them questions and offering understanding and respect. Really put yourself in their shoes.

- Gather as much information about the person and the situation as possible (using the connection characteristics above). This will help you to build up a better picture of what it feels like to stand in their shoes.

- Share similarities with the other person, but be careful (see below). If done in the right way, sharing commonalities can build a bond, especially if you share what you're feeling or show your vulnerabilities (watch Brené Brown's TED talk for more on this[19]).

- Pursue opportunities to volunteer or spend time with different people and experiences. Offer to help in a charity. Or if you're the leader of your company or senior in your organization, spend a day working on the shop floor, actually doing the job of your lowest-paid workers. This helps you to put aside stereotypes and judgments and to develop a greater level of understanding, empathy, and patience with people who live a different life to you.

- Write down who you've spoken to and what you've learnt over the course of a week.

   Week Tried (date): Score: /10

Observations:

A word of warning: making comparisons can unintentionally appear competitive or undermining, for instance if someone tells you they've just done their first 10km run and in your excitement you tell them about the fifth marathon you ran. Or, worse still, it can be disrespectful: if someone has just lost a parent, don't tell them you lost your grandparent, friend, or relative last year. Something as deeply personal as this is different for everybody and offering comparisons can feel hurtful and inappropriate. Instead, offer empathy, concern, and support.

CONNECTION CHARACTERISTIC 5: BE REWARDING TO DEAL WITH

Tomas Chamorro-Premuzic, professor of business at University College London, comments that "people who are more employable and successful in their career tend to be more rewarding to deal with."[20] I often say to hiring clients that, while we should do all we can to eliminate bias when assessing a candidate, when it comes down to it, the person who is most likeable will always have the balance tipped in their favor. Be more likeable, be cooperative and helpful, show more compassion toward others, be more friendly, trusting, and unselfish. Listen so that people feel like they've been heard. If you really listen with the right intentions, the person you are talking to will feel understood and valued. In return this will open doors for you. The more you try this and interact with different people, the more you will be able to refine your social skills.

How to do it:

- Make a commitment to smile at and talk to at least five people you don't know each day.

- Help someone out in some way every day.

- Give people the sort of attention you would like to receive: look them in the eyes, be attentive, and listen with intent.

- Write down who you've spoken to and what you've learnt over the course of a week.

Week Tried (date): Score: /10

Observations:

Rank how you found the connection characteristics in the list below. Then think through how you will commit to incorporating your number 1 ranking into your daily routine. Capture that as a statement, because writing it down will help you to engage with it. It will also give you something you can check back on to assess your progress or remind you of what you wanted to do.

My ranking of connection characteristics:

1.

2.

3.

4.

5.

I will incorporate the top-ranked connection characteristic into my daily routine by:

Starting on:

Whichever approach works best for you when it comes to connection, the key thing to remember is to make time and keep your reacting brain in check. Listen: listen to learn, listen to understand, and listen to feel. Let go of your own agenda and allow your remarkable brain to operate at its best. Amazing things will happen.

TOOLS OF THE SESSION

Putting It into Practice

Although you will get a sense of whether you are connecting with people better by doing the above activity, connection operates in two directions. The only way you're going to fully understand and have a benchmark from which to improve is to ask for feedback. Try the pointers above and then assess how you're doing by asking someone questions like these:

• Do you feel like I'm present when I'm talking to you?

• Do I listen effectively?

• Was it different to our normal conversations (i.e., when you were trying one of the techniques above)? How?

• What do I do well in conversation? What could I do better?

Work out what works best for you—build on the positives and work on any negatives. You may find it helpful to incorporate the outcomes of this into your statement above (i.e., "I will incorporate the top-ranked . . .").

Coming to the End of the Session

In this session, we've explored the topic of meaning, a huge subject that you started considering in the context of your values, passions, interests, and your story so far. These begin to build up a picture of what meaning means to you, which we'll explore further in Part III. We've also looked at the role that connection has in creating meaning, how important connection is, and how you can improve your connection with others, making time to block out the fast-paced world around you to allow your brain to work at its best.

In the next session, we'll be looking at your makeup using a psychometric test that measures the greatly researched and widely accepted theory of personality known as the Big Five. Psychologists use this measure globally to help people understand their psyche or makeup in more depth. It will help you to understand your strengths better and also work on your areas of weakness (or as I call them, areas for awareness and areas for development). We'll then use this together with the values, passions, and interests you have just identified to further define what meaning means to you.

PART II

Collecting

CHAPTER 5

Psychometrics

● ● ●

Psychometric measurement is a tool that psychologists use to get more insight into who someone is and how they approach things, either from a cognitive perspective in terms of working out problems (ability tests) or from the perspective of who they are as a person (personality). For the purposes of this book we're just going to look at personality, so you don't need to worry about brushing up your verbal reasoning or numeracy. Personality tests are preference based, they have no right or wrong answers; instead, they are simply a reflection of how you respond to different situations. As we have seen in the preceding sessions, by the time you have passed through emerging adulthood your personality becomes more consistent and therefore we're able to measure it more effectively. For example, someone you knew at university or college as being outgoing, creative, and strong willed is likely still to be outgoing, creative, and strong willed by the time they reach their 30s, 40s, or 50s. That's not to say, however, that you can't start exploring your personality using psychometrics earlier in life. They will provide you with useful insights and something to reflect back on over time regardless of when you complete them.

Psychometric tests are used in a range of environments, predominantly in professional, educational, criminal, and mental health settings. They are considered a hugely beneficial tool for businesses, being used by around 70% of UK companies with over 50 employees[1] and around 80% of the Fortune 500 companies in the US.[2] When looking specifically at personality, they can help to find out a person's preferences and motivational drivers, and provide a prediction of how they will behave in different contexts. And when used by psychologists as part of profiling, they can provide information that will help decipher who will thrive in a given role or situation, as well as pinpointing where individuals need help and support in terms of development.

In this session, you will get the opportunity to complete a psychometric tool and receive an individually tailored output. It will be constructed by a computer program using advanced algorithms, so, although it's going to provide an in-depth look at your personality, it will be completely confidential. No one will see it except for you—unless of course you want someone else to take a look. It's not the typical questionnaire you will find online (we'll look at why in a little more detail below) and would normally not be available without expensive intervention by a psychologist or trained practitioner. In that sense this test is unique: it is a rare opportunity to access an advanced tool, with a bespoke output, without the need for assistance. The report provided is expertly constructed and will give you the chance to build on the insights you have reflected on so far, boosting your self-awareness and refining your focus for development and growth.

Psychometrics and Psychological Measurement

Psychological measurement is a hugely complex practice, so much so that some people focus their whole academic career on the study and development of psychometrics. Psychometric assessments are not just questionnaires or quick quizzes like you find in magazines, they are put together through rigorous and advanced statistical analysis, considering vast amounts of data on behavior to create tests that on the surface are straightforward and easy to use, yet measure highly complex variables. To be academically and professionally recognized, tests need to have reliability and validity. Reliability means that the measure has been statistically tested to ensure that it's consistent across time, different individuals, and different situations. Test validity means that it measures what it sets out to measure, so if part of a test intends to look at extraversion, for example, that is indeed what it measures, rather than mixing that up with other aspects of personality such as conscientiousness. Psychometric assessments are also based on rigorously tested theories of personality. As a result, they require trained practitioners or psychologists to interpret them and give feedback on them, making access to the tool you'll be using here a valuable opportunity. The good news is that what you have to fill in is not at all complex, and the process should be both enjoyable and interesting.

As we're looking specifically at personality, it will be useful to provide a definition. Going back to the early roots of its study, it is defined as:

[a] set of relatively stable and general dynamic, emotional and affective characteristics of an individual's way of being, in his/ her way to react to the situations in which s/he is.[3]

Your personality is what distinguishes you from the next person, what makes you unique. It's the part of you that lies at the core, the bit that feels more genetic and less adaptable. You can modify your personality, but it will take a great deal of focused effort, effort that could be more usefully employed paying attention to areas for awareness, areas for development, or simply refining the way in which you do things. As well as highlighting your strengths and even hidden assets, the test you're about to take should allow you gain a better understanding of the less positive aspects of your personality, so that you can modify them or understand the impact they have on other people and try to mitigate that.

There are a range of personality models, but the vast majority tend to agree on the fact that there are five stable dimensions of personality that are relevant cross-culturally. These are sometimes known as the Big Five dimensions or the Super Traits, Openness to experience, Conscientiousness, Extraversion, Emotion, and Agreeableness, which I describe in more detail later in this session. If you've taken psychometric tests before you may have come across different labels or representation, but these underpin the majority of tools. The psychometric assessment you have access to via this book, known as Credo, is consistent with this model.

Credo

Credo is a personality measure that is designed to collect and summarize information about your preferences, interests, emotions, and style of relating to others in line with the Big Five. It is available to you for free as a reader of this book at the link below. It has been developed by Tests Direct, a group of chartered psychologists and professionals who have extensive experience in assessment, development, and psychometric test construction. Credo is distinctive in how it maps and analyzes personality, looking in particular for elements essential in leadership such as assertiveness, emotional intelligence, and resilience to stress, and it's also able to detect signs of burnout, obsessiveness, and even narcissism. The senior leaders I work with often have a good understanding of their basic makeup, having been through various assessment and development situations throughout their career. So it can be useful for them to look beyond the biographical part of the profile to explore aspects of how they behave under pressure, how they respond to stress, what risks are associated with their behavior, and how they are likely to behave in certain circumstances that are relevant to successful leadership. This information is useful for anyone wanting to gain a deeper level of self-insight.

When you go to the link you will work through the Credo test considering various statements, which may or may not apply to you, and indicating how you feel about each of them. It will take you about 25–30 minutes to complete, but there is no time limit and you won't be measured on how fast or slow you are. It is generally better to undertake it all in one go, but you can spread the test over two or more sittings if necessary, saving your answers from one session to the next. In order to get the most accurate representation of who you are, try not to spend too long deliberating on any of the questions and be as truthful as you can. There aren't any hidden meanings, so avoid thinking about any of the questions too deeply—if in doubt, go with your first reaction.

To register for the test, go to

https://www.tests-direct.com/defining-you

The Credo test is provided to you by Tests Direct Ltd.

You will need to fill in some information about yourself. The use of this information falls under the UK's data protection laws and will be held securely and confidentially.

THE CREDO QUESTIONS

Box 5.1 is an example of the type of question you can expect to encounter. In each case you will be asked to indicate the extent to which you agree or disagree with a statement by clicking on the button to the left of your selected response. If you select an answer and then wish to change it, you can do so by clicking on the new answer instead, but you won't be able to alter your response once you have moved on to the next question.

MY IMAGINATION OFTEN RUNS AWAY WITH ME

○ Agree
○ Tend to agree
○ Neither agree nor disagree
○ Tend to disagree
○ Disagree

Box 5.1 Sample question

When you have answered all of the questions, you will receive a personalized report that affords you an opportunity to explore your personality without the need for input from a qualified psychologist or professional. This instrument employs an expert system that produces the reports using a complex, multilevel algorithm, which means you are able to go through results without guidance. Don't worry about the complexity, though: the report itself is written in user-friendly language and includes questions to help you explore your outputs in more depth if you want to. Boxes 5.2 and 5.3 give examples of the summary output and one of the detailed pages to give you a feel for what the report looks like.

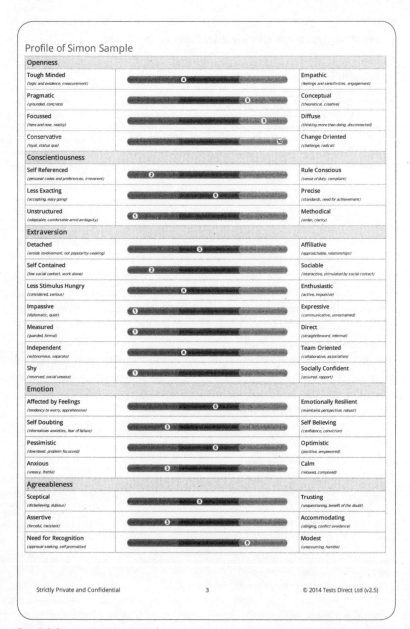

Box 5.2 Summary page example

Relationship Building

At work people typically operate within a team, or among a broader group (or network) of colleagues and contacts. This area relates to interacting effectively, and contributing towards the attainment of goals in agreement and co-ordination with others. People vary in the extent to which they accommodate others' ideas, demonstrate warmth, and are committed to a team ethos, and personality can significantly influence these behaviours. Relevant scales are shown below.

Detached	5	Affiliative
Assertive	3	Accommodating
Independent	4	Team Oriented
Measured	1	Direct
Self Contained	2	Sociable
Tough Minded	4	Empathic
Need for Recognition	6	Modest

You describe an average level of need for involvement with others. This suggests that, whilst clearly not being aloof or indifferent, you are likely to be fairly pragmatic in the way you build relationships. This is of course not unusual. You are likely to put effort into maintaining and enhancing relationships if there is some objective, role-related reason for doing so. The quality of your relationships with others may therefore vary from one person to the next.

The way you describe yourself here suggests you make a fairly clear distinction between your professional and personal existences. You are not likely to over-identify with others to the point where your judgement is undermined by sentimental considerations, or on the other hand to come across as distant and unapproachable.

From a developmental perspective it may be useful to consider:

Q. Are there times when I need to put more effort into enhancing relationships than comes naturally to me?

Responses elsewhere suggest you may be driven more by a need for power and authority than for affiliation per se. Your relationships with others at work are therefore likely to reflect a concern to influence rather than a desire for involvement. There is a suggestion here that a degree of competitiveness may at times characterize your working relationships. Though you might do it, it would probably go against your instincts to suspend your own agenda to accommodate a colleague.

Box 5.3 Example of detailed content

As you will see, the detail that sits behind the summary explains the output in more depth and encourages you to explore your results through further questions.

While I did not write this psychometric test and do not work with Tests Direct, we have agreed to collaborate for the purposes of this book. I strongly endorse the rigor and approach of Credo and the way in which the reports are written. Psychometric assessments can risk boxing people in, saying people are something that doesn't feel at all like a match with who they are. If that happens it's essential that they are explained by someone who understands them, you, and the context in which they are being applied. Credo avoids this danger by its thoughtfully constructed breakdown and questions that enable you to have control over exploring the outputs.

THE BIG FIVE DIMENSIONS

As I explained earlier, Credo is based on what are known as the Big Five dimensions of personality. Being aware of what each of the dimensions on the first Credo scale is considering will help you with your interpretation.

Openness

This dimension refers to openness to experience: how imaginative, cultured, curious, original, broad-minded, and artistically focused you are. It has also been described as reflecting the depth and complexity of your mental life and experiences,[4] how willing you are to try new things, to think outside the box, and to challenge accepted ways of doing things, as well as how prepared you are to experience your emotions rather than shutting them down by focusing predominantly on logic. If you are low on the Openness scale, you are more likely to prefer routine, concentrating on the reality of situations, sticking to what you know, and conforming to the status quo.

Conscientiousness

If you are high on the Conscientiousness scale you are likely to be more rule conscious, wanting to comply with expectations of how things are done, to be more precise and have high standards and a need to achieve specific goals, preferring order and clarity. If you fall at the other end of the spectrum you are probably more laid back, easygoing, unstructured, able to cope with ambiguity, able to adapt to different circumstances, and happy to make your own rules.

Extraversion

This is the dimension with which people are generally most familiar, although its true meaning can be misconstrued. Extraversion and introversion are about where you get your energy from, not how socially adept you are. For example, it's possible to be introverted and gregarious, outgoing, and socially adept, but because you are introverted you prefer to recharge your batteries by spending time alone. Equally, an extravert can be quiet and unassuming, but love being in the middle of crowded social interactions, because that's where they get their energy from. Credo helpfully breaks this dimension down into a range of sub-elements to prevent it from being misunderstood. The report looks at how much you avoid contact with other people or how far you get stuck into social situations and relationships, to what extent you prefer to work alone or prefer social contact when you're working, how considered you are or on the other hand how impulsive, whether you are quiet or more chatty and unable to keep your thoughts to yourself, if you are guarded about yourself and personal information or more open, and how shy or socially confident you are. This breakdown gives a much clearer understanding of what introversion and extraversion mean to you personally.

Emotion

Some people describe Emotion as relating to how comfortable you are in your own skin. If you are high on this scale, you are more likely to worry or become anxious, to be self-critical and doubt yourself, and you may also be more pessimistic. Typically, these are seen as less positive traits when it comes to succeeding, but I see these factors (with the exception of pessimism) frequently in senior leaders. The worry and anxiety drive them to succeed. I'm not suggesting this is a good way of operating, especially not when it comes to mental well-being, but I would highlight that these factors shouldn't necessarily be seen as adverse when it comes to achieving in life.

Agreeableness

This is the final dimension of the Big Five. If you are high on the Agreeableness scale you are more likely to be trusting of others, to give people the benefit of the doubt, to be accommodating, to avoid conflict, and to be more modest, unassuming, and humble. If you are lower on this scale you are more likely to be skeptical of others' intentions, be more forceful and insistent on your own perspective, and have a higher need to be recognized by others for what you have achieved.

INTERPRETING YOUR RESULTS

With any of these scales, try not to get too hung up on the language. If one of your scales highlights something you don't recognize in yourself or doesn't strongly resonate with who you are, it could be that you have a different understanding of the wording. You'll have a chance to explore any anomalies with someone you trust in a way that's explained in the next session, "Gathering Insights." Also note that high scores are not good or bad, and nor are low scores; they are simply a way of describing where you lie on a scale of preferences. However, if you are at the far end of a particular scale, realistically it will be more difficult for you to shift to the other end of the scale.

Psychologist Paul Sinclair, who pioneered and co-launched the UK's first Big Five personality profiling system in 1990, also cautions that it's the combination of these factors, not the individual scales or sub-scales, which defines someone's personality. He explains:

> *Looking at a single scale in isolation tells us hardly anything, and can be very misleading.*
> *For example:*
> *Although a creative (nonconformist) has the intellectual ability to be creative, if their nonconformity is combined with introversion and low confidence, they may not express their creative thoughts and ideas.*
> *A creative (nonconformist) who is also extravert, confident and unstructured (low detail-conscious), will not only express their ideas but may also propose quite impractical suggestions . . .*
> *Be careful not to read too much into these single-word descriptions—they provide a rough guide.*[5]

Any insight that emerges from a psychometric assessment needs to be explored in the context of the individual and the environment, because these factors can dramatically change the outcomes. Take someone who comes out as an introvert on the Big Five scale: you cannot immediately assume from this that they are shy, quiet, or reserved. People are often surprised to find out that I am mildly introverted, because I'm gregarious, talkative, love parties, will chat to anyone, and am comfortable with public speaking. But I also prefer time alone to recharge, like to talk to people one to one if I get the chance, and dip in and out of group and team activities. When you look at your own output you need to consider these different nuances rather than just taking it at face value—a lot has to do with how you piece the information together and what context you are looking at it within. The Credo results will help you do this by asking questions, which also supports how I use psychometrics. In profiling sessions, I use such measures as much as a point for exploring hypotheses with the client as to offer an answer to specific questions around leadership. In short, you shouldn't view the output of psychometric testing in a black-and-white manner, but rather explore it based on yourself as a person and the situation you find yourself in. That way it can be hugely helpful and positive in providing you with further insights into who you are.

Coming to the End of the Session

This session has considered psychometric tests and how they differ from questionnaires you may find on the internet or in a magazine. We've also explored the dimensions of the most widely accepted measure of personality, the Big Five. Most importantly, you have now had the chance to explore your own personality directly using the Credo psychometric measure, which aligns with the Big Five.

In the next session, we'll be looking at how you can gather insights into your behavior from people you interact with regularly. This will be particularly helpful in terms of exploring the outputs captured in your personal Credo report and thinking through the impact they may have on the way you operate on a day-to-day basis: what you do well, what you need to be more aware of, and what you may want to think about modifying. The report will also provide you with data to build on in Chapter 7, where you will pull together core themes in your personality, values, passions, and the areas you would like to focus on developing in order to achieve your goals and overall vision.

CHAPTER 6

Gathering Insights

• • •

So far you have explored your past and searched your story for patterns and meaning, examined your capabilities in a whole range of areas, and invested a great deal of effort into understanding yourself better. This has hopefully given you a better level of insight and self-awareness to build on further. The next step is to look beyond your own opinion to gain insight into others' viewpoints.

In order to get a really honest and balanced perspective, to gain accurate self-knowledge about who you are, you need to know what other people see. You're going to shift from looking inward to looking outward by asking people for their feedback. This can feel daunting, but you'll most likely find that in a number of areas other people have a much more positive view than you have of yourself. This will help grow your confidence and understanding of your strengths. On the other hand, there may be areas in what they say that highlight blind spots, behaviors that you're not conscious of and haven't been aware of their impact on other people. For example, you may have unwittingly been doing something very minor that is undermining someone else's confidence. The knowledge means you can do something about it.

The key reason why it's important to understand how others see you is to align your internal view with the external reality. This improves your self-awareness, which will help you build on your strengths and understand how to work on your areas for development. A higher level of self-awareness also provides a platform from which to grow your emotional wisdom, and as such can dramatically improve your ability to influence, because accurate self-awareness makes it much easier to navigate social situations effectively. In turn, this has a positive impact on skills critical to leadership and also to success and fulfillment in life more broadly. Let me give you an example.

About Me

When my observing brain is keeping my reacting brain in check, I'm pretty good at reading other people; it is, after all, what I do for a living. But when I'm out socially, my reacting brain can get a little overexcited by the situation (after all, I'm not at work, it's my playtime). I am quite a passionate and animated person and I know from what friends have told me that when I'm socializing I can unintentionally interrupt people and talk over them. Had I never had feedback on this, I might have remained unaware of this tendency, but because I am aware of it I can work hard in those situations to keep my observing brain in the driving seat; and if I slip up, this awareness means that I can at least apologize for my tendency. This is much better than continually talking over people.

The information you gather through this session may mean altering the way you construct your own narrative or lead to you changing your behavior, so that you represent yourself to others in a way that more closely aligns with your self-identity. However, you can see from the example that this information should be more about fine-tuning than anything that comes as dramatic news to you. Research shows that on average we see ourselves in a way that aligns with how other people see us, but that given different circumstances and people the view will alter and the precise detail will differ.

We'll go into a little more depth about why you should ask for others' views, then walk through some tips on how to gather them in a way that gives you constructive information. Asking people for their opinion on you can feel quite scary, but there are ways of doing it that make the actual act of requesting it easier, as well as minimizing the chance of getting messages that you may struggle to deal with. We'll explore how to ask for more personal feedback, and I'll encourage you to discuss the psychometric output you obtained in the previous session with someone you trust. It's worth making the effort to do this, as the techniques that enable you to understand people's opinion of you will provide you with tools that you can use for the rest of your life.

Why Get Feedback?

Put simply, if you don't get feedback, you don't know if you're going in the right direction to achieve your goals. That goal could be anything from picking up a dirty top from the floor to becoming leader of an organization. For example, my prime goal is to help people gain a better understanding of psychology. Although this is my work goal, it's also my broader vision and has an influence in every area of my life. So if I talk over everyone in every social situation, it's going to negatively affect my progress toward my goal, whereas knowing about my tendency and its impact helps me realign my behavior to engage people more effectively when I'm "on topic."

There's a classic experiment used in team-building workshops that clearly demonstrates the need for feedback to achieve goals. A volunteer is positioned in front of a basket and blindfolded, then they are turned around a few times to disorientate them. Next the volunteer is given three balls to throw into the basket. No one else in the room is allowed to say or do anything to help them. Typically, all three throws will miss; once they have been blindfolded and turned around, the volunteer has no idea where the basket is. The exercise is repeated, but this time the other members of the group are able to give them verbal instructions. On the second attempt the volunteer will usually get at least one ball into the basket, and often all three. It's a quick and simple way to demonstrate that we cannot operate blind, with no information from others. Unless someone is telling us where we are when it comes to our goals and behavior, we don't know how or what to alter in order to get things right, to achieve what we want, or to be how we want to be.

Feedback is essential to performance in all walks of life, from sport (e.g., the score in a match, video analysis of an athlete in action), to business (e.g., how the company is performing in the marketplace, what a boss says about an employee's work), to our personal lives (e.g., comments on our appearance, a partner telling us what they want from the relationship). It's also critical to our well-being, optimal performance, and success in whatever we pursue.

FEEDBACK, PERFORMANCE, AND THE BRAIN

The study of feedback is called cybernetics, which comes from the Greek word for "to steer" (this makes sense if you think about the example of steering the person toward the basket). Norbert Wiener is renowned for bringing cybernetics into the modern world, writing a book in 1948 entitled *Cybernetics: Control and Communication in the Animal and Machine*,[1] which asserts that with feedback we (or artificial intelligence in the case of machines) can control the outcome to achieve our desired goal. Feedback promotes learning, and that learning can be focused on controlling an action in pursuit of a specific goal.

When it comes to behavioral feedback, it isn't as straightforward as simply directing someone to throw a ball into a basket. Neuroscience is allowing us to see what types of feedback work and what don't. The traditional form of performance management in business is now known to be incompatible with our brain, for example. Ranking and rating people against one another are threatening to the primitive, reacting part of our brain and create a flight-or-fight response. While in sport this allows increased activation of muscles and a physical response, in an environment where that physical release isn't possible (e.g., sitting at your desk) it creates high levels of stress and diverts blood flow away from the helpful, rational, observing brain. This in turn impairs judgment and prevents the very change in behavior required to perform more optimally, because the part of the brain that needs to alter the behavior isn't in control.[2]

The other problem with many existing performance management systems is that they look at behavior from the perspective that talent and intellect are fixed. Yet this is not true. We are all, within reason, capable of growth and change, given the right motivations and understanding. And approaching feedback with what Stanford University psychologist Carol Dweck has famously termed a "growth mindset" enables the information received to have a positive impact.[3] Dweck uses neuroscientific research to explain that there are two possible mindsets: fixed and growth. With a fixed mindset, we approach feedback from the belief that our performance is based on capabilities that are dictated by our intelligence and talents, that they are part of who we are and unchangeable (i.e., reflecting traditional performance management systems). We are fearful that we'll be compared to others, that we'll be rejected from the group for not being good enough (which creates a threat response in the primitive brain), and that we are not in control. When we approach with this mindset, we are in survival mode, our brain is looking to protect us, so we are less open to or even capable of learning, because we are operating from our reacting rather than our observing brain.

At the other end of the spectrum, if we accept the research that shows our brain is still moldable or plastic whatever our age, then we can adopt a growth mindset. From this perspective, we understand that our performance is based on hard work, experience, and effort rather than something that is out of our control. This allows us to approach feedback from the observing brain, to take it on board and learn from it, adapt our behavior, and be less afraid of taking risks and making mistakes, both of which are critical for growth. It's important for you to keep this in mind when you're thinking about the information you gather on yourself. We'll also look at a method for collecting it that enables more of a growth mindset response.

My Moments of Feedback

A number of years ago I was running a workshop for about 30 people which involved presenting to the whole group between breakout sessions. The presentation was given in an open room, with the audience spread out in three wide rows facing the front. After one particular presentation, we broke into smaller groups with the aim of getting feedback from one another. I included myself in this to demonstrate that you don't have to have known someone very long to give or receive feedback, and also to show that it isn't as daunting as it might feel.

More than one person gave me the same piece of data, which was simple but immensely helpful. Throughout the workshop, I had only been presenting to the right-hand side of the room, completely missing any eye contact with people sitting on the left. I had been oblivious to this and was slightly stunned by the revelation.

When we went back into the main session, I made a conscious effort to speak to the left-hand side of the room as well as the right. What was interesting was that it did take effort, it wasn't simple, which told me that I must have been doing this for some time, possibly over the many years I'd been presenting, yet no one had told me. If I hadn't asked for feedback I still might not know, but having asked I've since been able to change my behavior.

P.S. If you ever see me present and notice I'm only focused on the right-hand side of the room, feel free to tell me!

TOOLS OF THE SESSION

Asking for Feedback

There are many different ways of asking for feedback, but I recently came across one that I've found really helpful as a simple yet effective method for getting constructive pointers. It's from a book called *The Success Principles* by Jack Canfield and Janet Smitzer.[4] I introduced this to a CEO I'm working with and he's used it with the company's owners, nonexecutive directors, his direct reports, and people who work for him throughout the organization. He finds it easy and incredibly helpful.

On a scale of 1 to 10, how would you rate _____ during the last week?

Insert in the blank whatever you'd like feedback on, for example the service I've provided you with, the way I present to the board, how I come across to customers, how I am as a parent. You can also use whatever timescale works for you.

You can vary the question to focus on whatever you're looking to get input on, for instance:

- On a scale of 1 to 10, how would you rate the meeting we just had?

- On a scale of 1 to 10, how would you rate me as a manager since our last review?

- On a scale of 1 to 10, how would you rate me as a parent?

- On a scale of 1 to 10, how would you rate me as a teacher this year?

- On a scale of 1 to 10, how would you rate this deal?

- On a scale of 1 to 10, how would you rate this book so far?

For any answer that gets less than 10 ask:

What would it take to make it a 10?

This gives people the opportunity to explain why it's not a 10 and to give helpful and constructive information without worrying about offending you.

For example, one Sunday morning while writing this book, I asked my husband: "On a scale of 1 to 10, how would you rate the morning so far?" His response was 6.5. So my next question was: "What would make it a 10?" His answers were:

- Having had breakfast together

- You having had more sleep so you weren't so tired

- The lawnmower not breaking

This was really useful information. First, I had no idea that my husband wanted to have breakfast together; the second point made me realize that he is aware that I'm tired and cares about that; and the third—well, there's not much I can do there, but at least I understand his frustration.

BEFORE YOU GET STARTED

Consider who
Think about who you ask for feedback, especially until you get into the swing of things. You want people who are not going to squirm with discomfort, who aren't just going to give you a 10 (which may feel nice, but isn't going to help at all), who understand what you're asking of them, and who want to help.

Set the stage
Help the person giving you input by explaining why you are asking them for it and what you hope to do with it. For example, you might want to say:

I'm working on my personal development and it would really help me to get some honest feedback about how I can improve the way I do things. Do you mind if I ask you some questions? I'm interested in your opinion, and would appreciate it if you can be as honest as you can.

Engage your observing brain

Try not to argue or debate. Some of the information may feel like a personal criticism, but it isn't. Try to remember that you asked for their views for a reason: arguing or debating is not going to help you learn, and will also make the person providing their thoughts feel uncomfortable and reluctant to give you their views again. Listen and keep your reacting brain in check. If you don't agree with what they say, just reply, "I really appreciate you telling me that." If you don't fully understand, don't be afraid to ask for more information. But overall, the best response is usually simply to say thank you (it's really important to show your appreciation, because giving feedback isn't easy).

If you get stuck with any of what they tell you, it might be useful to ask yourself: How does this information help me to improve? How can I use this to become better at what I want to do, or move toward my goal or purpose? Try reframing the information you've been given to be within your control.

TOOLS OF THE SESSION

Turning Feedback into Action

For small pieces of feedback like the tips I was given on presentation, you can do something with it straightaway. This immediately brings a greater level of impact and makes it more likely that change will take hold. If it's something that you do every day, then put a reminder in your phone or calendar to prompt you to do it.

For feedback that requires a greater level of behavioral change, for example having more gravitas in meetings, use the development plan in Chapter 7 to help you turn the information you've gathered into actionable outputs and make changes.

Discussing Your Psychometrics

Start with the less personal type of feedback before going into elements that are very specific to who you are as a person. It's best, for example, to stick with the first two scales, conscientiousness and openness, asking questions like:

- "How effective is my approach to organizing?"

- "How focused on routine do you think I am and what's the outcome of that?"

You may find this easier than going straight in to how you come across at an interpersonal level and what your impact on others is (i.e., the extraversion, emotion, and agreeableness scales).

In a typical profiling session, the client would spend time discussing their psychometric results with the psychologist to help them understand what they mean, the patterns, and what they want to do with the output. If you have completed the psychometric test in the previous session, it would be really helpful for you to go through the results with someone you trust and feel will be supportive but honest with you. This will give you another perspective on the output. For example, if your results reveal that you're less conscientious than you think of yourself as being, they may make you feel uncomfortable or disappointed, but if you discuss this with someone else you might uncover the reason for the discrepancy. For example, you may find that it's because you're feeling disengaged at work at the moment, not because you have become less focused on things that really matter to you.

If you haven't filled in the psychometric test, you can move straight on to the following section, "Asking for More Personal Feedback," which will also provide you with some really helpful insights.

TOOLS OF THE SESSION

Discussing Your Personality

Go through your psychometric results with a pen or highlighter. Mark the parts that really resonate with you with + or your chosen color of highlighter, and the parts that make you feel uncomfortable with – or a different color.

Give a friend a blank copy of your results and ask them to do the same, putting + (or the same color as you've chosen) for the parts that resonate with them about you, and – (or the second color) by the parts that don't.

Take a look at the results from your review and your friend's. Do they look the same?

Where the results overlap, discuss the elements marked with + that are really true to who you are. What are the implications of that? How do these areas make you special and unique?

Are there any negative implications—do these factors hold you back in any way or upset other people (which in turn will hold you back)? Is there an easy way for you to modify this behavior, or is it something that is integral to who you are?

If you can modify it, take note so you can explore it in more detail later in the book. For now, just having a greater awareness of it will help to mitigate any negative impacts, even if it's something you may struggle to change.

Are there any differences between your review and your friend's? Discuss why this is the case and what it may tell you about yourself. Maybe it's because your friend only sees you in certain circumstances, or because they have their own biases that are influencing the way they view things. Or maybe there is a discrepancy between how you think about yourself and how other people see you. It may be worth exploring this further with other people, asking for specific feedback using the approach discussed in the last section.

Tip: If you feel that the feedback you're given represents something that you really cannot change, consider doing the following.

Explain the tendency to people. Then ask someone close to you, either at work or in your personal life, to check you when you're doing it. When they do so, take a deep breath and try to think before reacting.

Where you both have marked responses as not sounding at all like who you are, it may be that you misunderstood the question that was being asked by the psychometric test, or that it doesn't give the whole picture of how this behavior displays itself in you.

Where there are differences between your review and your friend's, ask them to explain where they have seen this behavior. Try not to get angry with your friend for telling you: they are there to help you and provide you with the information (although it's easy to see them as the source). Instead, consider and discuss why you may see this behavior differently to the way other people do.

This might be an area you want to explore further by getting more feedback from people, you might prefer to reflect on it and decide what you want to do with it, or you may opt to leave it. It's up to you. This is your journey.

Asking for More Personal Feedback

If you have found this session useful so far, you may want to take your feedback further still, requesting opinions on more personal aspects of who you are (i.e., when it comes to the Credo, elements that refer to extraversion, emotion, and agreeableness). This may mean asking questions such as:

- "Would you say that I come across as worrisome?"

- "Do you think I'm more of an optimist or a pessimist? What impact do you think that has on the people around me?"

- "Would you describe me as someone who is impulsive? When have you seen me being like that and how does it make you feel when I am?"

This isn't for everyone, so if it makes you feel very uncomfortable then don't do it. However, if you do decide to pursue further information on your personality, be careful, quite simply because it is so personal. You're doing it to help you improve and grow, but you don't want to fall apart in the process or it will all become a pointless exercise. Equally, remember you need to consider the feelings of the person you're asking: giving someone feedback isn't easy, which is why we don't do it more naturally.

The benefits of asking for more intimate feedback are twofold. First, you gain from understanding more about yourself, which will help you grow as a person and move toward your self-development goals. Second, it creates a greater bond between you and the person you're asking. It shows that you value their opinion and you trust them. In fact, if you ask for their views and respond in a constructive way by altering your behavior, it will build the self-esteem of the person you're asking. They will see that you have enough respect for what they say to actually take action on it.

Think through who you get feedback from. Choose someone you trust, but also be careful not to ask someone who tends to see life as a glass half empty—this could and probably will unduly skew the information they give you. Also consider whether the person you're asking has their own agenda: maybe they're envious of you, or they're someone who doesn't know you well enough to comment. Such people are best avoided for this exercise.

TOOLS OF THE SESSION

Asking for Personal Feedback

Remember to set the stage and engage your observing brain, as you did in the earlier activity.

These questions are a useful guide to asking for more personal feedback:

- What am I good at?

- What am I not so good at?

- What three adjectives describe my best traits?

- What three adjectives describe my worst traits?

- What role do I play in people's lives?

The conversations that stem from these questions may be tough and bring to light views that are disconnected with how you see yourself. This will naturally make you defensive, but remember to try to keep your reacting brain in check and employ your observing, listening brain. Ultimately, you'll gain a lot more from this exercise if you do. Ask more questions to understand what specific situations have led the person to describe you in this way. That will help you to understand more fully and then make a decision (using your observing brain) if you would like to work on modifying that behavior or leave things as they are.

The SARAH Model

I sometimes use a particular model as a way of helping people understand how they may respond, adapt to, and integrate feedback into who they are, into their narrative and identity. Originally adapted from the Kubler-Ross change curve, the SARAH model[5] (Figure 6.1) is an abbreviation for the following stages:

Shock
Anger
Resistance
Acceptance
Hope

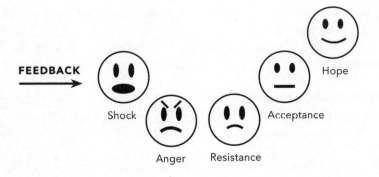

Figure 6.1. The SARAH model: Possible stages of emotion passed through following feedback

Typically, when encountering news that is a little unsettling, people pass through the phases shown in the model from S to H. However, you may move between different stages, skip stages, get stuck, or even jump straight to the last two.

SHOCK
You may react with shock or denial when you first hear something about yourself that doesn't fit with your internal narrative or personal identity.

ANGER

Once the shock has passed, you may feel angry or upset, take the comments to heart, or feel like you are being criticized. This is an emotion and you need to ride it out the best you can. Use the emotion surfing technique from Chapter 3 and try to observe your reacting brain, rather than engaging with it.

RESISTANCE OR REJECTION

You may become defensive. Although you've asked for the feedback, the actual message could be difficult to swallow. The primitive part of your brain wants to protect who you are, so survival mechanisms move into place and you respond with your reacting brain. Your observing brain will engage with your reacting brain to start producing reasons why it's not your fault and preparing you to reject what you've heard. However, this won't let you move forward and grow. Give yourself a bit of time out doing something you enjoy, preferably being physically active and being outside, such as going for a walk or a run. If that doesn't appeal, then find something else you like doing, such as social-izing with friends or even watching your favorite film. Then put the information aside for a few days and reconsider it at a later date. This will give your brain a chance to process it at a subconscious level and see it from a more objective perspective when you return to it.

ACCEPTANCE

Once you have come to terms with the feedback and you are ready to do something with it or live with it, you reach the acceptance stage. This enables you to start integrating the information into who you are. You may go straight to this stage without passing through any of the others.

HOPE

At this point of the cycle, you are able to move forward and act on the feedback. Yet it's still important to remember that change takes time. Once you've accepted the information you've been given and are doing something with it, it will still take a little time for the neural pathways in your brain to adapt. You may well keep going back to the old behavior, but that's OK, it's just a case of persistently addressing it until you create new neural pathways in your brain.

What to Do with the Feedback

You may not react emotionally to the views you are offered, or you may to some pieces of feedback but not to others. Regardless of how you respond, when you are ready to use the information, consider the following areas.

STRENGTHS

Don't rush over comments given to you on your strengths. People are typically so keen to see what they can improve or what they're not doing right that they skip right over what is working well. Your strengths are a critical part of defining who you are, they are what you're going to build on to become an even better version of yourself. In the next part of the book you'll be using them to help you work on the changes you want to make. So take time to think about your strengths, what they mean to who you are, what you've learnt about yourself, and what makes you unique and someone worth knowing.

POINTS FOR DEVELOPMENT

Try not to dwell on the areas where you need to improve. The key thing here is not to make them bigger than they actually are. You've probably lived with them so far without problems and we all have areas for development, it's about what we do with them that matters. Equally, try not to search for reasons to validate your behavior, otherwise you'll never learn from feedback or grow as a person.

VALIDATE

Make up your own mind about the feedback you receive. It's up to you to decide whether someone else's opinion is valid or not. If a number of people are saying the same thing, then it's likely that it's more of a universally held truth than when it's just one person giving you a specific viewpoint. In the latter instance, it may be more useful to understand why they think that and the others don't. Do they make you feel or respond in a certain way? Do they see you in a different context to other people?

REFLECT

It can be helpful to reflect on the feedback you've received for a while, to let it settle. This will allow your subconscious to work through things that you're not even aware of, putting you in a better place to decide on the next steps. Then leave it for a few days again. Don't rush. Think about the following:

- What patterns do you see emerging?

- Why do you think these things have become part of who you are?

- Which parts do you want to modify?

Write a summary of the patterns you can see emerging. For now, turn this into a list of three core areas you want to work on addressing over the next six months. For example, "I would like to become better at saying 'no' to people when I don't have time to do something" or "I would like to start being more organized with my time." You will complete this in greater detail in the next part of the book when you write your development plan, so for now these are just notes for you to refer to.

Revisiting Feedback

At a later date, once you've put together your development plan and taken action to change the behaviors you want to, it's worth going back to the people who gave you the original feedback to check in with them again. This will signal your desire to really grow and develop, and importantly the value that you have placed on what they've told you. In turn, this will give you further support for your continued growth.

Coming to the End of the Session

In this session you have worked through how to gather an understanding of who you are and how you come across to other people by using feedback to build on your self-knowledge, better understand your strengths, and raise awareness of any blind spots. If you completed the psychometric test in the previous chapter, you may also have had the opportunity to share the outputs with someone you trust, which has hopefully built a greater level of understanding of what the results tell you and what you can do with that information. Even if you haven't completed the test, you will have delved into your personality in greater depth, asking for more personal feedback that will have improved your self-awareness.

Next we'll be considering how you can start pulling together all of the material you've gathered, focusing on how that defines who you are now and how you want that to evolve over time. This will reflect the areas you have explored so far, including your true strengths, values, and passions, and also put them within the context of your purpose. Don't worry if you're not yet clear on your purpose, we'll do an exercise that will help you to gain more clarity over where you're headed. This will provide the backdrop for you to think through what and how you need to develop in order to best fulfill your life goals. Finally, to ensure you feel fully equipped to take action on your development and achieve the goals you outline, we'll be looking at how to increase your confidence and ways to overcome psychological barriers that may otherwise hold you back.

PART III

Doing

CHAPTER 7

Defining You

● ● ●

By this point in the book you've delved deep into your psyche, allowing you to really get under the skin of what makes you tick. The following group of three sessions is called Defining You, because it pulls together all the elements you've explored in one place, allowing you to think through who you are now, who you want to become, and how to do that. First you will summarize the themes relating to your core personality, values, passions, and strengths, and look at defining your purpose, all of which describe you. Then you will move onto "Developing You," thinking through how to achieve your goals in a way that builds on your strengths and helps you move toward your purpose in a pragmatic way. Finally, in order to achieve your goals you will need to get past any psychological barriers that could trip you up along the way. This is the focus of "Confidently You," which will help you identify obstacles and equip you with the tools to move beyond them, in order to fulfill your true potential.

Research shows that combining the elements you have defined as "you" in a way that aligns with your purpose will make you happier, more psychologically healthy, and better able to achieve your goals and ambitions. So, these sessions will not only provide you with clarity and coherence, but do so in a way that underpins both your life satisfaction and your future success.

Session 7A

Describing You

Now, you're going to do an exercise that pulls everything we've covered so far into a single model. This will make it easier for you to access and mentally summarize the work you have done. We will then take a look at why understanding your purpose is so helpful, and how it forms

the framework for everything you do and have explored about yourself
so far. You'll complete an exercise called "Interviewing your future self"
to help you define and pull out the essence of what you are striving
for in life and outline your purpose more succinctly.

TOOLS OF THE SESSION

Pulling It All Together

In this exercise, you'll start by capturing your core personality, looking
back over the information you've discovered through the sessions so
far. Following this you'll bring together your values, passions, and
interests. You'll then gather the information that is relevant to your
strengths and explore it in a little more depth, seeking to understand
how better to leverage your strengths and which of them stand out to
define who you are.

At each stage, you'll write down the main elements on a model made
up of concentric circles (see Figure 7.1). You may find it easier to draw it
on a larger sheet of paper. Think of these as elements of yourself, with the
inner circle denoting the core of who you are, on which everything else
hangs. As the circles radiate outward, the part of you they represent becomes
more influenced by life events. The outer circle, your purpose, holds all of
you together. At a broad level this remains constant throughout life, but
it is also continually evolving, morphing and flexing to fit with the opportunities, threats, and events that you encounter. Your areas for development
and your goals (which we'll expand on in the next session) fit outside of
your central makeup, but within the purpose you are striving to fulfill.

THE CORE OF "YOU"
The inner circle in Figure 7.1 represents the tendencies, preferences,
and personality traits that your friends and family would recognize as
being truly you. Use the guidelines that follow to help you pull together
everything you've discovered that's relevant to this circle. Note your
thoughts on a piece of paper and then pick out the most central themes,
writing a heading for each on the lines within the circle in Figure 7.2.

- **What did you identify in Chapter 2?** What tendencies did you pick
  out that are still true today? Which areas of your personality did
  you realize are possibly more genetic and integral to who you are?

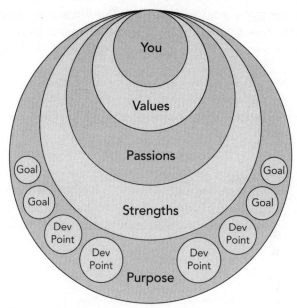

Figure 7.1 Defining you

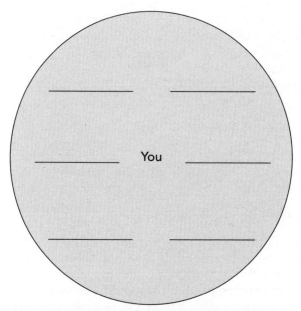

Figure 7.2 Your core tendencies and preferences

- **What did you identify in Chapter 3?** How do you deal with stress and setbacks? What sort of people motivate you and what sort of people annoy or derail you? What does this tell you about yourself?

- **What did you identify in Chapters 5 and 6?** Was there any feedback from the psychometric test or that people gave you that highlights specific behavioral tendencies and preferences? Capture key areas on Figure 7.2.

YOUR VALUES

Write down the values you identified in Chapter 4 on the lines in Figure 7.3. This is a good opportunity for you to go back and revalidate what you captured, making sure that they really represent your deepest values.

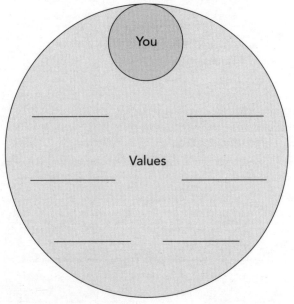

Figure 7.3 Your core values

YOUR PASSIONS AND INTERESTS

You also explored your passions and interests in Chapter 4. Other deeply held interests and passions may have come to mind since then. Write those you hold most centrally on the lines in Figure 7.4.

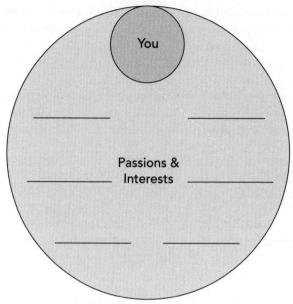

Figure 7.4 Your passions and interests

YOUR STRENGTHS

You've worked through a lot of information regarding your strengths, which may make it more difficult to pinpoint your "strongest strengths." Don't worry if you can't do this part all at once: like everything else, you can come back to it. There are pointers in what follows to help give you some clarity over what you may want to include here.

Go through each chapter, looking at your notes and your storyline to help you pull out your strengths. If it helps, just list them to start with, then you can refine them as a next step.

- **What did you identify in Chapter 1?** Looking through "Observe, Don't React," were there any parts that you read and thought "Ah yes, I already do that"? Which areas of the curiosity measure did you score highest on? Which sections of the self-awareness measure did you do best on?

- **What did you identify in Chapter 2?** What were you good at as a child? Is that a strength you have built on through your life? Maybe there is something that you weren't good at as a child but that has become a strength as an adult.

- **What did you identify in Chapter 3?** Which areas of emotional wisdom do you think you're strongest at? Can you identify strengths in how you have dealt with major life events? Did any of your positive life events come about as a result of a particular strength?

- **What did you identify in Chapter 4?** Do the things you love doing and your values coincide with your strengths? Are you good at connecting with people? If you are, what is it that makes you good?

- **What did you identify in Chapter 5?** If you completed the psychometric test, what emerged from it that highlights your strengths? If you shared your psychometric results with a friend, which of the strengths did they also see as strengths?

- **What did you identify in Chapter 6?** What came out of the feedback from other people that points to particular strengths?

Once you have an initial list of strengths, you can work through it and pare it down to key headings to write on the lines in Figure 7.5.

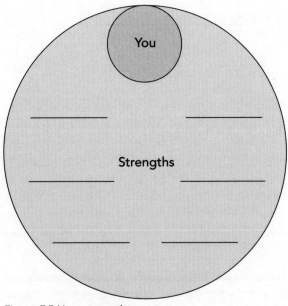

Figure 7.5 Your strengths

As you are working through your strengths, try to define what they mean. How do they help you in life? Understanding your strengths will help you to leverage them more effectively, partly because it makes you more aware of them, but also because your mind will help you move toward them if that's what you're focused on.

Identify what your strongest strength is, sometimes called a **signature strength**. It highlights who you are at your best and is unique to you. What is it that really stands out for you? What have people said about you that you think is unique? If you're struggling with this one, then look through all the strengths with a friend and ask them to help you.

Once you have decided which is your strongest strength, highlight or underline it on the model. You should now have everything you've learnt so far in one place.

Defining Your Purpose

You are now going to move to the outer circle of the model to build on the work you've already done on meaning, taking the values and passions you identified and thinking through how they make up your broader purpose in life. To start with, we will revisit what this means in a little more depth and look at why it's so valuable to know about.

Psychologists Joo Yeon Shin and Michael Steger from Colorado State University have reviewed the research on meaning and explain that to understand our purpose, we first have to have a coherent understanding of ourselves: our values, passions, strengths, weaknesses, preferences, and how we fit into the world.[1] You've been piecing this together throughout this book and have reached a point where you can now pull it all together. The next step is defining and working out what your reason for being is, what your long-term aspirations amount to, and what your life is all about. You may find it more helpful to think of this as your mission or vision—whatever works best for you. The thought of trying to define your "reason for being" may sound somewhat daunting, but while it is an immense concept, it's important to understand that it isn't something you *have* to do. It's your choice, and you can take your time coming back to it while you read through the remainder of the book and keep revisiting it in the months and years to come. Also, once you've decided your purpose, it doesn't have to remain fixed throughout your life.

Considering all this is helpful in the context of where you have reached in your personal exploration, because it provides an overarching framework. Once clear, all your other goals, aims, and objectives start falling into place, helping to guide everything you do with a greater sense of meaning. Psychologists Patrick McKnight and Todd Kashdan from George Mason University have done extensive research in this area and describe it as follows:

> *Purpose directs life goals and daily decisions by guiding the use of finite personal resources. Instead of governing behavior, purpose offers direction just as a compass offers direction to a navigator; following that compass (i.e., purpose) is optional.*[2]

Research has also shown that having an understanding of purpose and pursuing it through your daily activities has huge benefits to both your brain and your body. For example, Majid Fotuhi at Johns Hopkins Medical School has reviewed studies showing that people who have a higher sense of purpose also have better cognitive function, live longer, sleep better, have better cardiovascular fitness, and experience better mood. Fotuhi cites one study in particular showing that having a sense of purpose reduced cognitive decline in the elderly by as much as 50%. Other studies have demonstrated that it even protects against brain atrophy, stopping areas of the brain from dying off.[3]

One of the key reasons that purpose helps to protect the brain is that it relates to and engages the more advanced, higher-level functions, keeping neural networks ticking over and active as we go through life.

Purpose is about your intrinsic motivations, the things that are internal to you, that keep you going in spite of whatever else is happening, that are central to who you are. As a result, it's not related to status, position, the recognition of others, or rewards. Nor is it about doing things because you feel you have to, ought to, or would let someone down if you didn't. Once defined, the internal source of motivation, the bigger picture and perspective that purpose provides, will enable you to weather the storms of life, the obstacles, stress, and strain. It will effectively offer you hope on gloomy or tough days and help you not give up when things go wrong. It remains a guiding light, or a heartbeat if you like, that is steady and protected from external demands.

Society puts certain pressures on us: we're expected to complete further education, to leave home, to search out bright lights and big cities. But that's not right for everyone. It's important to remember that success is about what makes us feel fulfilled, our intrinsic motivations, not about what other people expect of us.

The four core needs of our advanced brain are connecting with others, finding a sense of meaning, continually learning, and giving back to society. As well as making use of our values, passions, and strengths, purpose also provides us with a vehicle from which to fulfill this fourth need, giving to something bigger than ourselves. Meeting this need provides us with an underlying sense of well-being and contributes strongly to life satisfaction. Yet this doesn't mean you necessarily have to go and work in a developing country and give up all your worldly possessions. Nor does it mean that you have to work for a charity, become a philanthropist, or give up your whole life to a bigger cause. It can simply mean spending more time with and giving to your family and friends, caring for children, helping other people, committing to your religion, volunteering in your community, or even looking after a pet. The options for fulfilling this need are immense in both scale and approach. It's up to you to choose something that works for you.

So, purpose provides direction and helps you to organize yourself around that direction. It enables you to leverage all of the parts of yourself you've explored: your preferences, values, passions, and strengths. It also provides a framework and context to your future life that you can use as a "compass" to guide you in making optimal use of who you are, and from which to identify which goals you want to pursue and how you want to develop. Let me give you an example.

How Purpose Helps Define You

Tom, the son of a friend, recently left college after completing one year of his studies. He wasn't struggling academically, he just didn't really like the course. With free time on his hands, he did some odd jobs for us and we started chatting about what he wanted to do. He felt a bit lost: nothing seemed to fit with him and he didn't know which way to turn next.

One afternoon we spent some time talking through his options. As you can imagine, I started with his core preferences and values, moving on to his passions and interests, and highlighting his strengths. Discussing this out loud helped Tom to clarify his thoughts, and it transpired that his core preferences and values centered around being at home with his family. He didn't want to be with hordes of students or to work in teams, he liked his own time and space. This was the main reason he wasn't enjoying college life, combined with the structure of the course he'd undertaken, which involved a lot of group work.

His interests are focused around nature and the outdoors. He had started doing a course in graphics, choosing the best he could find, but again he struggled with the course structure and being away from family. This left him feeling even more lost and confused.

Once Tom had freed himself of societal expectations and accepted where his personality, values, passions, and strengths lay, we investigated courses that better suited his more introverted nature and would allow him to stay at home. This meant predominantly carrying out distance learning with an element of lecture time.

Tom's purpose is to work with nature to create a more sustainable environment. He also knows what that looks like, for example in an ideal world, one that suited his preferences, he would offer this as advice in a one-to-one consulting setting, while spending a lot of time outside in nature. Defining this has allowed him to look at what the next steps could be. He needs to get the required qualifications (this is one of his goals) and he will have to develop his confidence to enable him to go out and gain the relevant experience and attract clients (an area for development). But all of this will be easier in the context of knowing why and what that should look like for him (for example, choosing a course that has the capacity for distance learning or one that's close to home and doesn't involve a high level of group work). While this will challenge him, none of it will take him too far from his core personality or values. And knowing what his overall purpose is will help him to overcome obstacles in order to fulfill his shorter-term goals.

You may find that your purpose is more straightforward like Tom's, or even crazily ambitious like mine:

I want to improve lives through helping people across the world to better understand behaviour, and provide the mechanisms to help people to live happier, healthier, more fulfilled, and successful lives.

That statement has taken me some time to come up with. I started studying psychology when I was 18 years old, but I can honestly say that I've only crystallized my purpose in the last year or so. What is more, I'm still working on it and may never fully achieve it, but it gives my life a sense of meaning that I can center my goals around.

Finding your purpose isn't something you will crack in just one sitting, and you shouldn't expect to—you are, after all, looking for your meaning in life—but give the next exercise a go and then start experimenting. Research suggests that it takes a degree of trial and error and an active approach to search out and find what really feels right for you. It's important that the interests you identify as being true to you really resonate with who you are and your values. What I'm about to share with you is quite a fun way of starting the process of experimentation and search. First, some background.

WHAT WILL YOU HAVE BECOME?
In the exercise that follows, you're going to use your imagination to project yourself into the future and envisage what, in an ideal world, you will have become. It's helpful to have a mental model based on someone who's "been there and done that." Someone may come to mind for you, and it doesn't need to be a prominent person, but I'm going to refer to naturalist and broadcaster Sir David Attenborough, because he's a great example of someone who has lived his life with purpose, based on his values and making use of his strengths and preferences. Attenborough's life has been centered around his devotion to the natural

world and a passionate desire to communicate and share that with the general population.

Now in his 90s, Attenborough is still working and enthusiastically contributing to society's understanding of the natural world and human impacts on it. He has been interviewed worldwide on talk shows, at universities, and even in the Oval Office by Barack Obama at the time of his presidency.[4] The following exchange really reflects how he has lived out his lifelong passion:

> *Obama: "How did you get interested in nature and wanting to record it? . . ."*
> *Attenborough: "Well, I've never met a child who's not interested in natural history . . . Kids love it. Kids understand the natural world and they're fascinated by it. So the question is, how did you lose it? . . . How did anyone lose the interest in nature? . . . And certainly I never lost it."*

Attenborough has kept his childhood interests alive and fully employed over the years, engaging them to pursue his life goals. He lives in alignment with his desire to communicate with and educate people about the importance and beauty of the natural world. He also effectively leverages his strengths and core personality, for example:

- Naturally inquisitive and open to exploring

- Open-minded about different technologies (to create cutting-edge presentations about his passion)

- Great communicator and storyteller

- Engaging and likeable personality

- Strong ability to connect authentically

- Confidence combined with humility

All of these factors have enabled him to fulfill his life purpose, contributing to something much bigger than himself along the way. As he commented: "People must feel that the natural world is important and valuable and beautiful and wonderful and an amazement and a pleasure."[5]

Yet as a young man Attenborough wasn't sure what he was going to do, he just knew what he loved and was confident enough to pursue that, taking up and forging opportunities along the way.

Try not to think of yourself as too old to start something new (remember, your brain is plastic). Research shows that the effects of finding purpose are beneficial whatever your life stage. Sometimes it's difficult to think about beginning a new phase or achieving once you have lived a bit of life, but there are plenty of examples of people who have:

- Donald Fisher was 40 (and had no experience in retail) when he opened the first Gap store in San Francisco.

- Jo Pavey won her first Olympic gold aged 40.

- Vera Wang became a bridal wear designer aged 40.

- Samuel L. Jackson had his first big film role aged 43.

- Charles Darwin published *On the Origin of Species* aged 50.

- Julia Child made her television debut in *The French Chef* aged 51.

- Daniel Defoe published *Robinson Crusoe*, his first novel, aged 60.

- Harland Sanders was 62 when he franchised Kentucky Fried Chicken.

- Ranulph Fiennes climbed Everest aged 65.

- Sir William Crookes invented the first instruments to study radioactivity aged 68.

- Lord Palmerston became prime minister of Great Britain aged 71.

- Mary Wesley had her first novel for adults published aged 71.

- John Glenn traveled into space aged 77.

- Gladys Burrill from Hawaii ran her first marathon aged 86.

And don't worry if your ambition is on a much smaller scale than Attenborough or any of these people—they are helpful examples, but there are many more who won't be well known for what they've done. It's about your purpose and what will make you satisfied. This is about what feels right to *you*.

TOOLS OF THE SESSION

Interview with Your Future Self

For this exercise, it's important to suspend disbelief and imagine life without any barriers or obstacles in the way—as if money was no object, there was no chance of failing (in other words, imagine that you are guaranteed success), and you had no life commitments (e.g., no mortgage, elderly parents, children to look after). Also, be sure to focus on what *you* really want rather than what other people expect of you. Keep checking back on this as you work through the exercise to ensure you're capturing your dreams rather than living up to others' expectations.

Imagine yourself at the age of 90 being interviewed about your life. This doesn't have to be about changing the planet: it could, for example, be about having a happy family, a beautiful garden that other people can share, or giving back to your local community. You could be being interviewed by a great-niece or -nephew, on a local radio station, or by a world leader—the choice is yours. Write the answers as if you're in the present, as if you were relating your story to the interviewer and audience right now: I am . . ., I have . . ., I enjoy . . ., I will . . .

> Tip: Try to have fun with this exercise—the more free and creative you are, the better the outcome will be. Really think through your responses. If you were being interviewed you wouldn't just give a few words as an answer, you'd explain and expand. Try to do that now and let your imagination run free.

STEP 1

Think through how you would be introduced. Here are some examples of how David Attenborough has been introduced:

> *"We have the actual king of the jungles, and the deserts and the oceans, and the Antarctic and all those places . . . Ladies and gentlemen, I'm so excited, I'm always thrilled that he agrees to come on this show, it's an honour to sit and talk with him and to listen to what he has to say. The words 'broadcaster' and 'naturalist' simply don't do him justice, but the words 'national' and 'treasure' do. Will you please welcome Sir David Attenborough." (Jonathan Ross[6])*

> *"Sir David Attenborough, I have been a huge admirer of your work for some time. I have to say when I heard you dove into the Great Barrier Reef again, 60 years after you first did it, that impressed me." (Barack Obama[7])*

STEP 2

Consider the following questions. You don't have to answer all of them, just choose the ones you find easiest to respond to. Write down anything and everything that comes to mind (the more you can answer, the easier you will find it to pin down what the essence of your purpose is). Remember to answer as if you are 90 years old looking back.

- Who has inspired you? Who would you say your role models are and why?

- What have you enjoyed most on the journey to where you are today? What have been the high points?

- How would you define a "successful life"?

- What do you consider to be the biggest contribution to society you have made?

- What accomplishment are you most proud of?

- What do you like to do in your spare time and how do you have fun?

- Do you feel differently about yourself now from how you felt when you were younger? How?

- What's the highest honor or award you've received and how did that feel?

- What's the best compliment you ever received?

- What's the most memorable phone call, email, or text you ever received?

- What would you say the turning points have been in your life and why?

- Do you have a philosophy of life? Can you share it with us?

- What advice would you give to someone just setting out in life about living the best life they can?

- If you won the lottery tomorrow, what would you do with the money and what would you do differently with your life?

- If you had the power to solve one and only one problem in the world, what would it be and why?

- What is your greatest hope for the future?

- What is your greatest fear?

- What would you like your children and grandchildren or other relations to remember about you?

- How do you think people outside of your family will remember you?

STEP 3

Go back through what you've written in response to these questions and, using a different color of pen or highlighter, mark your core personality, values, passions, strengths, and overall purpose. Are all of these areas represented? Are there any that are missing or don't have much emphasis? If so, add them in. Have you written anything that you could put into your circles in terms of the core headings you captured before? If this is the case, go back and include it.

STEP 4
Summarize your purpose in two or three sentences. Make this overall statement positive and ensure that it includes the true essence of you. You may find the following examples helpful as a guide:

> *"To have fun in [my] journey through life and learn from [my] mistakes." (Sir Richard Branson, founder of the Virgin Group)*

> *"To be a teacher. And to be known for inspiring my students to be more than they thought they could be." (Oprah Winfrey, founder of OWN, the Oprah Winfrey Network)*

> *"To use my gifts of intelligence, charisma, and serial optimism to cultivate the self-worth and net-worth of women around the world." (Amanda Steinberg, founder of Dailyworth.com)*

> *"To improve lives through helping people understand human behavior." (My own)*

Remember, your purpose is not an end point or a goal in itself and it will shift and alter as time passes.

Tip: When it comes to purpose or life in general, we need to be prepared for setbacks and disappointments. What is important is to get up when we are knocked down and keep going. The more we expose ourselves to in life, the more setbacks we face. Take J.K. Rowling, who was turned down by 12 publishers before she signed with Bloomsbury. If she'd given up, she would never have inspired the imagination of millions of children worldwide with her tales of Harry Potter. If we approach setbacks in the right way, with the right mindset, they can teach us some very important lessons.

Finally, put your purpose somewhere that you can see it every day: write it as a screensaver for your phone or laptop, frame it and put it on the wall, write it on a piece of paper and put it in your wallet. Do whatever will ensure you keep seeing it and remembering it throughout your daily life.

Coming to the End of the Session

You have now pulled together the fundamental elements of "you," defining your core personality, values, passions, strengths, and purpose. In the next session, we will look at how to make use of your purpose as a framework from which to bring meaning to your life, specifically focusing on turning your development points and goals into action. Following that, we'll consider how you take this forward with confidence, and how you deal with the setbacks and the fears you may face in the development process.

SESSION 7B

Developing You

You have already developed more than you're consciously aware of simply by working through this book. Research shows that having a better understanding of your story and piecing together your meaning helps you make more sense of your life. In one study, for example, social psychologist Roy Baumeister and colleagues found that the more people feel their activities are consistent with their core themes and values, the greater meaning they perceive.[8] Meaning is also related to developing a personal identity and "consciously integrating one's past, present, and future experiences." That is what you have been doing up to this point in the book.

As you've worked through what is core to defining you, you will have come across areas that you'd like to tweak or develop. Maybe these are things that you've known about for a long time but haven't gotten around to working on. Or possibly new areas for development have come up through self-reflection, the psychometric tool, or feedback from others. This session is about helping you construct a plan that will address the development points that are core to becoming the person you want to be and living out your purpose. You'll put together a detailed plan of action on your development areas, concentrating on factors that research has shown to be crucial for goal attainment. This will provide you with a clearer sense of how to invest in yourself so that you can achieve more, reach your potential, be happier, and live a more fulfilled life.

Development Points and Goals

You're going to be capturing both your development points and your goals. They may sound like they're the same, but they're not. A development point is more focused on behavioral change through learning and enabling you to grow as a person, improving your talents and potential. It's less about the destination and more about the process of gaining skills and knowledge. On the other hand, a goal is something that has a specific and tangible outcome or end point. You can think of some goals as staging posts toward your development points, while other goals may be longer term and reach beyond your current development plan.

We'll start by exploring your areas for development. When it comes to developing and altering your behavior, it's important to remember that it is possible to adapt your neural pathways (as I've said before, your brain is plastic). Even things that may seem impossible to overcome can be altered with focused attention and persistent action. Having said that, it's important to distinguish which behaviors are absolutely core to who you are and which are more peripheral. It's not a good idea to try to change aspects of your personality that are central to your makeup or genetic. Attempting to develop or alter these would be like pushing water uphill—utterly exhausting and something that could even derail you (which is definitely not the aim of this book). When it comes to these latter areas, it's more important to be aware of them and to understand their impact, so that you can learn how to modify and mitigate that rather than the behaviors themselves.

For example, if you are someone who is naturally very trusting and sometimes get taken advantage of as a result, you may want to become more aware of how to prevent this. You don't, however, want to change to being someone who is at the other end of the spectrum—that is, skeptical and disbelieving of others—because that would fundamentally change your personality. Instead, you could make sure you ask more questions before taking someone at their word, or ask what other people whose judgment you believe in think of someone, or simply try to remind yourself to slow down and collect more evidence before forming an opinion. This will help you to mitigate any negatives felt as an outcome of your tendencies, rather than trying to change who you are.

TOOLS OF THE SESSION

Identifying Your Core Development Points

Your core areas for development sit within your purpose, enabling personal growth in a way that it is meaningful to you. In this section, we'll be looking through the information you've pulled together throughout this book, this time in order to help you define the areas you're most motivated to develop. Initially just list information in response to each of the following prompts, which you can then refine into three or four key areas to work on.

- **What did you identify in Chapter 1?** Looking through "Observe, Don't React," were there any parts that you read and thought "I'm a long way off doing that"? Which areas of the curiosity measure did you score lowest on? Which sections of the self-awareness measure did you score lowest on?

- **What did you identify in Chapter 2?** What did you struggle to get to grips with as a child? Have you improved since then, or do you feel this is still an area that trips you up?

- **What did you identify in Chapter 3?** Which areas of emotional wisdom do you struggle most with? Is this something you would like to develop? If so, what steps can you take to improve? Did you learn anything from any major life events that illuminated an area you would like to work on?

- **What did you identify in Chapter 4?** Do the things you identified as not liking coincide with an area for development? Or do you dislike these things so much that trying to develop them would be fruitless? Could you improve how you connect with other people? If so, what approach will you take to do it?

- **What did you identify in Chapter 5?** If you completed the psychometric test, what emerged from it that highlights areas for development? If you shared your psychometric results with a friend, which of the areas for development did they also see as needing work?

- **What did you identify in Chapter 6?** What came out of the feedback from other people that you may want to work on?

REFINING YOUR DEVELOPMENT POINTS

You should now have collected a good deal of information on your areas for development. Look through all of this and pull out the development points that you are most motivated to work on.

First, separate out areas for awareness (those things that are central to your makeup that you don't think it would be possible to change, but that you may want to modify) from areas for development and capture them in Table 7.1, thinking about what action you can take to mitigate any negative impact of that behavior. Look at the core themes and patterns that are strongly ingrained throughout your storyline. These factors are those most central to your makeup. If they have a negative impact on either you or other people, they should become an area for awareness that you will try to modify (rather than the focus of any major change or development).

TABLE 7.1 YOUR AREAS FOR AWARENESS

Area for awareness	How it manifests	What I can do to moderate the behavior
e.g., Talking over people	Getting overanimated in conversation and butting in	Apologize Warn people in advance and explain that nothing is meant by it Give them permission to tell me to be quiet Take a deep breath and slow myself down to gain control of my reacting brain

Once you have defined your areas for awareness, look at your areas for development. Work through the information you gathered by answering the earlier questions and pull together three or four key headings that represent the areas you would like to work on. Write them in the circles in Figure 7.6.

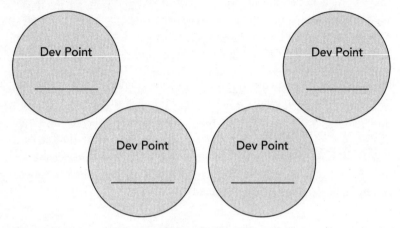

Figure 7.6 Your areas for development

TIPS FOR DEFINING YOUR DEVELOPMENT POINTS

- Don't try to change too many behaviors at once. It just won't work, and the sense of failure you will inevitably feel as a result could prevent you from living out your purpose effectively.

- The changes you are aiming to make should take you out of your comfort zone and stretch you, but shouldn't push you to extreme discomfort (into your panic zone; more about this in the next session). It's better to take smaller, successful steps than a giant leap.

- Pick the things that you feel intrinsically motivated to work on (as opposed to doing it because you feel you ought to or someone else has told you to) and that you feel will really help you take your life forward in a way that is in tune with your purpose.

TOOLS OF THE SESSION

Writing Your Development Plan

Now you've identified the areas you want to develop, it's time to construct your development plan. You will find a blank development plan at the end of this chapter. Here I'm going to work through it area by area, offering an explanation and some examples of how you might complete it, using the example development area of "Becoming more empathic." There is a little space for you to write your own examples under each question, or you could write them onto a separate piece of paper or in your notepad.

AREA FOR DEVELOPMENT
Example development area: Becoming more empathic

The more specific you can make your area for development, the easier it will be to fill out the remainder of the plan. For example:
I am going to work on the skills I have around empathy to become better at relating to other people when I'm feeling stressed and under pressure myself.

Which values underlie this development area? How does it align with my purpose?
Consider the development point you have picked and ask yourself whether working on it aligns with your values.

For example:
Core values: Being fair and just
Purpose: To become a better leader, to improve performance of the company I work for, and/or to improve the lives of people I interact with
Doesn't align with values: Being empathic to people who have done something wrong
Does align with values: Being empathic when people are distressed through no fault of their own
Values it aligns with: Being just and fair
Elements of purpose it aligns with: Improving relationships with my followers

What will success look like and what will the positive outcomes be?

Becoming a more effective influencer and making more informed judgments built through positive relationships and better understanding the undercurrents of what is going on around me.

What obstacles may I come up against and what can I do about them?

Internal obstacles may include thoughts and feelings, e.g., feeling demotivated, having self-doubt, fear, anger, anxiety. —
Frustration and impatience. Action to overcome: create a trigger that reminds me to take a step back and use my observing rather than reacting brain, and also practice emotion surfing on frustration and impatience.

External obstacles may include factors such as lack of money, lack of time, lack of skills, health constraints.
External obstacle—people don't understand what I'm trying to do. Therefore need to gain skills in the area of influencing other people and communicating more effectively.

Which strengths can I make use of to help me develop?

Interest in other people
Ability to listen
Desire to develop and grow as a leader
Social awareness

Action and by when? How can I break down my development area into smaller steps (goals)? How can I action those steps, and by when?

Take the overall area for development and make it into something that you can carry out a step at a time and build on over time as your skill level progresses. It's helpful to tie the action to something that you already do as part of your routine. It's also very important to make your actions time-bound, setting a day, date, and even a time for each of them where you can.

1. Make sure that I am consciously listening to people at least once a day. Start doing this in my first meeting of the day from tomorrow and continue for two months, until April 27.

2. Show empathic curiosity, really try to understand what the other person is saying and putting myself in their shoes. Continue doing step 1 and from April 27 build in step 2 once a day for two months, until June 27.

3. Go on a communication and influencing course by August 15.

4. Bring the understanding I get from the course into my everyday communications—continue with steps 1 and 2 and build the information into the board meeting and company presentations on August 31, thinking through how best to get the message across so that people can connect with it.

5. Use the greater level of awareness to think through how I influence people more effectively and consider the impact of the knowledge on decision making—continue with steps 1, 2, and 3 and list out all the points I've learnt by October 31.

What will the measurement/review mechanism be?

You need to know how you're doing against your specific goals, otherwise you don't know how close or far away you are from achieving them. Measuring behavior change can be tricky, but there are some simple methods you can use, like rating yourself, asking for feedback, and logging progress.

- Check I've completed the actions above by the specified date.

- Ask for feedback from people who work with me on how I'm progressing.

- Make a log in my diary of the interactions I have every day.

- Rate myself out of 10 in terms of how I think I'm progressing.

CREATE A SUMMARY DEVELOPMENT PLAN

Once you've filled in your detailed plan using the template at the end of this session, in order to give yourself a simpler version and a visual aid you can fill in a summary plan too (Table 7.2). You may want to write this out on an index card that you can carry around with you, or take a photo of it to keep on your phone.

TIPS TO HELP WITH DEVELOPMENT

- **Create reminders**—You need to put a reminder for your specific actions somewhere that you will see frequently, e.g., on your daily to-do list, in your diary, an alarm on your phone. This may seem like a minor step, but it is critical and represents the difference between making something happen and just having it as something you'll do one day.

- **Create a cue**—Tie the actions into something you do every day, e.g., if your goal is to start flossing your teeth, use the act of brushing your teeth as a reminder.

- **Reward yourself**—Every time you achieve success, however small, you should reward yourself. The reward should be something that will really provide you with personal satisfaction. You may want to have small rewards for smaller steps and a bigger reward for when you maintain the behavior over a longer period.

- **Enlist social support**—Ask a friend, relation, colleague, or even a member of the community to encourage and support you.

- **Persist**—Repetition is key to making a behavior stick. Research has shown that it can take from 15 to 254 days to truly form a new habit.[9]

If you feel overwhelmed by the amount you need to do having filled in one development point, stagger your development: start with one area, and once you feel satisfied with your progress with that, begin a second one. There is no need to (in fact it's not helpful to) try to do it all at once.

Over the longer term, you will need to keep coming back to these development points, adding new ones and assessing your progress on older ones. If there are some behaviors that you've tried to change but had limited success addressing, you may need to move them onto your list of areas for awareness. Then think through other ways of handling those aspects of your personality.

Area for development Underlying values: What success will look like:	
Actions	Complete by
How to cope with obstacles	

Table 7.2 Summary development plan

Defining Your Longer-term Goals

You will have captured short-term goals in your development plan (when determining how you can break a development point down into smaller steps), but you should also take this opportunity to think through the longer-term goals that sit between your development plan and your purpose. In other words, what do you want to achieve within the next three, five, and ten years? These kinds of goals take some thought and planning, and may include things like completing a college course or setting up a business.

Take a look through what you wrote in your "interview with your future self" and think about objectives that will help move you in the direction of your purpose. It may help to visualize where you want to be in ten years and work backwards from there. You can also break down the vision of where you want to be at each stage by considering the following:

- Where you want to be living?

- What job or career do you want to have?

- How do you want to be spending your free time?

- What do you want the relationships with your family and friends to be like?

- Who do you want to be spending time with?

The more information you can include under each question, the more specific and focused you will be able to make your goals. For more detail on what Jack Canfield and Janet Switzer call the "Vision Exercise," take a look at their book *The Success Principles*.[10]

Write your overall goals in Table 7.3. If you have captured details using the questions above, write them underneath your main goal. Rewrite your purpose as a reminder of the framework that these sit within. Don't expect to do this in one sitting (although you may)—it takes time to consider this kind of bigger life objective.

TABLE 7.3 LONG-TERM GOALS

My 3-year goal is:

My 5-year goal is:

My 10-year goal is:

My purpose is:

Be sure to come back to these long-term goals and adjust and update them as time goes by. You may not have complete clarity at first, but as you progress on your journey they will become clearer. Achieving any long-term goal takes perseverance, but it will be much easier to overcome the tough times if you keep reminding yourself of your ultimate purpose.

Coming to the End of the Session

You've now looked at how to take all of the information you've pulled together about yourself to create an action plan underpinned by your values and in the service of your purpose. You've also headlined your longer-term goals as a statement of where you want your life to go in the next three to ten years.

In the next session we'll be looking at how to take this forward with confidence, what confidence means, and how to build your own confidence. Bolstering your confidence will help you to achieve your development points, grow as a person, and communicate yourself to the world in a way that aligns with what you truly stand for.

Development Plan Template

AREA FOR DEVELOPMENT

WHICH VALUES UNDERLIE THIS DEVELOPMENT AREA? HOW DO THEY ALIGN WITH MY PURPOSE?

WHAT WILL SUCCESS LOOK LIKE AND WHAT WILL THE POSITIVE OUTCOMES BE?

WHAT OBSTACLES COULD I COME UP AGAINST AND WHAT CAN I DO ABOUT THEM?

WHICH STRENGTHS CAN I MAKE USE OF TO HELP ME DEVELOP?

ACTION AND BY WHEN? HOW CAN I BREAK MY DEVELOPMENT AREA DOWN INTO SMALLER STEPS (GOALS)? HOW CAN I ACTION THOSE STEPS, AND WHEN BY?

WHAT WILL THE MEASUREMENT/REVIEW MECHANISM BE?

Session 7C

Confidently You

Now that you have established your core areas for development and the goals that will help you move in synchronicity with your values, passions, strengths, and purpose, you will inevitably want to take what you have learnt forward with confidence. But despite having grown your understanding of your abilities, qualities, and judgments, that still doesn't mean that you trust them. You've deliberately imagined moving forward without fear of failing, but in reality you, like everyone else, will have self-doubts and face obstacles in achieving your goals. This is where confidence comes into play.

In this session, we will be looking at the two core facets of confidence, self-confidence and self-esteem, and explaining the difference between them. We'll then consider how you can go about building both in order to help you pursue your purpose with greater faith in your capabilities. We'll also be exploring how to present yourself to the world around you in a more confident way, and how to tell the story of who you are to people you already know and people you've yet to meet in a positive and engaging way. This will help you enlist the support of others in achieving your goals, influence people you need to bring on board with your ideas, and build your connection with the people you come into contact with.

What Does Confidence Mean?

Confidence is an elusive concept. Most of us lack it to some degree, and few would argue they don't want to feel more confident, yet when it comes to defining how we could develop it we are at a loss. Having confidence rids us of the anxiety and doubts that hold us back from so many opportunities. It not only makes us feel better about ourselves, but also enables us to achieve more and inspire the conviction of others in our abilities.

Having said that, too much confidence is not a good thing. This is displayed in leadership, where an "overwhelming" self-assurance leads to something known as hubris syndrome. This acquired condition, which represents the extreme end of the scale, results in what Lord David Owen, a former MP and psychiatrist, defines as "disastrous leadership" that can "cause large-scale damage." It is marked by behaviors such as "impetuosity, a refusal to listen to or take advice and a particular form of incompetence when impulsivity, recklessness and frequent inattention to detail predominate."[11] The same behaviors are manifest in anyone who becomes too self-possessed. Consequently, you want to build your confidence to optimize your potential, but you also need to be careful not to take it too far.

There is a "sweet spot" you want to reach where your self-assurance is robust enough to allow you to take a balanced view on risks, make effective decisions, have influence, and effectively forge ahead with your purpose. Getting there is something we will explore in this session. Understanding what this means and where you are with it will form a strong platform from which you can move forward and fine-tune your own level of confidence.

Psychologists consider confidence in terms of two broad concepts: self-confidence (known technically as self-efficacy) and self-esteem. Self-confidence is about how much faith you have in your ability to achieve a specific goal in a particular situation. As such, it's not a given that being self-confident with one task means you'll be equally self-confident with another. For example, you may be confident that you can cook a good meal or play a strong game of tennis, but still lack confidence when it comes to your ability to run a marathon or play a piece of music on the piano.

Although self-confidence is task specific, one person may have an overall higher level than another. Someone with higher levels of self-confidence will approach all new challenges in a more forthright way. For example, they might throw themselves down a mountain when learning to ski, confident that they'll get the hang of it, and approach another task, say scuba diving for the first time, with the same vigor. On the other hand, another person who is less self-confident may be very fearful of any novel task. It's this overall level of self-confidence that you'll be working on in this session.

Self-esteem differs in that it is more internally focused. Rather than being based on the successful completion of tasks or challenges, it's about how much you value yourself or how much you like and accept who you are. An easy way to assess your level of self-esteem is to listen to your internal dialogue. How do you speak to yourself: are you kind, accepting, and appreciative (e.g., well done, you did a great job with that), or harsh, cutting, and critical (e.g., you idiot, why did you do that again, when will you learn)?

People frequently strive to make themselves feel better by chasing the more tangible aspects that relate to self-confidence—external rewards such as awards, academic achievements, or sporting success—while neglecting to work on their self-esteem. Celebrities often fall into this category, looking to the outside world for reassurance about their self-worth and getting that by achieving public recognition, awards, or notoriety. However, they can often be the loneliest people, feeling empty because their higher-level needs are not being met, such as their ability to like and accept themselves. This leads to destructive behaviors such as taking drugs, drinking to excess, and overeating.

Both self-confidence and self-esteem are important to well-being and to the pursuit of your goals within the context of what makes you unique and special as a person. One without the other is not helpful. Once you've built your self-confidence and self-esteem, they need to be continually nurtured to enable optimal performance.

Self-confidence

A lot of self-confidence rests on your ability to deal with the unknown. You don't know whether you can achieve something you've never done before, but you have to have faith that you will be able to, otherwise you won't even try. This feels scary, since failure, whether physical or mental, hurts, and humans have evolved to avoid anything that's painful. As a result, your reacting brain jumps into action in an attempt to try to protect you, telling you that it's safer and much more comfortable not to try anything new. That way nothing bad will happen.

The problem with remaining comfortable and safe is that it prevents you from fulfilling your higher-level need to grow and develop. In order to get better at anything, to achieve anything, you have to take a leap of faith into the unknown. Taking that first step requires courage: courage to overcome your reacting brain and to accept that you probably will fail, or at least encounter setbacks along the way.

Moving Beyond Shy

As a teenager and in my 20s, I had pretty low self-esteem, but I did have self-confidence in my ability to carry out certain tasks. I knew that if I threw myself headlong into things I would get there in the end, while learning and growing in the process. Each time I attempted something new I had to take a massive leap of faith: with low self-esteem the knocks hurt more and are more of a mental setback. Nevertheless, I was compelled to keep trying (I have my parents to thank for my persistence and determination).

At 16, I was quite shy, so I stood for music captain, which involved "selling myself" to 400 pupils at a new school, explaining why they should vote for me. This was a deliberate attempt to overcome my fear of talking to people. I forced myself beyond my comfort zone in order to grow.

While the dislike of standing up in front of people had started to wane by the time I got to university, the thought of singing in front of massive crowds made me feel sick. But when I was asked to sing in a band (after some deep contemplation) I agreed, with the same objective: to overcome my shyness. Gradually, through forcing myself into these performance situations, I have become quite comfortable standing up in front of people, even presenting to hundreds. And I'm definitely not shy any more.

To build self-confidence you need to take a few risks. You have to have the courage to take that first step and be prepared to fail, because otherwise you will never get any closer to fulfilling your potential or living out your purpose. Psychiatrist, philosopher, and writer Neel Burton says:

in the absence of confidence, courage takes over. Confidence operates in the realm of the known, courage in that of the unknown, the uncertain, and the fearsome. I cannot be confident in diving from a height of 10 meters unless I once had the courage to dive from a height of 10 meters.[12]

And whether or not you are self-confident currently, it is the courage to take that first step that you need to build.

TOOLS OF THE SESSION

Measuring Your Courage

How much courage do you have? How willing are you to take that first step into the unknown? Use the Courage Scale on the next page to see where you are with this currently.

How accurately does each statement describe you? Think of yourself as how you generally are now, not as you wish to be in the future. Total your scores and then check the information in Table 7.4 to determine your level of courage.

COURAGE SCALE
· ·

Instructions: Rate the statements below for how accurately they reflect the way you generally feel and behave, then circle the appropriate answer. Do not rate what you think you should do, or wish you do, or things you no longer do. Please be as honest as possible.

1—Very inaccurate
2—Moderately inaccurate
3—Neither inaccurate nor accurate
4—Moderately accurate
5—Very accurate

1. I have taken frequent stands in the face of strong opposition   1 2 3 4 5

2. I avoid dealing with uncomfortable emotions   1 2 3 4 5

3. I don't hesitate to express an unpopular opinion   1 2 3 4 5

4. I can face my fears   1 2 3 4 5

5. I avoid dealing with awkward situations   1 2 3 4 5

6. I speak up in protest when I hear someone say mean things   1 2 3 4 5

7. I do not stand up for my beliefs   1 2 3 4 5

8. I am a brave person   1 2 3 4 5

9. I don't speak my mind freely when
there might be negative results   1   2   3   4   5

10. I call for action while others talk   1   2   3   4   5

Total your scores from each row, making sure you swap the scores for statements 2, 5, 7, and 9, so that if you have put a 1 it becomes a 5 and a 2 becomes a 4.

Total your overall scores in the adjacent box.

Source: L.R. Goldberg, J.A. Johnson, H.W. Eber, et al. (2006) The International Personality Item Pool and the future of public-domain personality measures, *Journal of Research in Personality* 40: 84–96. Public domain.

TABLE 7.4 THREE LEVELS OF COURAGE

Total	Level	Definition
10–21	Low	You may struggle to take the first step when it comes to exploring new things and find it difficult to step out of your comfort zone.
		You may fear the emotions that you'll experience if you take a step into the unknown or try something new.
		You may fear the outcome of undertaking new situations or challenges.
		You don't like the potentially negative outcomes of standing up against something.
22–36	Typical	You will try new things and step beyond your comfort zone, but this may not be something that you will do in every situation.
		You most likely stand up for others and for your beliefs, but this will depend on the situation and your level of comfort.
		You may fear the unknown and the uncertain to an extent.
37–50	High	You see new opportunities as an exciting challenge and an opportunity to grow.
		You stand up against opposition and are happy to state your personal opinions and beliefs.
		You're unlikely to have any issue with the negative emotions that can come from pushing yourself out of your comfort zone. You may enjoy those emotions or not even experience them.

Taking the First Step

Once you take that first step toward action, you'll create a new level of assurance of "I did it once so I can do it again." But to get out of the starting blocks, you need to be prepared to live with the discomfort of your emotions and the prospect of setbacks and failure.

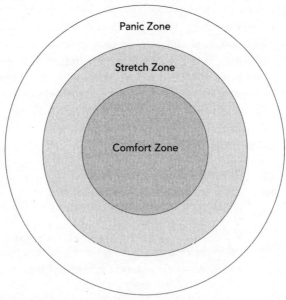

Figure 7.7 The Learning Zone model

Source: J.L. Luckner & R.S. Nadler (1991) *Processing the Adventure Experience: Theory and Practice*, Dubuque, IA: Kendall/Hunt.

The Learning Zone model (Figure 7.7), developed by John Luckner, (whose focus is special education), and psychologist Reldan Nadler, is a really helpful way to explain and understand the challenge of stepping beyond your comfort zone. When you are in your comfort zone, you don't have to take any risks, you know what to expect, and you have a sense of safety and security. That feels nice: it literally feels comfortable. To learn and grow as a person, you have to step into your stretch zone, pursuing situations that create a degree of discomfort, which takes courage. In your stretch zone, you'll experience emotional and potentially even physiological discomfort. Going into the stretch zone is known as a "borderline experience," because you are at the edge of your abilities and limits. Being in this space offers challenges, but also the chance to live out your curiosity, discover opportunities, and develop your capabilities. It's described as somewhere that you'll feel "eustress," a beneficial stress, which puts you in a heightened level of awareness and gives you competitive advantage.

Having courage isn't about constantly operating outside of your comfort zone, however. It's very important that you're able to return there after trying something new. Your comfort zone provides a safe haven, giving you a mental and physiological break. It also provides the essential breathing space for your brain to reflect and assimilate your learning. Nor is having courage about crossing into the panic zone, the third of Luckner and Nadler's zones. While the occasional trip into the panic zone can provide a helpful nudge (e.g., jumping off the 10-meter diving board for the first time or singing in front of a crowd), it's not somewhere you should ever be for too long. It's mentally draining, causes stress and fear, and is physiologically taxing, which (when it comes to active pursuits) leads to injury risks. Being in the panic zone also prevents rational thought. It puts you into survival mode, blocking off the opportunity to learn and grow.

So you need to push yourself out of your comfort zone in order to live out your purpose and feel fulfilled in the longer run. You have to take a deep breath and jump into things, give new activities a go so that you grow and develop. But you also need to be careful not to go too far.

You may find it helpful to look at this model in terms of yourself, using the information you collated in Session 7a. You, your values, passions, and strengths, all sit within the comfort zone (Figure 7.8). They are well established. Your development points and opportunity to grow sit in the stretch zone and may occasionally stretch into the panic zone, but never for too long. Your purpose encompasses both your comfort zone and your stretch zone.

TOOLS OF THE SESSION

Building Your Self-confidence

If you are at the lower end of the spectrum on the Courage Scale, or simply want to bolster your level of self-confidence when it comes to a specific task, this exercise will help you to take that first step.

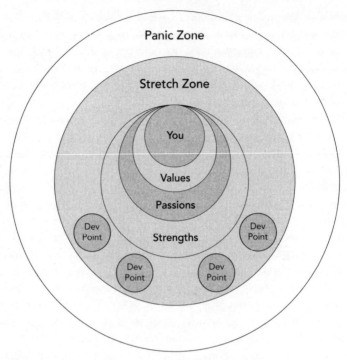

Figure 7.8 "You" in the Learning Zone model

Think of a challenge, task, or goal that you've been putting off because it worries you, or something that you know stretches you and creates a certain level of anxiety. With that task in mind, work through the following points.

1. What does it feel like when you think of this task and imagine yourself outside of your comfort zone (e.g., physiological— increased heart rate, sweating, etc.; and/or psychological—fear, panic, anxiety, excitement, etc.)?

2. While still thinking about stepping into your stretch zone with this specific task, use "emotion surfing" to sit with any physiological or psychological responses you have. Try not to engage with, respond, or react to them, just observe where they are in your body. Get comfortable with the discomfort.

3. Practice this once a day for several days before attempting the task and taking that first step you have been putting off. When you are ready to take the step, use emotion surfing to prepare yourself. If it helps, ask someone to support you, to come with you, or to be ready to discuss how it went.

4. Celebrate your success even if you don't achieve the outcome the first time. Celebrate your attempt and your effort, and recognize any obstacles that you've overcome. If someone is supporting you, ask them to do the same.

5. Repeat, repeat, repeat until this once daunting task falls within your comfort zone.

Don't expect perfection from yourself: failure and setbacks are inevitable in the stretch zone and are essential to growth and learning. Try to focus on setbacks as part of the process, rather than worrying about how you look to other people. For more on this, read Carol Dweck's *Mindset*.[13] Also focus on your purpose, since keeping your greater meaning in mind will help you to pull through setbacks.

It's important to realize that self-confidence isn't about never feeling inadequate or never having worries and anxieties; rather, it's about what we do with those emotions. If you can surf them rather than engaging with them, it will help you to move into a different realm.

TOOLS OF THE SESSION

Adjusting Your Development Points

Next, review your development points and the goals you've defined in light of your results on the Courage Scale and your understanding of the Learning Zone model. Are the goals stretching enough? Or are they unrealistically stretching, taking you too far into the panic zone? Tweak them if you need to so that they have the right balance between stretch and unrealistic. Placing them in the right zone will enable you to grow your self-confidence through proving your capability to yourself.

Self-esteem

Self-esteem is a more inward-facing facet of self-confidence. It's fundamental to who you are, what you believe, and what you tell yourself.
Self-esteem is closely related to intrinsic factors and less dependent on
external influences. In this sense, it's a little more difficult to achieve
than self-confidence. It takes reflection and self-belief, which is not as
easy to quantify as the achievement of goals and tasks. However, doing
things that focus on self-development—like working through this book
and reflecting on your journey—will help build your self-esteem.

Paul Gilbert and his colleagues at Kingsway Hospital have
demonstrated that self-esteem, self-criticism, and self-
compassion can be traced to three interacting emotional
systems in the brain.[14] Our ancient ancestors evolved to
protect themselves from any form of threat, which included a
threat to self-esteem. If they were sent off course because of
an obstacle or if they felt undermined by another group
member whom they perceived to be better, their fight-or-
flight mechanisms would be activated. These same networks
exist in our brain today.

Gilbert suggests that when we feel threatened (and respond
in fight mode), we verbally attack ourselves or the other
person who is making us feel threatened (although this may
not be out loud). Take a situation where someone puts you
down in a social setting. You may fight by criticizing yourself:
"Oh, they're right, I'm such an idiot, why did I say that?" or by
attacking the other person: "How dare you say that?" But you
could also flee from acknowledging your faults: "Well, that's a
load of rubbish, so I'll just ignore it." None of these responses
is helpful: the first undermines your self-esteem; the second
damages a social relationship; and the third creates an
incorrect level of self-awareness. But there is another system in
the brain that can, if we choose, act as an alternative to
activating the fight-or-flight mechanism. Gilbert refers to this as
the "contentment, soothing, and social safeness" system.

When we are not under threat, we go into a state of
contentment, feeling calm, peaceful, and with a sense of
well-being. From an evolutionary perspective, when our

ancestors were not fighting or fleeing an enemy, this system was triggered to enable attachment and caregiving of children and to other members of the social group. Within the brain, this represents an alternative response to fight or flight, triggering a different network and diverting thought patterns away from self-criticism. Hence it offers a way in which to build self-esteem.

To continue the above example, triggering the "contentment, soothing, and social safeness" system would involve a fourth response: "It's OK that they think that, it doesn't mean that's what I am, I just need to consider whether I've done anything to elicit that response." A great deal of research points toward us being able to trigger this system to override the fight response of self-deprecation. But to do so involves bringing your thoughts into conscious awareness, and also using self-compassion, which people can find very uncomfortable.

Psychologist Kristin Neff is a world leader in self-compassion research and has developed a program in affiliation with Harvard Medical School. She explains how having compassion for ourselves is really no different from having compassion for others. We need to go through the same steps to recognize and act on someone else's suffering as we do to notice and do something about our own. Seeing it as something we feel for others also helps to distinguish what self-compassion is not: it is not self-pity or self-indulgence. Neff outlines the three elements involved in compassion for others (and therefore ourselves) as:

- Noticing that someone is suffering (you could equate this with noticing that your internal dialogue is negative).

- Feeling moved by their suffering, to have empathy for it, and to understand it, responding with warmth and consideration.

- Understanding that suffering, failure, or imperfection is part of "the shared human experience," it's something that we all feel.[15]

Society portrays self-compassion as a bit "fluffy," soft, weak, and even selfish. On top of this, it triggers a different network in the brain from self-criticism. When we chastise ourselves, it activates an error-processing network that indicates to the brain there may be danger. This overrides the networks associated with self-compassion in an attempt to keep us safe, which creates a negative cycle. For example, if someone tells you to speak kindly to yourself and say "I am a lovely, caring, kind person," your response may be to think "That's a load of nonsense, I'm not going to bother with all that." That is automatically diverting signals in the brain to the fight response and away from the self-compassion network. So if you want to learn how to make effective use of the self-compassion network, you need to make a concerted effort to override this negativity. It's worth doing: there's a great deal of evidence showing the benefits of being more self-compassionate, including becoming a better leader, fulfilling your potential, and simply being happier.

TOOLS OF THE SESSION

Developing Your Self-compassion and Self-esteem

The next two exercises are taken from Kristin Neff's work. For more tools and research, go to http://self-compassion.org.

HOW WOULD YOU TREAT A FRIEND?
Take a piece of paper and answer the following questions:

- Think about a time when a close friend has felt really bad about him- or herself or has been really struggling in some way. How did you respond to your friend or how would you respond if you were "at your best" (or in other words, behaving like someone with a high level of self-compassion)? Write down what you would do, say, and note the tone in which you would talk to your friend.

- Now think about a time, any time, when you have felt bad about yourself or are struggling. How do you typically respond to yourself in these situations? Write down what you typically do, say, and note the tone in which you talk to yourself.

- Did you notice a difference? Why do you think the responses are different? What factors or fears come into play that lead you to treat yourself and others so differently?

- Write down how you think things might change if you responded to yourself in the same way you typically respond to a close friend when you're suffering. Try treating yourself like a good friend and see what happens.

IDENTIFYING WHAT WE REALLY WANT

Think about the ways in which you use self-criticism as a motivator. Is there any personal feature that you criticize yourself for having (being too overweight, too lazy, too impulsive, etc.) because you think being hard on yourself will help you change? If so, try to get in touch with the emotional pain that your self-criticism causes, giving yourself compassion for the experience of feeling so judged.

Next, see if you can think of a kinder, more caring way to motivate yourself to make a change. What language would a wise and nurturing friend, parent, teacher, or mentor use to gently point out how your behavior is unproductive, while encouraging you to do something different? What is the most supportive message you can think of that's in line with your underlying wish to be healthy and happy?

Every time you catch yourself being judgmental about your unwanted feature or trait in the future, first notice the pain of your self-judgment and then give yourself compassion. Try to reframe your inner dialogue so that it is more encouraging and supportive. Remember that if you really want to motivate yourself, love is more powerful than fear. Fear simply disables our observing brain and prevents us from growing, learning, or thinking rationally.

TOOLS OF THE SESSION

Making It Stick!

Doing exercises like these is one thing, changing the habits (and neural pathways) built up over a lifetime is quite another. To help make these particular changes stick, the following activity has been adapted from the work of professor of clinical psychology Paul Gilbert, who I have referred to above.

COMPASSION UNDER THE DUVET

Ideally you should try to practice "becoming the compassionate self" every day to ensure it really becomes a habit and retrains your brain. If your life is busy (which I'm sure it is), you can start by learning what Gilbert calls "compassion under the duvet." When you wake up in the morning and you're still in bed, stop and listen to your internal voice and what you are saying to yourself. Respond with warmth and consideration. Think about what you have coming up in your day, and talk yourself through it with reassurance, as if you were encouraging a friend or someone you love. Gilbert also suggests practicing in other places for just a couple of minutes at a time, when you're standing at the bus stop or in the shower for example. Even two minutes a day of this, if done every day, will have an effect on the neural pathways of your brain.

PRACTICE BY DOING

Another helpful way to begin to develop your mind to think differently is to change your behavior. Try to do one compassionate thing for yourself and somebody else each day, even if you don't feel like it. It actually doesn't matter! For example, if you regularly exercise even on those days you don't want to, you will still get fit because you're using and strengthening certain muscles in your body, including your heart. The same is true of habits and strengthening neural pathways in your brain. Now, you might say: "But if I don't feel compassionate then my behavior is not genuine." Yet it's often behaving compassionately even when we don't really want to that makes it even more compassionate. The point is, until you have more fully developed the neural pathways in your brain, how can you feel them? So you could, for example:

- Hold the door open for someone, even if you're in a hurry or the person you're doing it for looks really grumpy.

- Offer someone a lift, even if you'd prefer the silence of your own company.

- Compliment someone, even if they only ever criticize.

You can become more of what you would like to be when you practice. Just consider how you are going to "feed" the different neural pathways in your brain and practice paying attention to what goes through your mind, stopping it before it becomes overly self-critical. Try to keep in mind the need to practice and use mindfulness or emotion surfing, to help prevent you from getting caught up in your feelings and moods without taking notice.

> Tip: It's important to remember that our brain usually comes up with more negative emotions as a way of keeping us safe in a world in which we no longer exist. We can become despondent about having these thoughts, but they really aren't our fault. It is the way our brain has evolved. In effect, you're learning how to deal with an organ that's not well suited to the modern environment we all live in.

A PRACTICE DIARY

A practice diary is a way to keep notes about the exercises you practice while also helping you to see how you are getting on. As for the notes you have been writing on yourself throughout this book (e.g., on your timeline, in response to questions, in describing you), they provide a point of reference and enable you to pause and reflect. A practice diary is specifically used for working on self-compassion, as it's a way to help train your brain to think differently every day, for example, to focus on what you are grateful for. This will also have the added benefit of helping you to progress your other development points by giving you a greater level of self-esteem. You can even use this practice diary to capture thoughts about actions you have in your development plan. For example: "I was compassionate toward myself when I didn't manage to carry out one of the actions on my development plan," and then under observations, "I realized that I was pushing myself too hard and focusing on the wrong things today, which didn't allow me the space to live by my values." People often keep a diary to think, reflect, and write about their thoughts. It can also be useful to retain notes on and celebrate your successes, no matter how small. This will help to keep you focused and motivated to achieve your goals, not only when it comes to being self-compassionate, but also in fulfilling your development plan.

There's a template for a practice diary in Box 7.1.

BOX 7.1 EXAMPLE PRACTICE DIARY TEMPLATE

Practice Diary   Date:

5 things that brought me peace today were:

I feel happiest when:

I felt best about myself when:

The best part of today was:

3 things I am grateful for today are:

I was compassionate toward myself when:

I was compassionate toward someone else when:

Observations about today:

Presenting You With Confidence

We've discussed confidence as far as you and your approach to getting things done is concerned, but what about how other people see you? While building on your self-confidence and self-esteem will help you to fulfill your potential, the edge will come when you present your confident self outwardly to the rest of the world.

Presenting a confident persona is critical for leaders: without it they quickly lose the engagement and belief of their followers. However, it's really important for everyone else too, to get across the parts of you that you really want to share, to show who you are to the world, to give an accurate representation rather than blurting out random information that you later regret. How you position yourself with other people is what you are known for, and how you are known is critical to achieving your purpose. And while it may seem incredibly unjust, it's important to realize that everyone you meet judges you, and does so very quickly.

Psychologists Janine Willis and Alexander Todorov from Princeton University carried out research showing that it only takes a tenth of a second for us to form an opinion about someone when we meet them.[16] This happens in our reacting brain, so has little rational judgment attached to it, but that doesn't stop the initial view from "sticking." Most people don't go into situations with "observe, don't react" in mind, and our brain inadvertently looks for information that backs up our irrational, lightning-speed judgments, meaning that we very quickly label people by the first impression they make. Equally, others very quickly label us. So it's really important to be clear in your mind who you are, and to think through how you come across to others. This will ensure that the "right" version of you is presented clearly to whoever you meet, even in that first split second.

Think about the volume of information you have reflected on through the course of this book. That's all part of who you are, but you're not going to repeat all of it to everyone you meet, especially not in a brief encounter. You could tell any part of your story, but a single element, without the whole context around it, will not make sense. For example, if you said you had a car crash when you were 21 followed by a period of heightened anxiety and nervousness, that's what people will take away—they will view you as a person who is nervous and anxious. From that piece of information, they will fill in the gaps (because that's what our brain does) with other assumptions: maybe that you're no fun to be around, that you don't like doing the sorts of things that they do, that you haven't done much with your life because of your anxiety, and so on and so forth. But if in contrast you only told them about a time when you went out partying every night at college, danced on tables, and went to bed at 2 am, then the impression they will get of you will be very different. These may both be facets of who you are, but in isolation they tell a very different story.

Having put the effort into working through this book and raising your self-awareness, it's now worth thinking about the parts of you that you want to share and how you will do that. That doesn't mean selling yourself in a way that's dishonest; it means presenting an authentic, balanced picture of who you are and what you're about, communicating the things that you do well (without overblowing them) and the things that you struggle more with (without overplaying them).

This presentation of who you are is sometimes referred to as "personal branding." This label risks negative connotations of self-promotion, but, as Hubert K. Rampersad, a leading expert on this topic, explains:

> *Your Personal Brand should always reflect your true character, and should be built on your values, strengths, uniqueness, and genius. If you are branded in this organic, authentic, and holistic way your Personal Brand will be strong, clear, complete, and valuable to others.*[17]

Personal branding is about carefully considering how other people experience you (e.g., on social media, in interviews, from your CV, by email, and in person), how you reflect what you believe in, how you enable meaningful perceptions about the values and purpose that you stand for. It's about considering the positive feedback you have received and conveying that more confidently to the world around you. This will open up new opportunities and help you to be in the right position to attain your goals.

TOOLS OF THE SESSION

Sharing You

Everyone needs to tell their story to the outside world, so you may as well do it in a good way. Here are some steps that will help you think through how you position your story:

- Establish what you want to share: go through the key things that you wrote on your circles in Session 7a and highlight the areas that you want to share with people, the things that really tell the story of who you are.

- Go back to the "interview with your future self" and carry out the same activity for yourself in the present, thinking through which aspects you want to convey, why, and how. If this feels like too

big a task, move on to the next step. You can always come back to
this at a later date.

- Write your personal brand statement: a summary, in one paragraph,
of who you are and what you stand for. This may
take several attempts. You may find it helpful to write it out as
a longer version or a "mind dump" of what you're thinking to start
with. Then go through and cut out the bits that feel less relevant.
Or it may be helpful and fun to work with a friend to come up
with your statement. However you go about it, when it's finished
you need to feel that it accurately represents you, that it's neither
an overinflation nor an understatement of your capabilities.

- Test out your personal brand statement with people you know
and trust. Ask them for feedback. Is it simple enough? Is it saying
what you want it to? Does it resonate with them?

- Practice using your personal brand statement when you talk to
people and when talking about who you are more broadly, honing
your message. Think about what you say and how you say it, how
you hold yourself, the tone of your voice, what you are trying to
convey. Do this with a friend and ask for feedback, or even film
yourself and watch it back to help you tweak and fine-tune.

How You Come Across

As a simple guideline to creating a greater impact, think through the
following.

- **Smile**—Smiling has an immediate, measurable, positive impact on
the brain of the person you smile at, casting you in a more
positive light.

- **Be aware**—If you have any nervous tendencies, try to stay in your
observing brain mode to keep these in check when you first meet
people.

- **Connect**—Use the skills we've explored in this book to ensure you
connect authentically and make a constructive, lasting impression.

- **Think about body language**—Are you inadvertently crossing your arms or looking down, for example? Watch the TED Talk "Your body language may shape who you are" by Amy Cuddy, an associate professor in social psychology at Harvard Business School.[18] You may also find her book *Presence* helpful.[19]

- **Find positive examples**—Think about people you respect and admire and how they come across, look them up online and watch clips of them. What is it that resonates with you about what they say and how they say it? Which parts of them are true to you that you could authentically replicate?

Mel Carson, author of the book *Introduction to Personal Branding: 10 Steps Toward a New Professional You,*[20] offers helpful advice for presenting yourself in the digital world.

Coming to the End of the Session

In this session, we've looked at how to build your self-confidence and self-esteem, and I've given tips on how to help embed these capacities at a deeper level over time. This will enable you to fulfill the goals and development points you outlined earlier, and also to fine-tune them to keep them within your stretch zone. We've also explored how to present yourself to the world around you with confidence, so that those first impressions give a message that reflects the person you have defined as being you.

In the next session, we'll be working on "Optimizing You," finding the right environment for you to thrive in, in a way that aligns with your values, passions, and strengths.

CHAPTER 8

Optimizing You

● ● ●

This group of three sessions is called "Optimizing You," because it takes all the reflections and plans you have made so far and puts them within your work context in "Finding Your Place," considers how to get your brain into the best shape possible to enable you to fulfill your potential in "Fueling Your Brain," and finally helps you think through how you will make all this knowledge about yourself something that lasts and enables you to carry on performing at your best in "Continued Growth." So in essence, this chapter enables you to think through how to optimize your capabilities and maintain the energy and mindset to fulfill your dreams.

Session 8A

Finding Your Place

An essential step in profiling someone is not only finding out who they are, but also how they fit into their environment, such as the workplace and its culture, the team they will work with, or the values of the company. After the effort you've put into defining you, you now have a good understanding of who you are, what your purpose is (even if this is still evolving), and how to take that forward. But what about the best environment to suit your needs? You don't exist in isolation of the world around you, and you need to ensure that as far as possible the situations you find yourself in on a daily basis allow you to live out your values and pursue your purpose.

In the case of a leader, on paper the best candidate for a job may not be the best fit at a given point in time or in consideration of the team they will work with: the circumstances and needs of the situation have to be right in order for anyone to flourish. I often use Winston Churchill to illustrate what I mean by this. Churchill went down in history as one of the greatest leaders of all time as a result of his actions as Prime

Minister during the Second World War. However, before the war he made a number of political errors, including the decision when he was Britain's First Lord of the Admiralty at the time of the First World War that resulted in his dismissal from the Cabinet Office and exclusion from the War Council. Then, following outstanding leadership during the Second World War and an approval rating in the opinion polls of 83%, he lost the subsequent general election. In short, these environments and situations were not a good fit for him to perform at his optimum. Churchill was known to be a determined and stubborn man, which arguably helped him see Britain through the war. However, it could also be said that this prevented him from listening to others' concerns, which led to the errors before the war. Subsequently, this same stubbornness meant that his party did not flex and change to keep up with the seismic social changes that were taking place. This example demonstrates that you can't perform at your best unless you are in the right place for you at the right time. While you're unlikely to be involved in the same kinds of monumental decisions as Churchill, it's important that whoever you are, you can find an environment in which to flourish. By discovering the right place for you and removing yourself from environments that don't fit your values and purpose, you will be better able to thrive. You're now in a position where you can take the first step, as you have greater clarity over who you are and what you want to achieve.

In this session, you will have the chance to look at which environments are best suited to you and your preferences. You'll also learn how to distinguish a positive work environment from one that is toxic, and the impacts that these different environments have on your brain. When it comes to toxic environments, we'll explore how to cope with and where possible remove yourself from such situations. You'll learn that while you can and should attempt to find an environment that optimizes your natural preferences, reality imposes some limitations on all of us. Although it's possible to find a great fit, no environment is exactly right for anyone, so you don't want to spend your life searching for something that you'll never achieve.

Your Best Fit

The environments that allow you to thrive are where "person–environment fit" exists, i.e., the extent to which your characteristics as an individual are compatible with the environment you work in.[1]

There are generally four elements to consider when looking at person–environment fit: the match between you and your job, you and your organization, you and your boss, and you and the group or team you work with. When assessing someone for a role, I'll have an understanding of all these elements (i.e., job, organization, supervisor, and team) before meeting the candidate. These are the same factors that you need to weigh up for yourself before taking on any job or joining an organization or group, even if that isn't in the context of a paid position. The critical considerations for each element of your "best fit" are as follows:

- **You and your job or role**—how far your needs and preferences are met by the job or role.

- **You and your organization**—whether there is a match between your values and those displayed in the culture.

- **You and your boss**—whether you have shared goals, compatible personalities, and values that are aligned.

- **You and your team**—similarly, whether there are shared goals, compatible personalities, and values that are aligned.

The work you have done so far through this book has allowed you to define your values and your goals, and to understand your personality and what type of people you get on best with. You've also looked at the environments that you've thrived in and the ones you've struggled with, which will have provided you with a broader understanding of what works for you and what doesn't.

Rob Goffee, professor of organizational behavior at London Business School, and his colleague Gareth Jones collected data from executives over a four-year period with the aim of working out, at a generic level, what elements the best possible workplace would contain.[2] As an output of their research (and recognizing that individual differences found in person–environment fit also play a part), they created the mnemonic DREAMS, which outlines the six broad areas applicable to an ideal work environment, or what we might call a "healthy culture." These add up to a company where:

- **Difference** is nurtured, allowing people to be themselves and express their individuality.

- **Radical honesty** is a given, and people know what is really going on without information being suppressed or spun.

- Extra value is added for employees through personal development opportunities.

- Authenticity is integral, so the organization stands for something that has meaning.

- Meaningful work is standard, in that the work itself has meaning.

- Simple rules apply equally across the board.

In a *Harvard Business Review* article called "Creating the best workplace on earth," Goffee and Jones outline what they mean by each of these areas.[3] To shed light on what you should be looking for in a work environment, I summarize them here. Although this is written as if it's a work environment, the same applies to any organization, community group, or collection of people you're looking to join.

DIFFERENCE
Nurturing difference doesn't mean extreme individualism, but rather an opportunity for people to express themselves within what's broadly a more collaborative culture. Goffee and Jones give the example of people being accepted whether they come in wearing a suit if they work for a "hipster" company or wearing shorts and flipflops if they work in financial services. When you're considering joining a particular company, watch out for signs of too much conformity. It may not bother you if you are someone who likes to conform, but if you are keen to express your differences, it's something important to look for.

RADICAL HONESTY
A transparent culture allows you to operate at your best. In contrast, a toxic environment is not transparent, and people are unaware of what's going on or are given misleading information, which is, in turn, disempowering. Take a situation where you are trying to sell your house and the estate agent never reports back to you after viewings. You have no idea whether you're closer to selling or not, and therefore whether you can move ahead with buying another property. Aside from making it difficult to get on with your aim of moving home, it feels incredibly frustrating and the ambiguity is uncomfortable and stressful. When you're investigating an organizational culture, try to get an idea of how much information is shared, whether people are misled by the infor-

mation, or whether the culture is transparent and upfront about what's going on. Find out by asking people who already work there.

EXTRA VALUE

Employees are given opportunities to grow and develop and personal development is invested in, in terms of both finances and time. The culture also enables growth opportunities, allowing the space for people to fail and learn from mistakes. Ask a hiring company what its view is on personal development and check with existing employees to make sure it does what it says.

AUTHENTICITY

This is about a company providing meaning and applying internally with what it represents to the world. It's critical to look beyond the obvious on this one. I can think of a company I once worked with that gave the impression of being fair, open-minded, flexible, and forward thinking to customers, but had an internal culture that was stuffy, bureaucratic, old-fashioned, and unyielding. So find out more about how the company you may be thinking of joining works on the inside and what meaning it provides for employees. If it has a mission statement and values, does it actually live by those?

MEANINGFUL WORK

The work itself has meaning for you personally and it aligns with your values and your purpose. No company is going to match exactly with what you're seeking: you are unique and the whole purpose of this book has been about defining that. But try to find a company that aligns as closely as possible. For example, as a graduate I joined a consulting company which engaged my intellectual curiosity, drive, and the opportunity to make a difference. Yet how it made a difference didn't align closely enough with how I wanted to. It was a fantastic company for bringing cutting-edge, innovative solutions to clients, but I wanted to fundamentally improve people's lives. I stayed for four years because I was working with people whose values closely aligned with mine, but it wasn't enough in the longer term. Take time to really consider a company's values and how they sit with your own before joining. In my experience, this is the most important factor you should be looking at. You can't live out every day in a way that is misaligned with the core of who you are. At the very least, ensure that the people you would be working with share your values, even if their personalities and preferences are completely different from yours. Shared values provide the foundation for really positive working relationships.

SIMPLE RULES

As companies grow in size, the number of rules tends to increase, creating levels of complexity that can be suffocating. Rules need to exist as guidelines to how people should operate and to keep people safe, nothing more. Check that any company you want to join does not have so many rules that it makes it difficult to get on with work. Ideally there should be clear objectives and expectations, with freedom within which to achieve them.

TOOLS OF THE SESSION

Understanding Where You Thrive

Look back at the storyline that you created in Chapters 2 and 3 and note down the answers to the following questions in Table 8.1.

YOU AND YOUR JOB

Look over your narrative and think about the jobs that you've most enjoyed. Try to isolate the job from the organization, boss, and team aspects. What was it that you particularly liked about it? For instance, was it responsibility, contact with clients, carrying out research, being given the freedom to operate? Write these aspects under "Me and my job fit" in Table 8.1.

YOU AND YOUR ORGANIZATION

Which organization you have worked for has had the best fit with your values? This may not only be a full-time job, it could have been a part-time job you had while studying, or a college or university environment. What were those values? List these under "Me and my organization fit." You should find that they slot under the headings of the core values you identified in Chapter 7. If they don't, think of anywhere that you feel comfortable and why that is, what it is about that environment, and whether it is something you could look for in a workplace.

TABLE 8.1 UNDERSTANDING WHERE I THRIVE

Me and my job fit
Me and my oranization fit
Me and my boss
Me and my team

YOU AND YOUR BOSS

Who was the best boss you ever worked for? Who was the worst? What were their values and what approach did they take? Use this information to help you list the values, personality, and approach of your ideal boss and write them under "Me and my boss."

YOU AND YOUR TEAM

Which team have you most enjoyed working with? This doesn't have to be in a work context: it could be at university or college, a sports team you were a member of, or any other group. What were the team values, the personalities of the individual members, and what was the context (e.g., were you working together toward shared goals)? List the factors you would like to have in a team, taking account of personality, values, and approach, under "Me and my team."

Finding Your Best Fit Moving Forward

Now you have a list of the factors that constitute your ideal person–environment fit. It's hard to factor in all of these variables when looking for a job, but you can use them as a guide to help you find the best possible fit. The next activity helps you think through what to investigate when you are deciding on a new job or moving to a different environment. This covers "meaningful work," but you should also compare any organization you're thinking of joining against the remaining DREAMS factors: difference, radical honesty, extra value, authenticity, and simple rules. Approach this investigation in an interested and curious way. People like to see that candidates for roles are properly engaged, but do be careful not to come across as too intense in your questioning, or they won't want to hire you.

YOU AND YOUR JOB

Compare the job description and what you have been told by the recruiters to your list under "Me and my job." Also consider what you want to see in this role: you may want more responsibility or stretch than you've had previously, for example. Be sure to question and get underneath the description of the job, as sometimes there's a mismatch between what's written and what the actual role entails.

YOU AND YOUR ORGANIZATION

Compare your list with what the organization says it does. For this one you need to look beyond the words themselves. Ask questions in the interviews, ask people who work there, look on glassdoor (www.glassdoor.com will connect you to the site relevant to your location) for company reviews. Remember that you may not find an ideal match with your values, but it's important to get as close as you can.

YOU AND YOUR BOSS

Compare the list you created for "Me and my boss" with what you see in your potential supervisor. Do their values align with yours (this is the most important factor)? Is their personality the type that you'd normally get along with? Is there anything that niggles, worries, or annoys you about them (take time to reflect on this, as it could become an obstacle once you're in the role)? Are they going to let you do what you need to (i.e., give you support and space to carry out the role, recognize a job well done, give you feedback, support your personal development)? Do you have a shared belief in the goals required for the role?

YOU AND YOUR TEAM

Ask to meet the team before accepting any job. When you do, compare your impression with your "Me and my team" criteria. While this is important, it's not the crucial factor, however. Team members will probably change, whereas the values of the organization won't and your boss is less likely to.

Environmental Mismatch

When you're in the right environment, you free up the mental capacity that allows you to develop at your optimum. Rather than trying to deal with obstacles, you can focus on achieving your purpose. However, sometimes the environment you are in can be less than positive, and might even be described as "toxic."

The human brain hasn't evolved to meet the demands of the fast-paced, structured, processed, technological, scientifically advanced world we live in now. Our ancient brain evolved to respond to an environment where humans only interacted with about 100–150 people over their lifetime, spent most of their time with their family, and existed in close-knit communities.[4] Our ancestors were surrounded by the peace of nature, slept when it was dark, got up when it was light, and primarily concerned themselves with surviving and protecting their family. A huge number of organizational environments today are a mismatch with our ancestral setting, the one our brain evolved to exist in, so in many respects we're on the back foot from the outset. This makes it even more critical that we recognize the very worst or most toxic environments and where possible extract ourselves from them. Although this may sound negative, it's important to understand in order to equip you with the awareness of when your environment is interfering with your performance and of the need to be proactive in finding somewhere better, or at least recognize the factors that are having a detrimental impact on your well-being.

The two factors that contribute most significantly to the formation of toxic environments are a negative organizational culture (which enables adverse group norms) and bad leadership or a strongly influential negative group member. Charmine Härtel, professor of human resource management and organizational development, has carried out extensive research on organizational culture. In a 2008 paper she highlighted the core aspects of healthy and toxic working environments, explaining that cultures fulfill the basic human need to belong and the higher-level need of understanding our purpose for existing, which as you know are closely linked to emotional well-being.[5] Healthy cultures provide a supportive framework and degree of psychological safety that enable people to deal with uncertainties. Toxic environments strip away these positive aspects.

Härtel outlines two types of toxic culture, both of which are a mismatch to our basic emotional needs: one is extreme collectivism and the other extreme individualism. She explains that in a culture that encourages **extreme collectivism**, people lose their individuality, suppressing their personality to fit the expected template of the typical employee. These environments not only strip people of their identity, but also prevent personal growth and development, leading to feelings of anxiety, frustration, and depleted self-worth. To make matters worse, these cultures often expect employees to hold back their emotions. In turn, this not only undermines self-confidence and mental well-being, but at its extreme has even been linked to heart disease and suppressed immune functioning.

At the other end of the spectrum lie cultures of **extreme individualism**. While these allow people to express their personality, they can also make employees feel isolated if they are unable to identify with the work they do or the organization they work for. This can lead them to feel neglect, isolation, loneliness, vulnerability, fear, and dejection. The individualistic nature of the culture also reduces the opportunity to build positive working relationships, leading to distrust. As well as being incredibly unproductive for the organization, this undermines emotional well being and individual performance.

No culture will be an exact fit with a person's needs, but these extremes are best avoided. A healthy culture sits somewhere in between, allowing people the chance to display a degree of individuality, expressing their authentic self and having the opportunity for personal development, while working in collaboration with other people. At the same time, it doesn't suffocate them with expectations of conformity.

Härtel describes the ethos of such cultures as enabling people to be "accepted as unique individuals who have their own identities and growth potentials that belong to one unified social entity."

Beyond the culture, some individuals make an environment toxic, and these tend to fall into the category of bullies. Although bullying may start with one individual, it can quickly get ingrained within a culture, with people inadvertently, behaving in a negative and demeaning way to new entrants and more junior people. Those doing the bullying are either unaware of their behavior, seeing it as the norm, or have adopted the thinking of "It happened to me, so why should it not happen to them?"

A large part of removing yourself from a toxic environment is about being aware of the environment you're operating in. Does it sound like your work culture fits the description of extreme collectivism or extreme individualism, for example? Or do you work in an environment that is dominated by a bully or where bullying is accepted? If so, you should seriously consider moving jobs, because none of these is something that you can personally change.

Toxic working

Although I work on the positive aspects of behavior, such as enabling better performance, I have come across a number of different toxic environments over the years. One particular company had both a culture of extreme collectivism and inadvertent bullying. Even though I was not there to help sort out this issue, I got personally frustrated at my inability to effect change, or help people beyond equipping them with strategies to cope or suggesting they leave.

I was brought in to work with the top team, who themselves were disempowered by the structure and bullying from the very top (deeply ingrained through a complex power dynamic). The organizational culture was "command and control," with clocking in and clocking out, even for the most senior leaders; there was an expectation that people would be at their desk or walking the floor, never out to lunch or having a coffee with a colleague, and certainly not working from home. Employees were expected to be loyal and committed to the organization, although managers did not give much back to engender such behavior. Hours were long and little recognition was offered for a job well done.

Managers had "grown up" in the organization, learning to treat people with a certain degree of disdain and expectation that they would follow orders. Ironically, the leaders would then get frustrated that no one showed initiative or offered alternative viewpoints. This in turn fueled their disdain for their followers, and so the cycle continued.

Although my remit was to work with the senior team, I got to know people at all levels and heard story upon story of people feeling disempowered, demotivated, and stuck. The culture had infected employees with the belief that they were "not good enough" and as a result they felt powerless to find a job elsewhere, believing that no one at all would want them. This culture had such a strong influence that even the most senior leaders, with years of experience and recognized for their capabilities, felt trapped, disempowered, and worthless.

If you are in this situation, you either need to find some form of meaning in it for you personally and protect yourself from the influences of your environment (see "Dealing with a toxic environment" below), or you need to get out as quickly as you can.

TOOLS OF THE SESSION

Is Your Environment Toxic?

Some aspects of your work environment may well feel toxic, but not to the extent that they derail you. Others will be an inevitable part of the world we live in. For example, there is a need for all of us to conform to a certain extent, even if we feel we want to do something different: it's sometimes the only way to get on in a group setting. However, if you are conforming to the point that it feels like it's going against the grain of who you are, preventing you from expressing yourself or growing, then it's time to rethink. Ronald Riggio, professor of leadership and organizational psychology at Claremont McKenna College, California, suggests that there are five warning signs that a situation is not right.[6] Check your environment against this list:

- **You have to keep your head down**—you try not to stand out in any way, from making mistakes through to making suggestions, because you're likely to get put down or attacked.

- **The bullies run the show**—there's a culture of putting down and belittling others.

- **It takes an act of God to get anything done**—there are obstacles in the way to achieving anything.

- **No matter what you do, you can't get ahead**—your performance, however good, receives no recognition.

- **It's all sweat, and no heart**—the organization is focused on money, profits, cost cutting, etc., without seriously considering the role of employees in achieving success.

If you find yourself acknowledging any of these points, then it's likely that your environment is having a negative impact on you. Sometimes there is little you can do immediately to remove yourself from a toxic environment. It may take time and planning: for example, there may not be another job to go to straight away. In the meantime, if you do find yourself in a toxic environment or at a mismatch with where you feel you should be, then the next activity should help you to manage.

TOOLS OF THE SESSION

Dealing with a Toxic Environment

- **Realize that it's not you**—People who are suffering as a result of being in a toxic environment generally believe that they are in some way to blame. This is because such environments undermine your self-esteem and confidence. It's really important to realize that you are not at fault and that you are still as capable as you always have been.

- **Regain your identity**—One powerful way to keep your self-esteem intact is to look at how you can fulfill your purpose and values outside of work. This might be volunteering, taking a course, getting involved in the community, spending more time with your family and friends, or doing anything that aligns with what you feel deeply about and allows you to express your strengths.

- **Find an outlet**—Do something every day that allows you to relieve your stress while expressing your interests or passions. For example, you may want to take a yoga class, go to the gym to work out, do some gardening, go for a walk, bake, listen to music, go for a drive: whatever it is that you find relaxing.

- **Learn what you can**—Working through your storyline, you will have reflected on the learning and growth you experienced during difficult periods in life. People almost always learn and grow as a result of negative experiences. Proactively look for things that you can learn in this situation: What sort of boss do you *not* want to become? How would you do things differently if you were in charge? If you're planning on starting your own company at some point, how would you make sure no one felt like this? If you're interacting with people in a community, how do you want to influence the group?

- **Find positive people to associate with**—Keep away from people who perpetuate the toxic environment, who are negative, moan, gossip, or respond in a helpless way. They will only serve to exacerbate the situation and how you feel, so try to find positive people to talk to, work with, and associate with.

- **Build your support outside of work**—Make sure that you have people who you can vent your frustrations to, discuss concerns with, and seek support from.

- **Let your emotions go**—When you do feel frustrated, angry, or dejected, or when you cannot get away from a situation or person who is constantly negative, then try to make use of emotion surfing. Holding on to these emotions will make them worse and eat away at you. Mindfulness is also an incredibly helpful tool to use in this or any negative situation. Try to practice mindfulness every day using one of the apps recommended in the Bibliography (try them out and use the one best suited to you) and be patient with it. Mindfulness has a cumulative effect, so you may not see the difference straight away, but you will with persistence.

- **Plan your exit**—If you feel that you're not getting anything from your role and it doesn't look like things are going to improve, then it's best to plan how you will get out. Get your CV into shape, talk to people about opportunities, and start thinking about what to do next.

Dealing with Bullies

Bullying is a serious problem and not something that should be ignored. However, it is important to realize that you can't simply confront bullying and be done with it, as it's often a complex issue that's intertwined with what are called macro, meso, and micro levels of an organization. Dealing with "surface symptoms" won't make the problem go away and could leave you far worse off. So you need to use the organizational processes to support you:

1. **Confide in someone you trust**—Tell someone at work who you feel comfortable talking to and who you trust not to share information about the situation.
2. **Get advice**—Talk to someone in HR, or an employee representative, or, if it's not your boss or supervisor causing the issue, discuss it with them.
3. **Keep a diary**—Write down every single incident that makes you feel belittled or afraid. If there was anyone else present who saw what happened, note their names. This is known as a contemporaneous record. It will be very useful if you decide to take action at a later stage.
4. **Make a formal complaint**—If you've had no luck in trying to solve the issue by talking to the bully or following advice from HR, you will have to make a formal complaint. To do this, you will need to follow your employer's grievance procedure.

N.B. If the bullying is affecting your health, make an appointment to speak to your doctor.

Coming to the End of the Session

In this session you've explored the elements critical to a good fit between you and your job, identifying the individual aspects relevant to you and gaining an understanding of the more global factors that represent a healthy working environment. This should help you to find a context where you are most able to thrive and grow while working in a way that aligns with your values. You have also looked at the elements that make up a toxic environment. You've explored tools to help you manage and protect yourself if you need them, and guidelines on how to deal with a specific individual if you are being bullied. The next session will consider how to look after your brain and body, specifically addressing sleep, exercise, and stress, and the impact these have on your performance.

Session 8B

Fueling Your Brain

In order to perform at your best, you not only need to know yourself and where to find the best environment for you to thrive, you also need to look after your brain and body. It's becoming ever more evident that mental performance is influenced by biological factors, especially sleep, exercise, and stress (we'll come to stress in the last session of the book).

An athlete needs training and rest to improve their performance and reach their potential, and in the same way so do you. All too often we neglect our recuperation time when we're striving to get ahead or even just busy living. Sleep has become underrated. Unlike our ancient ancestors, we do not and realistically cannot go to sleep when it gets dark and get up when it's light. This mismatch with our natural needs has a massive impact on our performance. The first part of this session will investigate the science and benefits of good sleep to help you understand why it is so critical to your brain and body, and the obstacles that modern life puts in the way. Then we'll take a look at how to optimize your sleep and wake patterns by examining your circadian rhythms. We'll use the data from this to put together a plan that helps you make the best use of your daily rhythms and your sleep time, given the reality of the world and your lifestyle.

When it comes to exercise, we're very much aware of the benefits of being active for health and performance, but it's not always that convenient to fit exercise into our daily to-do list. We have to make a conscious effort to focus on this so the need doesn't get lost in the process of life. This session will explore physical activity, outlining the science behind its impact on performance and well-being. I'll help you identify what may be getting in the way of you doing more physical activity and ways around those obstacles, and how to choose an exercise that works best for you.

Sleep

From a physiological perspective, we need to spend about a third of our life asleep.[7] Without sleep we aren't able to function normally, let alone have the space to function optimally, thinking through what we want from life and how we will go about achieving it. Nevertheless, most of us live busy and stressful lives, which leads us to ignore or brush aside our sleep requirement (while still complaining that we're tired the whole time).[8] This isn't helped by the "culture of success," where working long hours on little sleep has come to represent a badge of honor. As a result, even when we're tired, we push ourselves to stay awake, checking emails or having another drink at a party or watching one more episode on Netflix. We forget how important sleep is in order to remain self-aware, to keep our reacting brain in check, and to enable us to reach our potential on a daily basis.

The repercussions of lack of sleep can be worryingly severe. When we haven't had enough sleep we tend to get moody, our memory becomes impaired, we make poor decisions, we snap at people,[9] and, more significantly, lack of sleep is often a contributory factor to accidents and injury. Over a prolonged period, sleep deprivation can also have serious health implications, including an increased risk of diabetes, obesity, heart disease,[10] clinical depression, anxiety, and paranoia,[11] and at the extreme end of the spectrum psychosis[12] and even death.[13] Lack of sleep creates the same levels of cognitive deficiency as drink and drugs.[14] In the UK, four out of five people have disturbed or inadequate sleep,[15] a proportion that is higher still in the US, where according to the Centers for Disease Control one in three people doesn't get enough sleep.[16] A major problem with this is that despite being dangerously tired, many of us still think we are functioning at a normal level.

Sleep is worth investing in: optimal sleep is linked to better cognitive performance, increased energy levels, and better physical and athletic performance, as well as improved emotional and social functioning. In short, we need sleep in order to define who we are and fulfill our purpose in life. We need sleep to think clearly enough to pursue our goals, to network effectively, to have a good level of self-awareness, and to be able to perform in whatever capacity that may take.

Our brains haven't adjusted to the use of artificial light or to our modern way of life. In his book *At Day's Close: Night in Times Past*, Roger Ekirch, professor of history at Virginia Polytechnic Institute in Roanoke, outlined typical sleep patterns for our ancestors.[17] He found over 500 references to sleep in diaries, court records, and medical books that all pointed to the same sleep patterns: going to bed soon after sunset and getting up at sunrise. Until a century or so ago, people would also typically have a period of being awake in the middle of the night for about an hour. These findings were backed by research carried out in 1992 by a psychiatrist called Thomas Wehr.[18] He undertook a study to see what happened if eight men were kept in complete darkness for 14 hours a day for an entire month. By the fourth week, all of the men had fallen into the same sleeping pattern, which completely mirrored the pattern in historical records: four hours' sleep followed by one or two hours of being awake and a further four hours' sleep. There are a number of professionals, including academics and medics, who believe that fighting this natural rhythm of sleep and wakefulness is in part what aggravates insomnia. People wake up in the middle of the night and lie there getting more and more anxious, because they feel that being awake is unnatural or bad. This in itself exacerbates their inability to sleep.

Furthermore, our internal clock, known as our circadian rhythm, struggles to adapt to any major deviations from normal and biological sleeping patterns. Although the rhythm is affected by exposure to natural light,[19] and to a lesser extent by the time we go to bed, exercise, social cues, local time (depending on where we are in the world), and when we eat, it is slow to change. Yet we constantly shift our sleep time, and our body finds it difficult to cope. We can see this most obviously when we travel to a different time zone and are exposed to light at different times of day. Even with this dramatic change in when our body experiences sunrise and sunset, it takes roughly one hour per day for us to shift completely to a new local time.[20] Our circadian rhythm itself differs according to biological, genetic, psychosocial, and contextual components. Some of us are more alert in the morning—

known fondly as "larks"—and others are better in the evening—known as "night owls." We'll explore your own circadian type a little later.

Regardless of when we go to bed or get up, many people are almost proud of not having enough sleep because they are so busy. We equate busyness with importance and therefore it makes us feel valued. But it's much better to feel a sense of value from being able to live our life with meaning. Without sleep, we cannot do that effectively. The need to be busy is particularly true in the corporate world, where there is an expectation that to get ahead you just carry on and deal with sleep deprivation. Arianna Huffington is an example of someone who did just this, and suffered the consequences when in 2007 she collapsed from exhaustion. Now she works to promote the benefits of proper sleep by giving talks on the subject for the TED media organization, as well as ensuring that it is highlighted in editorials for her online magazine *The Huffington Post*. The chief operating officer of Facebook, Sheryl Sandberg, also used to prioritize work over sleep, but negative health consequences mean she now ensures she gets a minimum of seven hours a night. The former CEO of Microsoft, Bill Gates, who used to burn the midnight oil for work, has changed his working habits to allow for at least "seven hours sleep a night because that's what I need to stay sharp and creative and upbeat." More and more, successful executives are coming to understand how important sleep is. Let me give you an example of someone I've worked with.

What's Sleep Got to Do with It?

A client of mine, Alec, constantly traveled around the world for meetings, surfing time zones. While he said he was fine and that the travel didn't really affect him, his performance was far from optimal. He was given feedback that he needed to be more empathic with people, that he was always short-tempered and never had time to listen. This was particularly important because the company was going through some dramatic changes, and the staff were feeling unsettled and needed his leadership. Alec didn't see this feedback as a problem, claiming that he would just listen a bit more, time allowing. But in reality, he couldn't switch his behavior so easily, despite putting in a great deal of effort.

Working with him on this, it became clear that his behavior was simply and directly linked to his tiredness. None of these performance issues existed before he took on a role that required so much travel. Yet while his company recognized the need for him to connect better with people, they didn't acknowledge the demands they were placing on him through his travel schedule. Once this was appreciated and we had a chance to look at all of the factors influencing his sleep patterns, his performance began to improve.

The point is that it's up to you to recognize how much sleep you need, because your employer rarely will. And then you have to be realistic about your needs rather than carrying on regardless, as lack of sleep can dramatically affect your performance, your health, and have a negative impact on the people around you too.

TOOLS OF THE SESSION

Circadian Rhythm

The Morningness–Eveningness Questionnaire was designed in the 1970s, but is so robust that it is still widely used by psychological and medical researchers today. James Horne and Olov Östberg, who designed this measure, were interested in what time of day a person's circadian rhythm or biological clock would produce peak alertness. Some people are better in the morning, others in the evening, and some fall between morning and evening. Knowing when your peak alertness is can help you to understand how to make the most of your performance and when to schedule tasks that require your highest levels of attention and competence.

Complete the questionnaire and then check out what your score means in Table 8.2.

MORNINGNESS–EVENINGNESS QUESTIONNAIRE
SELF-ASSESSMENT VERSION (MEQ-SA)

For each question, please select the answer that best describes you by circling the point value that best indicates how you have felt in recent weeks.

1. What time would you get up if you were entirely free to plan your day?

[**5**] 5:00 am–6:30 am
[**4**] 6:30 am–7:45 am
[**3**] 7:45 am–9:45 am
[**2**] 9:45 am–11:00 am
[**1**] 11:00 am–12 noon

2. What time would you go to bed if you were entirely free to plan your evening?

[**5**] 8:00 pm–9:00 pm
[**4**] 9:00 pm–10:15 pm
[**3**] 10:15 pm–12:30 am
[**2**] 12:30 am–1:45 am
[**1**] 1:45 am–3:00 am

3. If you have to get up at a specific time in the morning (one that's different from your usual wake-up time), how much do you depend on an alarm clock?

[**4**] Not at all
[**3**] Slightly
[**2**] Somewhat
[**1**] Very much

4. How easy do you find it to get up in the morning (when you are not woken unexpectedly)?

[**1**]　Very difficult
[**2**]　Somewhat difficult
[**3**]　Fairly easy
[**4**]　Very easy

5. How alert do you feel during the first half hour after you wake up in the morning?

[**1**]　Not at all alert
[**2**]　Slightly alert
[**3**]　Fairly alert
[**4**]　Very alert

6. How hungry do you feel during the first half hour after you wake up?

[**1**]　Not at all hungry
[**2**]　Slightly hungry
[**3**]　Fairly hungry
[**4**]　Very hungry

7. During the first half hour after you wake up in the morning, how do you feel?

[**1**]　Very tired
[**2**]　Fairly tired
[**3**]　Fairly refreshed
[**4**]　Very refreshed

8. If you had no commitments the next day, what time would you go to bed compared to your usual bedtime?

[**4**] Seldom or never later
[**3**] Less than 1 hour later
[**2**] 1–2 hours later
[**1**] More than 2 hours later

9. You have decided to do physical exercise. A friend suggests that you do this for one hour twice a week, and the best time for him is between 7 and 8 am. Bearing in mind nothing but your own internal "clock," how do you think you would perform?

[**4**] Would be in good form
[**3**] Would be in reasonable form
[**2**] Would find it difficult
[**1**] Would find it very difficult

10. What time in the evening do you feel tired, and, as a result, in need of sleep?

[**5**] 8:00 pm–9:00 pm
[**4**] 9:00 pm–10:15 pm
[**3**] 10:15 pm–12:45 am
[**2**] 12:45 am–2:00 am
[**1**] 2:00 am–3:00 am

11. You want to be at your peak performance for a test that you know is going to be mentally exhausting and will last two hours. You are entirely free to plan your day. Considering only your "internal clock," which one of the four testing times would you choose?

[**6**] 8 am–10 am
[**4**] 11 am–1 pm
[**2**] 3 pm–5 pm
[**0**] 7 pm–9 pm

12. If you got into bed at 11 pm, how tired would you be?

[**0**]   Not at all tired
[**2**]   A little tired
[**3**]   Fairly tired
[**5**]   Very tired

13. For some reason you have gone to bed several hours later than usual, but there is no need to get up at any particular time the next morning. Which one of the following are you most likely to do?

[**4**]   Wake up at usual time, but will not fall back asleep
[**3**]   Wake up at usual time and will doze thereafter
[**2**]   Wake up at usual time, but will fall asleep again
[**1**]   Will not wake up until later than usual

14. One night you have to remain awake between 4 and 6 am in order to carry out a night watch. You have no time commitments the next day. Which of the following would suit you best?

[**1**]   Would not go to bed until the watch is over
[**2**]   Would take a nap before and sleep after
[**3**]   Would take a good sleep before and nap after
[**4**]   Would sleep only before the watch

15. If you had two hours of hard physical work and were entirely free to plan your day, considering only your internal "clock," which time would you choose?

[**4**]   8 am–10 am
[**3**]   11 am–1 pm
[**2**]   3 pm–5 pm
[**1**]   7 pm–9 pm

16. You have decided to do physical exercise. A friend suggests that you do this for one hour twice a week. The best time for her is between 10 and 11 pm. Bearing in mind only your internal "clock," how well do you think you would perform?

[**1**]   Would be in good form
[**2**]   Would be in reasonable form
[**3**]   Would find it difficult
[**4**]   Would find it very difficult

17. Suppose you can choose your own work hours. Assume that you work a five-hour day (including breaks), your job is interesting, and you are paid based on your performance. At approximately what time would you choose to begin?

[**5**]   5 hours starting between 4 and 8 am
[**4**]   5 hours starting between 8 and 9 am
[**3**]   5 hours starting between 9 am and 2 pm
[**2**]   5 hours starting between 2 and 5 pm
[**1**]   5 hours starting between 5 pm and 4 am

18. At approximately what time of day do you usually feel your best?

[**5**]   5–8 am
[**4**]   8–10 am
[**3**]   10 am–5 pm
[**2**]   5–10 pm
[**1**]   10 pm–5 am

19. One hears about "morning types" and "evening types." Which one of these types do you consider yourself to be?

[**6**]   Definitely a morning type
[**4**]   Rather more a morning type than an evening type
[**2**]   Rather more an evening type than a morning type
[**1**]   Definitely an evening type

_____ Total points for all 19 questions

Source: Adapted with permission from: J.A. Horne & O. Östberg (1976)
A self-assessment questionnaire to determine morningness–eveningness in
human circadian rhythms, *International Journal of Chronobiology* 4(2): 97–110.

**TABLE 8.2 WHAT TYPE ARE YOU IN THE
MORNINGNESS–EVENINGNESS QUESTIONNAIRE?**

Score	Type
16–30	Definitely evening (DE)
31–41	Moderately evening (ME)
42–58	Neither (N)
59–69	Moderately morning (MM)
70–86	Definitely morning (DM)

UNDERSTANDING YOUR CIRCADIAN RHYTHM

As mentioned earlier, morning and evening types are also referred to as larks and night owls. If you are a definitely morning type or a lark, you perform better mentally and physically in the morning. If you are a definitely evening type or a night owl, you perform better both mentally and physically in the late afternoon or evening.

The typical circadian rhythm range covers the N, MM, and ME types. These account for 70% of the population. If you are in this median range, you will normally wake up between 7 and 8 am and go to bed between 11 pm and midnight. You are most mentally alert in the morning and early evening and least mentally alert in the early afternoon. If you are an MM type, you could find it more difficult to work late into the night than ME or N types.

Only 10% of the population are DMs or extreme larks. If you fall into this category, you will be most productive at around 8–9 am and tired out by 9 or 10 pm.

The final 20% fall into the category of DE or extreme night owls. If this is you, as the term suggests you'll be able to work well into the night without any problems, but perform poorly first thing in the morning. You need to be careful, though, because having to get up at what society considers to be a "normal" time will gradually lead to sleep deprivation.

If at all possible, you should try to schedule mentally and physically demanding tasks to fit with your peak time, allowing you to get more done and to a higher standard. You may even want to consider shifting your sleeping time forward or back so that you're always able to make the most of your peak time. An example of someone who has understood his ideal times and made use of them is the Japanese novelist Haruki Murakami, who goes to bed at around 9 pm every night and wakes up naturally at 4 am. He has spoken about how this enables him to write optimally from waking up until midday. This is his peak performance window—following at least seven hours of sleep a night.

WAYS TO OPTIMIZE YOUR SLEEP

Along with optimizing your use of your circardian rhythm, it's useful to understand how to improve the quality of your sleep. Sleep coach Nick Littlehale has worked with a range of elite British athletes, including cyclists Bradley Wiggins and Chris Hoy, as well as football teams such as Manchester United. He teaches clients how to apply techniques to optimize their sleep in different situations.

Littlehale says that most of us are not only out of sync with our natural circadian rhythm, we also lack awareness of good sleep patterns and habits. He refers to 90-minute cycles as the method we should be concentrating on to optimize sleep. These cycles allow us to go through all the required phases of sleep, including REM and non-REM. He suggests that people use this length of time to work out when to sleep and when to wake up. Working on this principle, we should sleep for 6 hours, 7.5 hours, or 9 hours, which Littlehale explains can be shifted according to what's going on in our life to ensure we maximize our sleep. For example, he usually goes to bed at 11 pm and gets up at 6.30 am. If he has a night out and misses his normal bedtime, he'll try to catch his next window, going to bed at 12.30 pm but still getting up at the same time. He also says that we have three natural sleep periods during the day, which we should use if we want to catch up on any missed sleep. Interestingly, these ideas fit with our primitive sleep pattern of diurnal sleep with a nap during the day. Athletes are advised that extra sleep should be taken as a 90-minute nap between 1 pm and 3 pm or 5 pm and 7 pm.

In 2009, Littlehale coached the Sky cycling team in their sleep habits, seeking to maximize their recovery during the Tour de France race. They were advised to do the following:

• To ensure their room is at the best temperature (typically between 16 and 18 degrees Celsius).

• To eliminate sugary and fatty foods and to be careful about consuming caffeine later in the day. Alcohol is something to be avoided completely. Athletes are given a milk-based protein drink at bedtime to encourage drowsiness.

• To remove any electrical devices from their bedroom, but if that is not possible, they certainly shouldn't look at their mobile, TV, or computer in the 90 minutes before bed. The light emitted from them can affect the natural circadian rhythm and prevent sleep.[21]

Here are some other tips to improve your sleep:

• **Mindfulness and meditation**—Medical research is increasingly showing that meditation can be more effective than other interventions for the treatment of insomnia, while also improving sleep quality across healthy populations.[22] As little as 10 minutes a day can have a positive impact on sleep quality.[23]

• **Fitness wristband or sleep app**—Using one of these allows you to get a rough estimate of your sleep quality, how much time you're asleep for, and whether your sleep is calm or restless. This can help you remain aware of your sleep and organize your life so that you get enough when times are busy. But be conscious that these devices won't help solve a sleep problem or diagnose any sleep-related disorders.

- **Work considerations**—If you need to travel for work, Charles Czeisler, a professor at Harvard Medical School, advises that you should be allowed at least a day for your body to acclimatize to the different time zone after an international flight, before you even consider carrying out business or driving a car. Also, if you are a senior leader you should seriously consider postponing critical decision making to a time when you are well rested.[24]

While you don't necessarily have to do all these things, it helps to be more aware of how you should become attuned to your internal body clock, one of the most powerful parts of the brain. Many successful people have worked out how to use this primitive brain mechanism to optimize performance, to get the best out of themselves in sport or business, and so give themselves the edge by which they are able to beat the competition or fulfill their purpose. For tips on how to get to sleep more effectively, see a book by a good friend of mine, psychologist Suzy Reading: *The Self-Care Revolution*, specifically Chapter 1.[25]

Physical Activity

Regular exercise has many benefits, one of the less commonly cited of which is a boost in brain power through neurogenesis, whereby exercise actually protects the brain and stimulates its regeneration.[26] This is beneficial to everyday life, but also to aspects relating to performance such as decision making, learning, memory, thinking more clearly, and more effectively managing our response to the emotions from our reacting brain. Regular exercise also improves energy levels and productivity, enabling us to do more, engage better, and live life more fully.[27]

Our body developed a need to consistently engage in phyisical activity, in the same way that our brain evolved to survive in a very different world to that of today. Exercise can even reset our circadian rhythm when it is out of sync. That is not the only benefit of exercise, however. Research lists exercise as strengthening the heart and improving lung function, reducing coronary heart disease risk factors, reducing the risk of heart attacks, reducing the risk of type 2 diabetes, and reducing the risk of some cancers.[28] In addition to these physiological benefits there are mental benefits, which include reducing stress, alleviating anxiety, preventing cognitive decline, reducing the risk of depression, and boosting self-esteem, self-confidence, mood, sleep quality, and energy level.[29]

The benefits for all of us are clear. Moreover, when it comes to the leadership population or anyone wanting to succeed while under pressure, exercise provides a critical counter to the build-up of stress hormones produced by the nature of the role. The daily stressors that trigger a chemical release from our primitive reacting brain are immense. The following list covers some of the simple things that set off a reaction in our survival-driven reacting brain, which responds as if we are under threat. This usually happens without any conscious thought:

- Finding someone sitting in your chair.

- Someone bumping into us on a train.

- Someone pulling out in front of us in a car.

- Not being invited to a meeting.

- Being left off an email.

- Feeling compared to someone else.

- Being ignored by someone attractive.

And so on and so forth. Every day, hundreds of situations cause our reacting brain to release chemicals that would in our ancestors' time have been dispersed through some form of action, but in our modern world get trapped in our system. Once these chemicals have been released there is no pressure valve: we don't turn around and fight someone who is sitting in our chair, or flee when someone bumps into us on a train. As a result, the chemicals build up in our system, creating toxic levels of stress that clouds our judgment and the thought processes in our observing brain.

You want to perform at your best, even when you're under pressure. To be at your optimum it's critical that you can get rid of these chemicals, and the most natural way of doing this is through being active.

This may seem obvious—after all, we are repeatedly told by the media, healthcare professionals, government, and a host of other people that physical activity is good for us. The issue is actually doing it, particularly when we get overwhelmed with the stresses of daily life, and even more so when we're in a highly pressurized situation.

Staying Active Pays Off

Adelina was a naturally active woman who in her younger years had enjoyed rowing, cycling, tennis, running, and sailing, but as she became more senior in her role and life became busier with family and young children, activity took a back seat. She still walked and ran, but this was more of a "do when I can" approach than a regular occurrence. She ate healthily and was not overweight, and could not really be considered unfit, but at the age of 55 she had a heart attack followed by heart valve replacement surgery. This gave her a horrendous wake-up call, encouraging her to reassess the focus she gave to everything in life, including physical activity.

When she recovered, Adelina didn't want to take up running again and the opportunity to row, play tennis, or sail didn't appeal at the point she'd reached in life. She did, however, love to walk. She started taking a swift three-mile walk every day, regardless of the weather conditions, wherever she was in the world. She also cycled wherever she could, whenever she could. In addition, she factored in a ten-mile ramble across challenging terrain, with hill climbs, at least once a fortnight. Her cardiologist was continually amazed and impressed by her physical condition: 20 years after surgery she still didn't need a replacement valve (which at that time was usually scheduled for 10 years after the initial operation).

Adelina was one of the participants in the research I carried out on physical activity and its impact on combating cognitive decline in older adults.[30] As well as performing well on the tests of aerobic capacity, she also did very well on all the cognitive tests. The overall results once rigorously analyzed showed that physical activity, taken over a lifetime, protects the neural networks in the frontal lobes of our brain. Adelina was a prime example of this, with the mental agility of someone much younger than her, even in her later years.

However active we are, we all allow life to take over, but we don't need to. We shouldn't have to have a wake-up call to think through how we can incorporate regular exercise into our way of life. We deprioritize physical activity, even those of us who like it and may consider ourselves sporty, and that has detrimental effects.

When Adelina was forced to reassess her life, she actively incorporated activity into her plans, thinking through what she liked doing and what she could practically get on with given her age, where she lived, and other lifestyle factors that were important to her. This is what we all need to do. It may mean shedding an association with an old exercise—e.g., "I am a hockey player, so if I can't play hockey I won't do anything else"—and forming an association with something new, finding mechanisms to overcome excuses—e.g., "I've had a hard day so I won't exercise tonight"—and discovering activity that we really like.

Taking the premise that everyone reading this knows that it's good to be physically active, I'm going to encourage you to explore what's standing in your way and, if you're already active, what gets in the way of you doing more. Following that, you're going to consider what you can do differently, including thinking through how your personality may influence your preferences for different exercise. This isn't something that you may have consciously reflected on, or that's often discussed unless you see a personal trainer; even then, it tends to be within the confines of your preferences in the gym. Yet it's very relevant to defining you and enabling you to get the most from knowing more about yourself, so it's worth putting some time in here. It's also been shown that if a physical activity suits your preferences, you are more likely to stick with it.[31]

TOOLS OF THE SESSION

What Are Your Obstacles?

What gets in the way of your being physically active? Read each statement in the Obstacles to Physical Activity and indicate how likely you are to respond in that way when asked why you don't exercise. Circle the response that feels most like you.

OBSTACLES TO PHYSICAL ACTIVITY

Instructions: Rate the statements below for how accurately they reflect the way you generally feel and behave. Do not rate what you think you should do, or wish you do, or things you no longer do. Please be as honest as possible.

3—Very likely
2—Somewhat likely
1—Somewhat unlikely
0—Very unlikely

How likely are you to say . . .

1. My day is so busy now, I just can't
make the time to include physical   0   1   2   3
activity in my schedule

2. None of my family members or friends
like to do anything active, so I don't   0   1   2   3
have a chance to exercise

3. I'm just too tired after work to exercise   0   1   2   3

4. I've been thinking about doing more
exercise, but I just can't seem to get   0   1   2   3
started

5. I'm getting older so exercise can be risky   0   1   2   3

6. I don't get enough exercise because I
never learned the skills for any sport   0   1   2   3

7. I don't have access to a gym, jogging
trails, swimming pools, bike paths, etc.   0   1   2   3

8. Physical activity takes to much time
away from other commitments—time,   0   1   2   3
work, family, etc.

9. I'm embarrassed about how I look
when I exercise with others   0   1   2   3

10. I don't get enough sleep as it is. I just
couldn't get up early or stay up late to   0   1   2   3
get some exercise

11. It's easier for me to find excuses not to
exercise than to go out and do something   0   1   2   3

12. I know to many people who have hurt
themselves by overdoing it with exercise   0   1   2   3

13. I really can't see me learning a new
sport at my age   0   1   2   3

14. It's just to expensive. You have to take a class
or join a club or buy the right equipment   0   1   2   3

15. My free times during the day are too
short to include exercise   0   1   2   3

16. My usual social activities with family or
freinds don't include physical activity   0   1   2   3

17. I'm too tired during the week and I need
the weekend to catch up on my rest   0   1   2   3

18. I want to get more exercise, but I just
can't seem to stick to anything   0   1   2   3

19. I'm afraid I might injure myself or have a heart attack   0   1   2   3

20. I'm not good enough at any physical activity to make it fun   0   1   2   3

21. If we had exercise facilities and showers at work, then I would be more likely to exercise   0   1   2   3

Enter the numbers that you circled on the Table 8.3 grid in the spaces under the corresponding question numbers. Then add the three scores on each line.

Your barriers to physical activity fall into one or more of seven categories. A score of 5 or above in any category shows that this is an important barrier for you to overcome.

TABLE 8.3 OBSTACLES TO PHYSICAL ACTIVITY SCORES

Obstacles to physical activity	Question numbers			Total
	1	8	15	
Lack of time				
	2	9	16	
Social Influence				
	3	10	17	
Lack of energy				
	4	11	18	
Lack of motivation				
	5	12	19	
Fear of injury				
	6	13	20	
Lack of skill				
	7	14	21	
Lack of resources				

Source: Adapted from Centers for Disease Control and Prevention (2007) *Overcoming Barriers to Physical Activity*, Washington, DC: CDC. Public domain.

OVERCOMING YOUR OBSTACLES

Simply recognizing what your obstacles to exercise are, raising your awareness of them, is a first step to overcoming them. When you can see what is holding you back, it gives you something to work with. The following are suggestions for what you can do to overcome a particular obstacle. Feel free to take your own approach: what is important is to work on overcoming what is holding you back.

If **lack of time** is the main obstacle for you, then try:

- Identifying the available time slots in your diary and scheduling in physical activity.

- Swopping a more sedentary activity (e.g., watching TV, surfing the internet) for exercise.

- Monitoring your daily activities for a week and identifying at least three 30-minute time slots that you could use for exercise.

- Adding physical activity to your daily routine (e.g., walk or ride your bike to work or to go shopping, exercise while you watch TV, walk up stairs rather than taking the lift or escalator, get off your bus a stop earlier, park further from your destination).

- Doing activities that are time efficient, such as walking, jogging, or lifting weights.

- If you're traveling a lot with work, finding ways of incorporating exercise, for example taking a resistance band in your suitcase, doing a yoga routine with online guidance, taking trainers and going for a run. Try to book a hotel that has a swimming pool or gym, or just run outside.

If **social influence** is the main obstacle for you, then try:

- Explaining your need for physical activity to family and friends and asking them to support you.

- Finding fun ways of exercising (e.g., dancing, Zumba, cycling) that you can ask your friends to join in with.

- Joining a club or class, e.g., walking, hiking, running, yoga.

- Spending more time with your friends or family members who are physically active and joining in with their activities.

- If you're lacking in confidence, use the tools in Chapter 7 to take that first step.

If **lack of energy** is the main obstacle for you, then try:

- Using your circadian rhythm results to help identify the times in the day when you're most energetic and scheduling physical activity into those time slots.

- Planning exercise and using approaches such as emotion surfing to avoid engaging with excuses not to exercise. Physical activity will increase your energy levels, but your reacting brain will tell you something different. Surf the excuses and don't engage with them, just get on and do it.

If **lack of motivation** is the main obstacle for you, then try:

- Planning exercise and using approaches such as emotion surfing to overcome excuses not to exercise when the time comes up in your diary. Note down the excuses you normally use and think through how you are going to respond to them ahead of time. For example, if you decide you are going to the gym but by the evening you feel too tired, write down that excuse—"I'm exhausted, I'll just go another day" or "I haven't got time today, it will make me late home"—then prepare a response—"I knew I would feel like that, that's OK, I'm going to do it anyway." Health professionals Joseph Ciarrochi, Ann Bailey, and Russ Harris talk about this in their book *The Weight Escape* and advise that every time the excuse comes up:

   especially when you don't feel like doing it . . . Ask yourself "Can I do this anyway, even though my mind if giving me lots of excuses not to?" The key is to recognise that you can carry your excuses with you but you don't have to obey them—you can have those words in your head and simultaneously carry out some health promoting action.[32]

- Asking friends to exercise with you: the commitment to someone else will increase the chances that you'll follow through, with the added bonus that it will also be more enjoyable.

- Joining clubs, exercise classes or groups where you make a commitment to engage.

- Considering your personality preferences. If, for example, you are extraverted, you may prefer to do a class of some sort rather than running on your own or exercising at home with a DVD.

- Doing things that you enjoy. For example, if you love dancing, find a way for that to become your exercise rather than something you just do on an occasional night out.

- Varying your routine. Moving between different activities will keep your interest peaked, e.g., jogging, swimming, and cycling.

- Using a wrist device, app, or diary to keep track of your exercise. Seeing how well you are doing will motivate you to do more. It's also a useful way of seeing what obstacles may be getting in the way of you achieving your targets: e.g., do you exercise less when you have slept less and if so, do you need to address your sleep habits?

- Setting yourself a goal, such as running a 5km race or joining a charity hike.

- Writing down and referring to the benefits that are most pertinent to you, e.g., better mental performance, protecting against heart disease.

If **fear of injury** is the main obstacle for you, then try:

- Learning how to warm up and cool down properly in order to minimize the chances of injury.

- Learning how to use the correct techniques in whatever exercise you choose to do.

- Not overdoing it: start slowly and build up, then never exercise to excess.

- Choosing activities that are low risk.

If **lack of skill** is the main obstacle for you, then try:

- Choosing activities that require no new skills, e.g., walking, jogging.

- Finding people who have the same skill level as you and exercising with them.

- Asking someone to teach you the new skills you need or get training.

If **lack of resources** is the main obstacle for you, then try:

- Choosing activities that require minimal facilities or equipment, such as walking, jogging, or yoga.

- Exploring local resources and finding inexpensive, convenient solutions (e.g., park and recreation programs).

TOOLS OF THE SESSION

Action Plan to Overcome Your Obstacles

Once you've identified which areas you want to work on, pick a solution and make a plan to take action using Table 8.4 to help you. The top cells have been filled in with examples.

BE PERSISTENT
Managing to include some form of physical activity in your life and persisting with it will make a tremendous difference to your health, well-being, and performance, so don't give up, keep trying until you find the right thing for you and the right way of overcoming anything that gets in your way. You haven't failed if something doesn't work: there's a bigger aim here and that's ultimately to fulfill your purpose. As long as you stay focused on how you're going to achieve that by being in top mental and physical form, then stopping one activity or giving up on a particular objective is not failing, it's discovering what works and what doesn't for you. As long as you keep on going with something else, then you're still moving in the right direction.

TABLE 8.4 OBSTACLES TO PHYSICAL ACTIVITY ACTION PLAN

Obstacle	Action	When by	How will I measure progress?
Motivation: I make excuses whenever it comes to doing exercise	Plan exercise putting everything in my calendar	22nd June	How many times I do the exercise I plan to in my diary and how many times I skip without a very valid reason
	Identify the excuses, write them down and emotion surf them	22nd June	As above
Motivation: It feels pointless doing exercise	Sign up to a 5km race in September	28th June	Training for the 5km race and doing it
	Write down all the benefits to my performance and health, and look at it when I can't be bothered	30th June	How many times I check in with my reasons. How readily my reasons come to mind with persistence

Coming to the End of the Session

We've investigated how critical sleep is to your performance and how acknowledging the needs of your brain and the environment it works best in can get the most out of your sleep pattern. We've also explored your personal circadian rhythm, whether you're a lark or a night owl, and when you perform at your optimum, whether that's on mental tasks or physical ones.

When it comes to physical activity, I outlined the familiar benefits and considered why most people don't do more. We saw that the answer lies in a number of different psychological and external obstacles, and explored what these may be for you, some options for overcoming them, and the structure of a plan of action.

Exercise reduces stress, but when you can't get out for a run, go to the gym or take a walk, you need other options to help you destress because stress interferes with optimal performance. In the final session, we will explore this in more depth in the light of giving your brain the chance to assimilate your learning and pursue your personal development. We'll also look at how making new connections and finding a mentor can really help to keep your performance at its optimum, through being in tune with the world around you and knowing how to respond and adapt, with help and support from others.

Session 8C

Continued Growth

As you move ahead in life, your story will continue to evolve and your journey will take unexpected twists and turns. As a result, you have to stay flexible and keep growing and adapting in order to live your life to the optimum. This requires ongoing balances and checks, both from a physiological perspective and in terms of your ability to keep performing in an ever-changing world. Personal development should always remain a priority, continuing to raise your self-awareness, understanding what makes you tick and what derails you. Senior executives typically have coaches and advisers to assist them with this ongoing growth, but while you may not be in a position to employ someone in this capacity, you can find a mentor and use your network to garner the help and support you need.

In this final session, we'll explore your physiology in more depth to understand why maintaining your optimum health is critical to performance. Space and time for reflection are necessary for everyone, not just to relax but in order for your brain to assimilate learning and to allow personal growth. Stress interferes with this, both from the perspective of performance and by clouding the mind. We'll look at what your key stressors are to help you plan for and cope with them more effectively. You'll also consider how to optimize your downtime, creating space to unwind and for your brain to embed learning.

Social connections are key to continued personal growth and for support in pursuing your purpose. We'll examine your broader network and the world around you, how you can stay in tune with changes in your environment by tapping into a network, and how you can go about growing your own connections. In amongst that network is the opportunity for you to find role models and mentors to help encourage you, stretch you, and keep you in check, in the same way as an executive coach or adviser would.

This will provide you with the icing on the cake, the ability to take everything you've learnt about yourself through this book and not only apply it, but keep applying it in a way that flexes to your own needs and those of your environment. You'll be optimally performing in whatever you decide to do in life, providing you with success and satisfaction, whether that's living off the land or running a multinational organization. Adding these elements to your personal toolkit will enable you to continually grow and develop.

Equilibrium

We all experience stress to some degree, therefore it's essential that you understand how you personally respond to stress and what your most effective stress releases are. There are a few good staples of stress relief, including sleep and physical activity (which we looked at in the last session), good nutrition, avoiding toxic substances (e.g., alcohol to excess, nicotine, drugs), and time management. Alongside this, we all have our own individual stress releases. Things that work as a release for you may not work for someone else: for example, I love walking outside in the dark, rain, and wind, but someone else may find that activity stressful. You need to identify what works best for you in your downtime, rather than taking on what others prescribe.

Stress isn't always detrimental—we need a certain amount in order to perform at our optimum—but too much is crippling. Cardiologist Peter Nixon developed a model called the Human Function Curve (Figure 8.1) that illustrates the balance of good and bad stress, with optimal stress and performance at the midpoint.[33] At a low level of stress, we may feel bored or disinterested, finding it hard to get ourselves going. As stress increases, so does our physiological and psychological arousal until it reaches an optimal level, enabling improved performance: for example, performing better in a presentation or exam, finding it easier to concentrate and get things done, or being more able to think on our feet. With too much stress, the demand becomes excessive, quickly tipping us into overload. Our performance follows a downward trajectory, leading to negative emotions and overall cognitive decline. Once we're snowballing downhill, our observing brain is flooded by stress

FIGURE 8.1 THE HUMAN FUNCTION CURVE

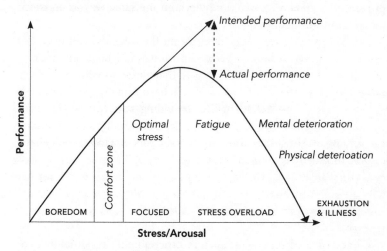

Source: Adapted with permission from P.G. Nixon (1981) The human function curve: A paradigm for our times, *Activitas Nervosa Superior* 3(1): 130–33.

hormones (e.g., cortisol, adrenaline) from our reacting brain, and we lose insight into how to get ourselves back into the more positive position of asking for help, getting rest, and making use of the stress release techniques that we know help us. This is why it's critical to:

- have a high level of self-awareness so you're able to tell when you're tipping over the edge;

- understand what your effective stress relievers are and have a plan in place for when they're needed;

- allow other people to provide support and give feedback on when they think you need time out or stress relief.

When you're learning something new, you will typically move to the right-hand side of the graph, making it even more critical to understand what your personal destressors are and how to move back to your comfort zone in order to assimilate your learning. Short bursts of stress, even when they're more toward the right, are not damaging. It's only when stress occurs unremittingly that it begins to wear you out mentally and physically. This can then lead to a plethora of illnesses (e.g., heart disease, headaches, digestive problems, insomnia, depression) and over the longer term damages your immune system.

Knowing Your Stressors

Identifying what triggers stress for you can help you anticipate circumstances in which you're likely to be more vulnerable, plan your response, consider your options for destressing, and know when to ask for help. Everyone gets stressed, it's not something you can escape, but it is something you can learn to manage more effectively and even use to your advantage.

Create a list of the situations and concerns that trigger your stress response using Table 8.5 as a prompt. You may find it easier to do this based on what's stressing you at the moment.

You'll notice that some of your stressors come from within (internal), while others are events that happen to you (external); some of the external stressors occur regularly, others are one-off or life events. Put your personal stressors into these three categories in Table 8.6.

Note: You may dismiss little stressors as insignificant, but in volume they can have just as much impact as a major life event.

Planning Your Response to Stress

Now that you have a list of stressors, you can think through how and when they may occur and how you will deal with them. This may seem obvious, but once you have moved to the right-hand side of the Human Function Curve, you won't be able to think straight, which risks stress becoming self-perpetuating and damaging. Look through the following suggestions with the list you've made in mind and see how they relate.

TABLE 8.5 POTENTIAL CAUSES OF STRESS

Internal	External	
	Regularly occurring	*Life event*
Attitudes Thoughts Fear Anger Anticipation Worry Memory Overall health and fitness levels Emotional well-being Amount of sleep and rest you get	Workplace stress Interpersonal conflicts Relationship/marital stress Balancing career and family Being a parent Noise – loud and constant low-level noise Poor work conditions (e.g. too much noise, lack of privacy) Commuting Lack of sleep Sexual difficulties Loneliness Poor nutrition Being a carer Paying a bill Running late	Death of a spouse Divorce Death of a close family member Personal injury or illness Being fired Retirement Major change in health of a family member Pregnancy Major change in financial status Death of a close friend Change in career Taking on a mortgage Taking an exam Change in school Moving house

TABLE 8.6 YOUR POTENTIAL CAUSES OF STRESS

Internal	External	
	Regularly occurring	*Life event*

CHOOSE YOUR MINDSET

Make use of the tools we've explored throughout this book—reframing, emotion surfing, mindfulness, and self-compassion—to help you live with anxieties, worries, and concerns rather than letting them control you.

It's important to be aware that although positive thinking is helpful, your brain will not allow you to turn all negatives into positives. Trying to do so will feel like an Herculean battle and could take you even further to the right-hand side of the curve. It's critical to learn to accept those emotions rather than fight to change them (for more on this, read *The Happiness Trap* by Russ Harris[34]).

ASK FOR FEEDBACK

Give someone permission to tell you when they think you're getting stressed. Once you are stressed, you won't be able to see things clearly and you'll need someone else to point it out.

TIME MANAGEMENT

Organizing your time is critical to optimizing your performance and alleviating stress. I've worked with CEOs who are struggling in their role simply because they haven't planned their time effectively—those who are completely on top of their game are always well organized and able to prioritize effectively. Here are some tips for time management:

- **Make date-assigned to-do lists**—Create lists of what you need to do and prioritize the tasks, then decide when you're going to do each of the tasks and write it in your diary. Doing this at the start of every week will help you feel more in control and ensure you get all that you need to do done, reducing the chance of additional stress.

- **Get assistance**—Think through where someone else can take things off your hands and ask for help ahead of time. Once you're stressed, your tendency will be to think you have to do it all.

- **Make use of your circadian rhythm**—Plan to do your most difficult tasks at your optimum time of day.

- **Factor in downtime**—Ensure that your weekly or daily plan always has downtime (more on this in the next exercise). Without time for reflection, you will lose perspective, struggle to align what you're doing with your purpose, and fail to integrate your learning into your broader understanding of who you are, which is essential for continued self-awareness and personal growth. Learn to recognize when you're at boiling point or when your energy levels are particularly low, so you can step back.

TOOLS OF THE SESSION

Understanding the Stress Relievers That Work for You

In order to optimize the downtime you plan, you need to have a good understanding of what stress relievers work for you. For example, while self-hypnosis is a proven technique for reducing stress, you may find that you just can't get on with it, so trying to do it over and over again will simply be counterproductive.

Read through the following suggestions and list the stress relievers that you find most effective. Include some that you haven't tried but are willing to experiment with.

- **Physical activity**—Plan to incorporate the type of exercise that you identified as your "best fit" into your weekly schedule.

- **Engaging your passions**—Professor of psychology Mihaly Csikszentmihalyi found that when people engage in an activity that they are deeply passionate about, they go into a state of consciousness called "flow", in which they feel "strong, alert, in effortless control, unselfconscious, and at the peak of their abilities."[35] The concentration involved acts as a stress reliever, because you simply don't have room for other thoughts, worries, and concerns. Look back to your passions and identify the things that put you into flow, whether that is writing, reading a good book, doing sport, singing, yoga, dancing, gardening, cooking, doing the washing up, walking in the rain, or something else entirely.

- **Getting outside**—A 2012 study published in *Biomedical and Environmental Health* examined the impact of cortisol on people who were sent into a forest for two nights.[36] The researchers found that stress levels in the forest group were significantly reduced compared to a group who remained in the city. Other studies have shown that walking in nature or even just looking out of a window at a pleasant view lowers stress. Our brain has evolved to live in a natural rather than an urban environment, so whenever you can, get outside, whether that's for a lunch break, a walk between meetings, or a weekend's camping.

- **Social support**—Connection with others is vital to maintaining a good level of mental health and reducing stress,[37] and we'll look at this in more detail later, but it's helpful here to recognize what this ideally looks like to you. Think through the type of person you are, and if you completed the psychometric test revisit the results and see what they say about your degree of introversion and extraversion. If you're introverted, you will probably need time alone or with just one close friend in order to unwind. If you're extraverted, you're more likely to be reenergized by spending time in a busy social environment with a group of friends. If you didn't complete the psychometric test, take some time to reflect on what makes you feel best: being with people, being with a few specific people, or being alone. Make sure you consider this when you need to refuel.

- **Finding your "evidence-based" stress release**—There are methods for reducing stress that are backed by scientific research, including the approaches we've discussed, such as mindfulness and emotion surfing. Other approaches include progressive muscle relaxation,[38] autogenic training,[39] the relaxation response,[40] biofeedback,[41] guided imagery,[42] and diaphragmatic breathing[43] (more information on each of these is available in the Bibliography). These all enable your body to counter the build-up of harmful stress hormones. Try them and once you've found the one that you are most comfortable with, practice it on a daily basis to avert stress and to make the technique more habitual so that it becomes more accessible to you when you need it most.

- **Watch what you eat**—Mealtimes should be downtime when you relax, so keep them sacred rather than eating on the go or at your desk. What you eat can also affect your stress through the production of stress hormones. For example, caffeine increases the level of cortisol,[44] whereas salmon, dark chocolate, berries, garlic, olive oil, turmeric, green tea, and chamomile tea are all proven to decrease cortisol.[45] Prebiotic foods, such as asparagus, bananas, barley, leeks, lentils, mustard greens, onions, and tomatoes, also reduce the level of cortisol.[46]

Now fill in the following questions based on what works for you to relieve stress:

• Thinking through what's written above and considering other methods you know work for you, write down your most effective stress relievers in the space below.

• Think through what techniques you may try to add to your 'toolbox'. What are they, write them down here.

TOOLS OF THE SESSION

Destress Plan

It is important to plan how you will minimize your stress levels and make the most effective use of your downtime. The following exercise creates a plan to help with this.

Thinking through how you will work on a planned approach to tackling stress at the start of your week, fill in the script below.

Every..................(e.g. Sunday) at...............(time) I will anticipate my most likely stressors in the week ahead and plan how to respond. I will also write my daily to-do lists for the upcoming week and block out downtime each day.

My most likely stressors this week are

I will respond by doing

I'll ask for assistance from

My most difficult tasks will be

I will schedule my most difficult tasks for

When I have downtime I will

What are the thoughts you have that pull you into a negative stress cycle? Try writing them down and how you will respond to them so you're better able to identify and manage them when they do occur. Don't worry if you don't manage it every time, just keep gently pulling your mind back to a more constructive mindset whenever you catch it. Fill in the text below to help you with this.

I will work on changing my mindset whenever I catch myself using harmful self-talk. For example when I say...I will do.........................(e.g., emotion surf) or reframe as.........................
....

Think through who could help you counter your stress or point it out to you, and write their name down.

I will ask (insert name)...................................to tell me when I'm getting overly stressed

To really address stress you need to be doing something every day. Write in what you're going to do.

I will do (insert evidence-based technique)

I will do this every day at

Planning what you're going to eat and when will help stop you from binging on "bad" foods and stick to a more healthy diet. Think through what you are going to eat and write it below.

I will eat healthy food including

I will aim to avoid

This level of detail may seem excessive, but it's very helpful to write it all down as it will help you maintain your peak level of stress, so that you're engaged and performing at your best. One senior leader I work with does every aspect of this exercise and also encourages it in his staff. He is a very successful and productive man who not only optimizes his own capabilities, but encourages the personal growth and well-being of everyone who works for him. See if doing the same is good for you.

Mentors and Networks

To truly optimize your capabilities and help you perform at your best over time, you not only need to take care of your physiological and mental health, you also have to have people to help you. Getting anything done requires the support of other people, and being connected opens doors and enables opportunities, while keeping you in check and aware of how you're doing. This involves both networks and mentors.

BUILDING A NETWORK

The recruitment company Reed describes networking as:

> *the process of speaking to professional contacts and sharing information with them. Networking can be formal or informal, and can take many different forms, ranging from exchanging business cards with clients at corporate events, through to simply striking up a conversation with someone you overhear speaking about your industry at an event.*[47]

Networking provides an additional vehicle through which to take your career or the pursuit of your purpose to the next level.[48] Research shows that networking enables personal learning, skill development, and career development through facilitating access to personal and professional resources. Brain Uzzi and Shannon Dunlap from the Kellogg School of Management focus specifically on how networks facilitate innovation. They give examples of breakthroughs in thinking that have been enabled via networks, including the work of psychoanalyst Sigmund Freud, artist Pablo Picasso, scientists James Watson and Francis Crick, and even Greek philosopher Pythagoras.[49]

I frequently explain to people how their decision making will be improved through networking. Talking to people from a wider sphere of influence provides you with a larger amount of data from which to draw information. It gives you a better and more "savvy" insight, allowing you to keep a "finger on the pulse," hearing about things and events that aren't documented anywhere or officially presented. This allows you to build up a more complete picture of what's going on in the world and, through generating a range of different viewpoints, take a more unbiased and balanced perspective and get buy-in for your thinking along the way.

Networks are therefore a worthwhile addition to your personal toolkit. The problem is that people often view networking negatively, seeing it as contrived, superficial, forced, or transactional. An article in *Administrative Science Quarterly* gives this away in its title alone: "The contaminating effects of building instrumental ties: How networking can make us feel dirty."[50] Its authors explain why networking has "unintended consequences for an individual's morality" because of the active way in which relationships are formed for personal gain. In my experience, people often put networking in the same pile as "being political," considering it something that just doesn't sit right with them. Yet it can also be approached in a far more "moral" way while still optimizing your success. To consider this in more depth, it's worth reading *21st-Century Networking*, co-authored by someone I have the pleasure of knowing and who, I can vouch, connects in the most genuine and authentic way.[51]

We discussed earlier in the book how connecting with others fulfills a higher-level need. Connecting using the approach advocated here involves giving, not just taking or being simply transactional, but rather forming meaningful associations. This is also the approach to adopt with networking, by being genuinely interested in every single person you meet: valuing their individuality, aiming to find out something about who they are and what their story is (be curious, be a detective), listening, being empathic, being helpful, showing a genuine interest and concern, putting aside your own thoughts and objectives to really connect. In doing so you will be giving back to that individual in that moment and it will also make you feel good about yourself. That's not to say you have to form a deep and lasting relationship with everyone you meet, but that the relationship you do have with them, however fleeting, is not superficial but has greater meaning.

If you've ever worked in the service industry, you will understand the difference between a brief connection and a mere transaction. When I was doing my postgraduate degree, I worked in a shop in central London. When you serve customers all day, every day, people unwittingly tend to treat you as part of the "machine," with no idea of who you are or what you stand for. They rush in and rush out, busy with their own agenda, in effect taking whatever they need from you in a very transactional way. Then every so often, one person makes the time to connect with you as a person, to look you in the eye and show genuine interest, to treat you as an individual rather than part of a corporate entity. They may not spend ages talking to you, but they make you feel valued for the moment that they do this, a feeling that in my experience leaves a lasting impression.

TOOLS OF THE SESSION

Defining Your Network

This activity is going to help you define your network, starting with looking at your current network to establish where there may be gaps. You can then go about filling those gaps.

Using the circles in Figure 8.2, plot the initials of contacts/friends/colleagues in the appropriate circle, indicating how close or distant they are from you by the length of the line that connects "Me" to them. When it comes to plotting the looser connections, you won't be able to put them all down, so just focus on the ones who are at the front of your mind or most significant. You can work out who to put in which circle by reading the definitions that follow.

FIGURE 8.2 YOUR NETWORK MAP

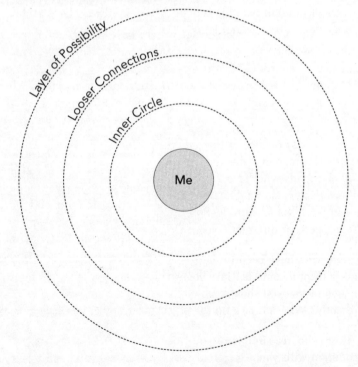

- **Inner circle**—this contains what Reid Hoffman, networking guru and co-founder of LinkedIn, calls "allies."[52] Hoffman describes these as the people you regularly seek advice from (e.g., a lifelong friend, close family member, community leader), share opportunities with (e.g., collaborate on a project, give away a spare ticket to a concert), talk up (e.g., promote their work or them as a person to other people, show pride in how they've dealt with a difficulty), and, should a conflict arise, people you would defend (and they would do the same for you). These are deeper relationships that tend to be few in number.

- **Looser connections**—this is your wider circle of friends, colleagues, interesting people, and helpful contacts. They are people you speak to infrequently and usually for a specific reason. Hoffman describes them as people "whom you have spent low amounts of low intensity time with but with whom you're still friendly." It's also those people you'd like to reach out to in order to form a more concrete relationship, but sometimes worry that they wouldn't reciprocate.

- **Layer of possibility**—this contains people you may have some connection to but do not know personally. They share your values, passions, interests, or are striving toward a common purpose. This layer may contain potential mentors who you are not yet in contact with but could potentially be introduced to.

Don't worry if you don't have a huge network, it's more important that you have people you have a genuinely deep connection with in your inner circle, and outside of that others who can help you achieve your purpose. Hoffman explains that having only 40 connections, each with 35 other friends who have 45 distinctive friends (i.e., the friendships don't overlap), creates a total of 63,000 (40 x 35 x 45) potential contacts you can reach via an introduction.

Using pens of different colors, circle the following people:

- **Those who have been brokers**—people who have connected you to other helpful contacts. Have you offered them something in return? If not, maybe you should. How much have you spoken to them recently? Why not pick up the phone or drop them an email?

- **Those who are similar to you**—people who share a lot in common with you, e.g., job or background. They may not be as helpful to your network, because they are less likely to bring knowledge, experience, and opportunities that are different to your own. They may, however, help to act as a sounding board or associate in the work you do.

- **Those who offer something different and diverse**—people from a different social circle or industry, yet who share similar interests, values, or purpose to you.

These different colors should help you to pick out people who are particularly helpful to you (brokers) in terms of facilitating your network, who to invest less energy in unless they are good friends (it sounds harsh, but your time isn't limitless), and who you should prioritize (those who offer something different and diverse). We'll come back to mentors in the next section. For now, have a go at the following action points, which are adapted from "Reid's rules". For more, read *The Start-up of You* (see Bibliography).

IN THE NEXT DAY
Look at your calendar for the past six months and identify the five people you spent the most time with. Are they people you choose to be in your inner circle? Are you happy with their influence on you? If not, how are you going to change the people you're interacting with most frequently?

IN THE NEXT WEEK
Identify two people in your network map who don't know each other but you think should do, and introduce them to one another. Help them understand why you are introducing them by explaining their shared values, or whatever it is that will offer a mutual benefit.

Think about a challenge you face and ask for an introduction to a connection in your layer of possibility who could help. Think of how you position yourself using the data you identified in Session 7c.

Imagine you lost your job tomorrow: who are the 10 people you'd email for help or advice? Keep each of these connections alive and email them or call them today.

IN THE NEXT MONTH
Identify two people in your looser connections who you'd like to build an alliance with or work with in some way. Get the opportunity underway by giving them something they may find helpful: forward an article to them, or make an introduction to someone else.

ONGOING

Hoffman recommends that you should be receiving or making at least one introduction a month. Make this something you put in your calendar or on your monthly to-do list.

Check that you are optimizing your network: revisit your network map and ensure you have enough people who are different and diverse, and people who broker connections with other people.

Keep your network alive: have coffees (one-to-one situations are usually best if you are introverted), accept invitations, make the effort to meet people from different walks of life by taking up social opportunities such as joining a sports club or team, voluntary group, professional body, or charitable foundation. Host your own networking events (you don't need to label them as that, just a social event where you bring people together who you think would have mutual interests). And most importantly, follow the guidelines in Chapter 4 on connection. In order to fulfill your higher-level needs, everyone you meet should first be a connection and someone you can help, and only secondly be someone who can help you to achieve your own purpose (adapted from "Reid's rules" in Reid Hoffman's *The Start-up of You*).

FINDING YOUR MENTOR

Building a network will assist you with accessing potential mentors. Mentors will also be useful in building your network.

There are many different definitions of what constitutes a mentor, but Brad Johnson, professor of psychology at the US Naval College, says this:

> *Mentoring is a personal relationship in which a more experienced (usually older) . . . professional acts as a guide, role model, teacher, and sponsor of a less experienced (usually younger) . . . professional. A mentor provides the protégé with knowledge, advice, challenge, counsel, and support.*[53]

While Johnson says "usually older," a mentor may also be the same age or younger than you. What is most important is to find the right match. Johnson provides an overview of the literature on mentoring, explaining how having a mentor brings a host of proven benefits, including development of professional skills, improved self-confidence and professional identity, enhanced networking, job satisfaction, and support and encouragement in helping you to achieve your purpose or dream. Other research shows mentors conferring further advantages such as a higher number of promotions, higher incomes, more career mobility, and more career satisfaction. The mentor enables this by providing the mentee with a sense of competence, acting as a sounding board, helping with problem solving and role modeling behaviors.[54]

A Mentor Helps You Find Your Own Path

My first meeting with Joseph was to assess him for a role within a particular organization. He was coming in at a senior level, but not right at the top of the tree, despite his capabilities. Joseph had great interpersonal skills: he was sociable, self-confident, and immediately engaging, quickly establishing rapport. He had a good level of emotional awareness of both himself and his audience: listening, showing respect, and seeking to understand. Together with this, he was someone who was always striving to do better, not afraid to take himself beyond his comfort zone, enjoyed being stretched and achieving, and had good judgment. Yet he hadn't reached the full potential of these skills, and was older than other people who had already achieved more in their career.

The core reason that Joseph's career had stalled was through lack of professional support (i.e., a mentor) and limited networking. This meant that he wasn't known in the marketplace as an industry expert, he couldn't benchmark himself against others to know how he needed to grow and extend beyond his current level, and he couldn't see where he could leverage his strategic and creative capability or influence people more broadly.

He had spent the majority of his career with one employer and hadn't sought to extend his network beyond that company; he also didn't like the concept of networking. Along with this came the feeling that he couldn't just pick up the phone or drop an email to senior people he had worked with previously, because he considered they wouldn't want to talk to him, which closed down opportunities to engage a mentor.

Joseph had a great network within the company he was

leaving and, after our discussion, realized that he could take the same approach as he had with former colleagues—getting to know them, treating them with respect, seeing what he could help with—out into the external marketplace. So he reached out to a few former colleagues who now worked elsewhere. He had thought they wouldn't be interested in speaking to him, in part because they were now at dizzying heights in their careers. But they were all delighted to hear from him, welcomed the opportunity to meet up, and offered career advice, guidance, and suggestions of continued contact and support, without him even having to ask.

To find a mentor, bear in mind the following guidelines.

HOW TO IDENTIFY A MENTOR

Finding a mentor can take a little trial and error. I have personally considered numerous people who I thought could be a good match, but who turned out to be wrong given my needs and theirs. That doesn't mean I don't stay in touch with them or remain friendly, rather that I've not pursued actually asking them to be my mentor. It's also important to realize that while you may form a very positive relationship with a mentor, they are not your friend: there is a formal and professional element to the relationship, however casual it may be, which is different from everyday friendships.

Think about what you want in a mentor: is it someone who can help with industry expertise, guidance on your chosen career goals, or networking? Is there someone who has your dream job or who you greatly admire? Is there someone with a great track record of success when it comes to fulfilling a similar purpose? You don't need to look within your current workplace or circle, it could be someone from a totally different walk of life who has pursued the sort of path you want to pursue.

Look at your network map. Is there anyone on it who shares your philosophy or has a similar value system to you? Is it someone you like? Do their strengths align with your needs? Are they passionate about personal development? This may show through in their own investment to personal development, and indicates someone who is far more likely to invest time and energy in your development. Is it someone who is authentic and well respected, who is empathic and supportive, yet will tell you the truth?

This is a lot to live up to, and you may not be able to find someone who ticks all these boxes, but they are important questions to ask. You may find that you need more than one mentor; for instance one who helps with networking who is outside of your industry, and another who helps with development in your profession or area of expertise.

HOW TO APPROACH A MENTOR

This is the part most people stall on, because they are afraid of asking too much or of being rejected. The key things to bear in mind are:

- **Self-confidence**—Remember how to step into your stretch zone.

- **Use your network**—If you're reaching out to someone in your "layer of possibility," the best way to connect is to ask for an introduction from someone who knows them, rather than going in cold. Do some research on the potential mentor so that you can talk about a shared interest, present a good reason for them to meet you, and also think about what you can give to them.

- **Preparation**—Before you meet them, think through what you're hoping they will bring to the relationship, and be prepared to share what you have learnt by working through this book: your values, passions, strengths, purpose, and importantly your development plan. This is the part they can help you with, so explain your goals, how you hope to achieve them, and what the potential mentor can do to help you. Ask them for their thoughts, and potentially reshape your development plan and goals accordingly. Also think about what you may be able to bring to the relationship.

- **Connection**—Be interested in the other person and use the skills you learnt in Chapter 4. Make an effort to really listen when you actually meet: that way you'll not only make your potential mentor feel valued, but you're more likely to find where you have shared interests and values, how you may be able to help them achieve their purpose, where it overlaps with your own, what they may be able to do to help you with your purpose, who you could introduce them to, and who they may be able to introduce you to. And always follow up, promptly and graciously, showing that you are grateful to them for having spared their time.

- **Reciprocity**—This is human nature, people like to help, particularly if they understand the purpose in personal development, in which case they will likely achieve a sense of personal satisfaction from seeing you learn, grow, and succeed.

- **Persistence**—If one person turns you down, don't give up, find someone else to approach.

MAINTAINING THE RELATIONSHIP

Once you've found the right mentor for you, it may sound obvious, but put regular meetings in your diary. These could range in frequency from every four to six weeks to every six months, depending on your needs and what you agree with your mentor.

Mentoring relationships can last for months, but often continue for years. Make sure you invest in giving back to your mentor in whatever way they value—that could simply be showing gratitude by saying thank-you or giving them an occasional bottle of wine, or they may appreciate introductions you can make for them or ask you for advice on something in an area where you have expertise. It doesn't matter what it is, just try to work out what will be most rewarding for them.

Coming to the End of the Session

You've now considered how to perform at your optimum, keeping up the level of challenge to ensure you are pushed enough, but understanding when to step back to stop stress becoming too much. You've also thought through what triggers your stress, your best stress relievers, and hopefully discovered some new options. Being more aware of this should help you to plan your week to minimize stress wherever possible.

You've also looked at positive and authentic ways for you to go about building a network, leveraging the skills you've learnt in other sessions through the book to enable reciprocal and helpful relationships. You have considered who may be a good mentor, and thought through how you are going to connect with and work with them moving forward. This will all serve to support your continued growth.

In the Conclusion, I will summarize the areas you've covered in the book as a whole and offer some thoughts for you to ponder.

Conclusion

● ● ●

What a journey—you've just taken a walk through your life, what makes you tick, what makes you *you*. It is the story of you. One thing is clear: making it this far shows that you are committed to growing and developing yourself, to highlighting the characteristics that make you feel like you, and to overcoming those things that frustrate you and prevent you performing at your best in life.

The key insight I hope you will take away from this book is that your journey doesn't stop here: it will continue to evolve. It is likely that your environment will change, your goals may become different, and the people you interact with almost certainly will alter. So you need to reassess yourself on an ongoing basis—not necessarily going through this whole book again, of course, but continuing to think about the changes that happen, making adaptations in the areas that will help you to fulfill your potential, and taking action. Remember those last two words: **taking action**.

Let's quickly recap on what we've done together to get to the point where you've started to make things happen. By beginning with reflection, you created your narrative, your storyline, and looked at how its different highs and lows have affected your life. You covered a lot of ground and probably felt a little daunted, but it helped create the foundation for this whole process, and it was probably one of the first times you had looked at yourself in this way. In fact, you covered more than you may have realized, including:

- **What defines you**, regardless of what goes on in the world outside. You investigated the parts of you that have been shaped by experience and those that are central to your makeup.

- **How your brain works**, understanding the difference between your more advanced, observing brain, which searches for purpose and meaning, and your fast-thinking, reacting brain, which is driven by primitive survival impulses. You also saw how these differences influence your daily interactions.

- **Why emotional wisdom** is important and how to work on your own emotional wisdom and resilience.

- **Why connections matter** to mental well-being, and why you need them in order to create meaning and to feel a greater understanding of your part in the world.

To go deeper still, you used the Credo report to help you get more insight based on your own inbuilt way of responding to the world, your preferences and predispositions. To balance this, you also gathered feedback from the people who know you best across all your environments. Were the results obvious? Perhaps, but gathering feedback isn't something most people do, and you now have this current and honest insight into how others see you.

Arguably, the most important thing you have done was to stick with this process and move to the point of taking action. By picking up this book, reading it, carrying out the exercises, and thinking about what and how you want to develop, you have made great strides toward fulfilling your potential. By following up the additional resources and ensuring you look after your mental and physical well-being, you will be able to continue to grow as a person, constantly working in line with your chosen purpose in life.

You have covered a huge amount of personal material as you've worked through this book and may only change your behavior on a few elements at a time, which is in fact the most effective way of approaching this. Your brain simply won't respond if you try to do too much in one go. You should use the development planning and goal-setting tools you've found here to help you practice and embed different ways of doing things, and then, once they have become a habit, move on to something new. Your purpose is something you may still explore further and take your time over defining. That's fine: there is no time limit, so keep reflecting on and working through the various aspects at your own pace. After all, your purpose is for you and no one else.

Moving forward, you can use the sessions in this book as a guide to your continuing development, revisiting the science and touching in on the information that you've collected about yourself, your story, and what defines you. Ideally you should keep the outputs alive on an ongoing basis, as a living guidebook to you and your life: updating your storyline; mapping your evolving strengths, achievements, insights; learning what stresses you, how you sleep most effectively, what exercise suits you, how your network is constituted, and what your goals are relating to your purpose. Your self-awareness should be constantly nurtured to ensure you are operating at your optimum: you are not static, so neither should your understanding of yourself stay the same. While the core of who you are remains true whatever course you take, the outer layers of your circles will continually adjust and evolve as you pass through life. It's only through maintaining your self-awareness and continuing to learn and grow that you'll get the most out of yourself and continue to feel fulfilled. Doing this will also consistently remind you of who you are and what you stand for, helping to build your resilience and keeping you true to yourself, whatever circumstances you encounter in life.

Alongside your understanding of you as an individual, I would also urge you to try to maintain the basic principles you've learnt about how the brain works as part of your thinking. Working with your brain rather than against it will free your mind up from niggles and struggles, providing you with the mental capacity and space to achieve more. This does take practice and persistence, but using approaches such as mindfulness or simply "observing, not reacting" can make a huge difference to your life in many ways. Each and every time you manage to observe, not react, you are fine-tuning your brain to work more constructively. Understanding and committing to work on this will help you to establish a virtuous cycle of self-awareness, confidence, and self-management, enabling not only success, but a greater sense of contentment and mental well-being.*

In concluding this book, I want to share my motivations with you. As part of what I do, I regularly hear stories of people that we'd think of as highly successful, those we'd typically expect to have an exceptional understanding of their own behavior and that of other people. Over the years I have seen time and again that such people have learnt how to do well in life in an ad hoc way, by watching others or by being guided by an accidental mentor, and that often, through no fault of

---

* N.B. If your emotions are causing you ongoing or sustained distress, then you should visit a doctor or counselor in order to get help. No one should suffer alone, and you need a person, not a book, to get you to a better place.

their own, their learning is incomplete. As a result, they may still struggle with problems that get in the way of them doing their job properly, misdiagnose the behavior or intentions of other people, or make faulty decisions based on emotional data. My point is that these are the privileged few, who arguably have more access to personal development resources than anyone else, so where does that leave the rest of us?

One of the obstacles that society faces with regard to understanding behavior is we can take for granted that learning about our conduct just happens through the course of growing up. As a consequence, there is a belief that we don't need to be educated about the way we interact, communicate, respond, or feel, because our knowledge of behavior is a matter of common sense. Unfortunately our understanding is not as natural as this, especially given the mismatch between our brain and the environment we live in. In reality, the more we know about psychology and behavior, the more there is to know and the more helpful it is to our lives. An improved knowledge won't make any of us infallible, but education about behavior and the brain, our own preferences and tendencies, will allow us to live a more fulfilled life, avoid misunderstandings, make more effective judgments, and optimize our health. Importantly, continual self-development and exploration not only facilitate better relationships with others, greater success in life, and better mental well-being, they also enable us to be more effective and helpful members of the global community.

At a collective level, a better understanding and optimization of who we are as humans would also help mitigate a myriad of global issues. For example, I know through the work I have done that leveraging knowledge of human behavior could have lessened the impact of a range of political issues we have faced in this century alone, including the election of poor leaders into globally significant positions and the world financial crisis. Among other things, it could also help resolve the obesity epidemic, reduce the risk we all face from terrorism, alleviate international conflicts, diminish global warming, and ease poverty. It could literally make the world a better place. However, to enable such an understanding, we cannot rely on people picking up a book to learn more about themselves. The general population needs to comprehend and acknowledge that learning what we need to do shouldn't be left to chance. To get society to that point, I believe that we need to begin education about the brain and behavior in schools. Children should be taught this subject in the same thorough way that they are taught to add up and read, and with the same priority as technological and scientific knowledge. If that happened, future generations could be capable of incredible things.

It is my intention that you will have finished this book feeling you have learnt about yourself and are better equipped with tools and techniques to help you achieve whatever your dream may be. As I alluded to earlier, personal development, defining who you are, and becoming more self-aware are part of an ongoing journey. To become a wise sage who has lived a full and satisfying life, fulfilling your purpose, involves recurrent challenge (in the right measure) and growth. It means continually looking at the world around you to see what's going on, what's changing, how events are changing you, and how you need to adapt yourself and your purpose to keep living at your optimum. This could be just the first step, but I hope you now understand your story with greater insight. Ultimately, this will help you to be successful, but also just as importantly to be satisfied, mentally fit, and to live a happier life.

The Credo Test

● ● ●

Detailed below are all the different ways of accessing the personality questionnaire, Credo, created by eminent author and Chartered Psychologist Peter Rhodes for Tests Direct Limited. The report you will receive is designed as a self-development tool but there is also a further version, using the same responses, that is designed for a selection/ assessment context (with probe questions).

As highlighted in Chapter 5 the quickest and easiest way to complete the questionnaire is by registering for the test on https://www.tests-direct.com/defining-you. However, if you prefer you can request access to the test by the following methods:

1. Email admin@tests-direct.co.uk
2. Telephone (+44) 0207 036 3883
3. Visit https://www.tests-direct.co.uk and go to the 'Contact us' page to fill in an online form

In all cases, to access this free test and report you will need to quote **Defining You/TDL**.

Tests Direct will respond to all requests within a maximum of two working days (usually much quicker). This offer is open for one year from publication of the book.

For help with any problems, contact by email support@tests-direct.co.uk

For those interested, Tests Direct have a further extensive range of psychometrics covering specific industries such as health care and aviation, and functions such as sales aptitude and customer service.

Acknowledgments

• • •

I would like to thank Emma Parkin and Jo deVries for believing in my mad ideas, Liz for pointing me in the right direction, Holly Bennion for making it all possible, Izzi for chasing permissions and never-ending positivity, Cheryl for reading it raw, Emma for keeping me sane, Charlie for being my rock, my brother just because, Libby and Polly for letting me write when you really wanted me to play, my Mum for having the girls so very often, and Chris for your suggestions, love, and eternal support.

Notes

● ● ●

Chapter 1

1 Statistics Iceland (2015) More than 42 thousand took part in lifelong learning in 2014, https://statice.is/publications/news-archive/education/life-long-learning-2014/

2 L.M. Giambra, C.J. Camp, & A. Grodsky (1992) Curiosity and stimulation seeking across the adult life span: Cross-sectional and 6- to 8-year longitudinal findings, *Psychology and Aging* 7: 150–7.

3 Ian Leslie (2014) *Curious: The Desire to Know and Why Your Future Depends on It*, Toronto: Anansi.

4 F. Borrell-Carrio, A. Suchman, & R.M. Epstein (2004) The biopsychosocial model 25 years later: Principles, practice, and scientific inquiry, *Annals of Family Medicine* 2(6): 576–82.

5 Matthew Lieberman (2013) *Social: Why Our Brains Are Wired to Connect*, Oxford: Oxford University Press.

6 PR Newswire (2015) Merck KGaA, Darmstadt, Germany presents first curiosity report in the U.S. to help drive innovation, http://www.multivu.com/players/English/7648551-merck-kgaa-smarter-together/

7 S. von Stumm, B. Hell, & T. Chamorro-Premuzic (2011) The hungry mind: Intellectual curiosity is the third pillar of academic performance, *Perspectives on Psychological Science* 6(6): 574–88.

8 G.E. Swan & D. Carmelli (1996) Curiosity and mortality in aging adults: A 5-year follow-up of the Western Collaborative Group Study, *Psychology and Aging* 11(3): 449–53.

9 M.W. Gallagher & S.J. Lopez (2009) Positive expectancies and mental health: Identifying the unique contributions of hope and optimism, *Journal of Positive Psychology* 4(6): 548–56.

10 F. Gander, R.T. Proyer, W. Ruch, & T. Wyss (2012) The good character at work: An initial study on the contribution of character strengths in identifying healthy and unhealthy work-related behavior and experience patterns, *International Archives of Occupational and Environmental Health* 85(8): 895–904.

11 P.D. MacLean (1990) *The Triune Brain in Evolution: Role in Paleocerebral Functions*, New York: Plenum Press.

12 B.J. Avolio & W.L. Gardner (2005) Authentic leadership development: Getting to the root of positive forms of leadership, *The Leadership Quarterly* 16(3): 315–38. V.K. Bratton, N.G. Dodd, & F.W. Brown (2011) The impact of emotional intelligence on accuracy of self-awareness and leadership performance, *Leadership and Organization Development Journal* 32(2): 127–49.

13 K.W. Brown & R.M. Ryan (2003) The benefits of being present: Mindfulness and its role in psychological well-being, *Journal of Personality and Social Psychology* 84(4): 822–48. C.R. Cloninger (2006) The science of well-being: An integrated approach to mental health and its disorders, *World Psychiatry* 5(2): 71–6.

14 M.D. Ferrari & R.J. Sternberg (eds.) (1998) *Self-Awareness: Its Nature and Development*, New York: Guilford Press.

15 Greg Ashley & Roni Reiter-Palmon (2012). Self-awareness and the evolution of leaders: The need for a better measure of self-awareness, *Journal of Behavioral and Applied Management* 14(1): 2–17. Also available at https://digitalcommons. unomaha.edu/cgi/viewcontent.cgi?article=1006&context=psychfacpub

16 Alain Morin (2011) Self-awareness part 1: Definitions, measures, effects, functions and antecedents, *Social and Personality Psychology Compass* 5(10): 807–23.

17 D. McAdams (2001) The psychology of life stories, *Review of General Psychology* 5(2): 100–22.

18 Lisbeth Nielsen & Alfred W. Kaszniak (2006) Awareness of subtle emotional feelings: A comparison of long-term meditators and nonmeditators, *Emotion* 6(3): 392–405.

Chapter 2

1 Jo Blanden, Paul Gregg, & Lindsey Macmillan (2006) Accounting for inter-generational income persistence: Non-cognitive skills, ability and education, CEE Discussion Paper, London: Centre for the Economics of Education, London School of Economics and Political Science.

2 A. Goodman, H. Joshi, B. Nasim, & C. Tyler (2015) Social and emotional skills in childhood and their long-term effects on adult life. London: Institute of Education.

3 T.E. Moffitt, L. Arseneault, D. Belsky, et al. (2011) A gradient of childhood self-control predicts health, wealth, and public safety. *Proceedings of the National Academy of Sciences* 108(7): 2693–98.

4 Goodman et al., op. cit.

5 M.B. Rutherford (2009) Children's autonomy and responsibility: An analysis of childrearing advice, *Qualitative Sociology* 32(4): 337–53. J.M. Causadias, J.E. Salvatore, & L.A. Sroufe (2012) Early patterns of self-regulation as risk and promotive factors in development: A longitudinal study from childhood to adulthood in a high-risk sample, *International Journal of Behavioral Development* 36(4): 293–302.

6 Goodman et al., op. cit.

7 D. Goleman (2003) What makes a leader?, in L.W. Porter, H.L. Angle, & R.W. Allen (eds.), *Organizational Influence Processes*, 2nd edn, Armonk, NY: M.E. Sharpe, 229–41.

8 University of Haifa (2007) The quality of a father–child relationship affects intimate relationships in adulthood, https://www.eurekalert.org/pub_releases/2007-02/uoh-tqo021907.php

9 K. Larson, S.A. Russ, B.B. Nelson, et al. (2015) Cognitive ability at kindergarten entry and socioeconomic status, *Pediatrics* 135(2): e440–8.

10 Lada Adamic & Ismail Onur Filiz (2016) Do jobs run in families? https://research.fb.com/do-jobs-run-in-families/

11 Goodman et al., op. cit.

12 Kathleen M. Jodl, Alice Michael, Oksana Malanchuk, et al. (2001) Parents' roles in shaping early adolescents' occupational aspirations, *Child Development* 72(4): 1247–66.

13 C.J. Hopwood, M.B. Donnellan, D.M. Blonigen, et al. (2011) Genetic and environmental influences on personality trait stability and growth during the transition to adulthood: A three wave longitudinal study, *Journal of Personality and Social Psychology* 100(3): 545–56.

14 Norman Doidge (2010) *The Brain That Changes Itself: Stories of Personal Triumph from the Frontiers of Brain Science*, Carlton North, Australia: Scribe Publications.

Chapter 3

1 J.J. Arnett (2000) Emerging adulthood: A theory of development from the late teens through the twenties, *American Psychologist* 55(5): 469–80.

2 J.L. Tanner & J.J. Arnett (2011) Presenting "emerging adulthood": What makes it developmentally distinctive, in J.J. Arnett, M. Kloep, L.A. Hendry, & J.L. Tanner (eds.), *Debating Emerging Adulthood: Stage or Process?* New York: Oxford University Press, 13–30.

3 Peter Salovey & John D. Mayer (1990) Emotional intelligence, *Imagination, Cognition, and Personality* 9(3): 185–211.

4 Daniel Goleman (1995) *Emotional Intelligence: Why It Can Matter More Than IQ*, New York: Bantam Books.

5 Robert A. Baron & Gideon D. Markman (2000) Beyond social capital: How social skills can enhance entrepreneurs' success, *Academy of Management Executive* 14(1): 106–16. M.A. Brackett, S.E. Rivers, S. Shiffman, et al. (2006) Relating emotional abilities to social functioning: A comparison of self-report and performance measures of emotional intelligence, *Journal of Personality and Social Psychology* 91(4): 780–95.

6 J. Ciarrochi, F.P. Deane, & S. Anderson (2002) Emotional intelligence moderates the relationship between stress and mental health, *Personality and Individual Differences* 32(2): 197–209.

7 Richard Boyatzis (1999) The financial impact of competencies in leadership and management of consulting firms. Department of Organizational Behavior Working Paper, Cleveland, OH: Case Western Reserve University.

8 D.C. McClelland (1999) Identifying competencies with behavioral-event interviews, *Psychological Science* 9(5): 331–9.

9 McBer, Hay (2000) Research into teacher effectiveness: A model of teacher effectiveness, London: Department for Education and Employment.

10 G.A. Marlatt & J.L. Kristeller (1999) Mindfulness and meditation, in W.R. Miller (ed.), *Integrating Spirituality into Treatment*, Washington, DC: American Psychological Association, 67–84.

11 Arnett, op. cit.

12 Meg Jay (2013) *The Defining Decade: Why Your Twenties Matter—And How to Make the Most of Them Now*, New York: Twelve.

13 V. Kumari (2006) Do psychotherapies produce neurobiological effects? *Acta Neuropsychiatrica* 18(2): 61–70. P.R. Porto, L. Oliveira, J. Mari, et al. (2009) Does cognitive behavioral therapy change the brain? A systematic review of neuroimaging in anxiety disorders, *Journal of Neuropsychiatry and Clinical Neurosciences* 21(2): 114–25.

Chapter 4

1 Sonja Lyubomirsky (2007) *The How of Happiness: A New Approach to Getting the Life You Want*, Harmondsworth: Penguin.

2 Daniel Kahneman (2011) *Thinking, Fast and Slow*, New York: Farrar, Straus and Giroux.

3 Jules Pretty (2012) *The Earth Only Endures: On Reconnecting with Nature and Our Place in It*, London: Earthscan.

4 M. Koizumi, H. Ito, Y. Kaneko, & Y. Motohashi. (2008) Effect of having a sense of purpose in life on the risk of death from cardiovascular diseases. *Journal of Epidemiology* 18(5): 191–6.

5 P.A. Boyle, A.S. Buchman, R.S. Wilson, et al. (2012) Effect of purpose in life on the relation between Alzheimer disease pathologic changes on cognitive function in advanced age, *Archives of General Psychiatry* 69(5): 499–505. P. Boyle, A. Buchman, L. Barnes, & D. Bennett (2010) Effect of a purpose in life on risk of incident Alzheimer disease and mild cognitive impairment in community-dwelling older persons, *Archives of General Psychiatry* 67(3): 304–10.

6 B.W. Smith, E.M. Tooley, E.Q. Montague, et al. (2009) The role of resilience and purpose in life in habituation to heat and cold pain, *Journal of Pain* 10(5): 493–500.

7 Gerben J. Westerhof, Ernst T. Bohlmeijer, Ilse M.J. van Beljouw, & Anne Margriet Pot (2010) Improvement in personal meaning mediates the effects of a life review intervention on depressive symptoms in a randomized controlled trial, *The Gerontologist* 50(4): 541–9. S. Robatmili, F. Sohrabi,

M.A. Shahrak, et al. (2015) The effect of group logotherapy on meaning in life and depression levels of Iranian students, *International Journal for the Advancement of Counseling* 37(1): 54–62.

8 M. Błażek, M. Kaźmierczak, & T. Besta (2015) Sense of purpose in life and escape from self as the predictors of quality of life in clinical samples, *Journal of Religion and Health* 54(2): 517–23. S.M. Schaefer, J. Morozink Boylan, C.M. van Reekum, et al. (2013) *PLoS One* 8(11): e80329.

9 C. Bamia, A. Trichopoulou, & D. Trichopoulos (2008) Age at retirement and mortality in a general population sample: The Greek EPIC study. *American Journal of Epidemiology* 167(5): 561–9. P.L. Hill & N.A. Turiano (2014) Purpose in life as a predictor of mortality across adulthood, *Psychological Science* 25(7): 1482–6. S.P. Tsai, J.K. Wendt, R.P. Donnelly, et al. (2005) Age at retirement and long-term survival of an industrial population: Prospective cohort study, *BMJ (Clinical Research Ed.)*, 331(7523): 995.

10 Viktor E. Frankl (1984) *Man's Search for Meaning: An Introduction to Logotherapy*, New York: Simon & Schuster.

11 R. Harris (2008) *The Happiness Trap: How to Stop Struggling and Start Living*, Boston, MA: Trumpeter.

12 Emma Seppala (2013) The compassionate mind, https://www.psychologic-alscience.org/observer/the-compassionate-mind

13 D. Umberson & J. Karas Montez (2010) Social relationships and health: A flashpoint for health policy, *Journal of Health and Social Behavior* 51(1 Suppl.): S54–66.

14 B.N. Uchino (2006) Social support and health: A review of physiological processes potentially underlying links to disease outcomes, *Journal of Behavioral Medicine* 29(4): 377–87.

15 H.J. Dour, J.F. Wiley, P. Roy-Byrne, et al. (2014) Perceived social support mediates anxiety and depressive symptom changes following primary care intervention, *Depression and Anxiety* 31(5): 436–42. H.R. Roohafza, H. Afshar, A.H. Keshteli, et al. (2014) What's the role of perceived social support and coping styles in depression and anxiety? *Journal of Research in Medical Sciences* 19(10): 944. G.D. Zimet, N.W. Dahlem, S.G. Zimet, & G.K. Farley (1988) The multidimensional scale of perceived social support, *Journal of Personality Assessment* 52(1): 30–41.

16 T.R.P. de Brito, D.P. Nunes, L.P. Corona, et al. (2017) Low supply of social support as risk factor for mortality in the older adults, *Archives of Gerontology and Geriatrics* 73: 77–8. J. Holt-Lunstad, T.B. Smith, M. Baker, et al. (2015) Loneliness and social isolation as risk factors for mortality: A meta-analytic review, *Perspectives on Psychological Science* 10(2): 227–37.

17 Adam M. Grant (2014) *Give and Take: Why Helping Others Drives Our Success*, London: W&N.

18 Tania Singer (2013) I'm OK, you're not OK, https://www.mpg.de/research/supramarginal-gyrus-empathy

19 Brené Brown (2010) The power of vulnerability, https://www.ted.com/talks/brene_brown_on_vulnerability

20 Tomas Chamorro-Premuzic (2013) *Confidence: Overcoming Low Self-Esteem, Insecurity, and Self-Doubt*, Toronto: Hudson Street Press.

Chapter 5

1 Psychometrics Centre (2013) Frequently asked questions about psychometrics, https://www.psychometrics.cam.ac.uk/news/news.25
2 Ben Dattner (2008) The use and misuse of personality tests for coaching and development, *Psychology Today*, https://www.psychologytoday.com/blog/credit-and-blame-work/200806/the-use-and-misuse-personali-ty-tests-coaching-and-development
3 G.W. Allport (1937) *Personality: A Psychological Interpretation*, New York: Henry Holt.
4 O.P. John & S. Srivastava (1999) The Big Five trait taxonomy: History, measurement, and theoretical perspectives, in L. Pervin and O.P. John (eds.), *Handbook of Personality: Theory and Research*, 2nd edn, New York: Guilford Press, 102–38.
5 Paul Sinclair (n.d.) The "Big Five" factors personality model, http://www.academia.edu/16028834/Big_5

Chapter 6

1 Norbert Wiener (1948) *Cybernetics: Control and Communication in the Animal and the Machine*, Hoboken, NJ: John Wiley.
2 David Rock (2009) Managing with the brain in mind, *Strategy+Business*, autumn.
3 Carol S. Dweck (2008) *Mindset: The New Psychology of Success*, New York: Ballantine.
4 Jack Canfield & Janet Switzer (2005) *The Success Principles: How to Get from Where You Are to Where You Want to Be*, New York: HarperCollins.
5 Liz Wiggins (2008) Managing the ups and downs of change communication, *Strategic Communication Management* 13(1): 20–3.

Chapter 7

1 J.Y. Shin & M.F. Steger (2014) Promoting meaning and purpose in life, in A.C. Parks & S.M. Schueller (eds.), *The Wiley-Blackwell Handbook of Positive Psychological Interventions*, Chichester: Wiley-Blackwell, 90–110.
2 P.E. McKnight & T.B. Kashdan (2009) Purpose in life as a system that creates and sustains health and well-being: An integrative, testable theory, *Review of General Psychology*, 13(3): 242–51.

3 Majid Fotuhi & Sara Mehr (2015) The science behind the powerful benefits of having a purpose: Purpose in life is one of the main components of quality of life, *Practical Neurology* Sept.: 32–3.

4 The Obama White House (2015) Sir David Attenborough and President Obama: The full interview, https://www.youtube.com/watch?v=NZtJ2ZGyvBI

5 Jack Shepherd (2017) David Attenborough: 15 of the naturalist's best quotes, *Independent*, http://www.independent.co.uk/arts-entertainment/tv/news/david-attenborough-best-quotes-birthday-a7724216.html

6 The Obama White House, op. cit.

7 *The Jonathan Ross Show*, series 5, episode 11. Broadcast 28 December 2013. The full interview, https://youtube.com/watch?v=3p63equuRG8

8 Roy F. Baumeister, Kathleen D. Vohs, Jennifer Aaker, & Emily N. Garbinsky (2013) Some key differences between a happy life and a meaningful life, *Journal of Positive Psychology* 8(6): 505–16.

9 D.T. Neal, W. Wood, M. Wu, & D. Kurlander (2011) The pull of the past: When do habits persist despite conflict with motives? *Personality and Social Psychology Bulletin* 37(11): 1428–37.

10 Jack Canfield & Janet Switzer (2005) *The Success Principles: How to Get from Where You Are to Where You Want to Be*, New York: HarperCollins.

11 D. Owen & J. Davidson (2009). Hubris syndrome: An acquired personality disorder? A study of US presidents and UK prime ministers over the last 100 years, *Brain* 132(5): 1396–406.

12 Neel Burton (2015) Self-confidence versus self-esteem, https://www.psychologytoday.com/blog/hide-and-seek/201510/self-confidence-versus-self-esteem

13 Carol S. Dweck (2006) *Mindset: The New Psychology of Success*, New York: Random House.

14 Paul Gilbert (2005) *Compassion: Conceptualisations, Research and Use in Psychotherapy*, London: Routledge. Paul Gilbert (2009) *The Compassionate Mind: A New Approach to Life's Challenges*, London: Constable-Robinson. Paul Gilbert (2012) Compassion-focused therapy, in W. Dryden (ed.), *Cognitive Behaviour Therapies*, London: Sage, 140–65.

15 K.D. Neff (2011) Self-compassion, self-esteem, and well-being, *Social and Personality Psychology Compass* 5(1): 1–12.

16 J. Willis & A. Todorov (2006) First impressions: Making up your mind after a 100-ms exposure to a face, *Psychological Science* 17(7): 592–8.

17 Hubert K. Rampersad (2008) A new blueprint for powerful and authentic personal branding, *Performance Improvement* 47: 34–7.

18 Amy Cuddy (2012) Your body language may shape who you are, https://www.ted.com/talks/amy_cuddy_your_body_language_shapes_who_you_are

19 Amy Cuddy (2015) *Presence: Bringing Your Boldest Self to Your Biggest Challenges*, New York: Little, Brown.

20 Mel Carson (2016) *Introduction to Personal Branding: 10 Steps Toward a New Professional You*, Seattle, WA: Delightful Communications.

Chapter 8

1 R. Su, C.D. Murdock, & J. Rounds (2015) Person–environment fit, in P.J. Hartung, M.L. Savickas, & W.B. Walsh (eds.), *APA Handbook of Career Intervention*, vol. 1, Washington, DC: American Psychological Association, 81–98.

2 Rob Goffee & Gareth Jones (2015) Why should anyone work here?, *London Business School Review* 26(4): 10–12.

3 Rob Goffee & Gareth Jones (2013) Creating the best workplace on earth, *Harvard Business Review* 91: 98–106.

4 R.I. Dunbar (1992) Neocortex size as a constraint on group size in primates, *Journal of Human Evolution* 22(6): 469–93.

5 Charmine E.J. Härtel (2008) How to build a healthy emotional culture and avoid a toxic culture, in C.L. Cooper & N.M. Ashkanasy (eds.), *Research Companion to Emotion in Organizations*, Cheltenham: Edward Elgar, 1260–91.

6 Ronald E. Riggio (2015) The 5 warning signs of a toxic work environment, *Psychology Today*, https://www.psychologytoday.com/blog/cutting-edge-leadership/201501/the-5-warning-signs-toxic-work-environment

7 Mariette DiChristina (2015) Science explains why we really do need to sleep a third of our lives away, *Scientific American*, October 1, https://www.scientificamerican.com/article/science-explains-why-we-really-do-need-to-sleep-a-third-of-our-lives-away/

8 M.M. Mitler, M.A. Carskadon, C.A. Czeisier, et al. (1988) Catastrophes, sleep, and public policy: Consensus report, *Sleep* 11(1): 100–9.

9 P. Alhola & P. Polo-Kantola (2007) Sleep deprivation: Impact on cognitive performance, *Neuropsychiatric Disease and Treatment* 3(5): 553–67. A.J. Krause, E.B. Simon, B.A. Mander, et al. (2017) The sleep-deprived human brain, *Nature Reviews Neuroscience* 18(7): 404–18. J.J. Pilcher & A.I. Huffcutt (1996) Effects of sleep deprivation on performance: A meta-analysis, *Sleep* 19(4): 318–26.

10 G.G. Alvarez & N.T. Ayas (2004) The impact of daily sleep duration on health: A review of the literature, *Progress in Cardiovascular Nursing* 19(2): 56–9. K.L. Knutson, K. Spiegel, P. Penev, & E. Van Cauter (2007) The metabolic consequences of sleep deprivation, *Sleep Medicine Reviews* 11(3): 163–78.

11 S.S. Yoo, N. Gujar, P. Hu, et al. (2007) The human emotional brain without sleep: A prefrontal amygdala disconnect, *Current Biology* 17(20): R877–8.

12 W.R. Gove (1970) Sleep deprivation: A cause of psychotic disorganization, *American Journal of Sociology* 75(5): 782–99. A. Kales, T.L. Tan, E.J. Kollar, et al. (1970) Sleep patterns following 205 hours of sleep deprivation, *Psychosomatic Medicine* 32(2): 189–200.

13 J.M. Mullington, M. Haack, M. Toth, et al. (2009) Cardiovascular, inflammatory, and metabolic consequences of sleep deprivation, *Progress in Cardiovascular Diseases* 51(4): 294–302.

14 A.M. Williamson & A.M. Feyer (2000) Moderate sleep deprivation produces

impairments in cognitive and motor performance equivalent to legally prescribed levels of alcohol intoxication, *Occupational and Environmental Medicine* 57(10): 649–55.

15 Sleep Council (2011) Toxic sleep: The silent epidemic, http://www.sleep-council.org.uk/latest-news/toxic-sleep-the-silent-epidemic/

16 Centers for Disease Control and Prevention (2016) 1 in 3 adults don't get enough sleep, https://www.cdc.gov/media/releases/2016/p0215-enough-sleep.html

17 A. Roger Ekirch (2005) *At Day's Close: Night in Times Past*, New York: Norton.

18 T.A. Wehr (1992) In short photoperiods, human sleep is biphasic, *Journal of Sleep Research* 1(2): 103–7.

19 J.F. Duffy & C.A. Czeisler (2009) Effect of light on human circadian physiology, *Sleep Medicine Clinics* 4(2): 165–77.

20 P.C. Zee, H. Attarian, & A. Videnovic (2013) Circadian rhythm abnormalities, *Continuum: Lifelong Learning in Neurology* 19(1): 132–47.

21 Gary Morley (2014) Sport sleep coach's top tips to improve your slumber, CNN.com, http://edition.cnn.com/2014/11/12/sport/golf/sport-sleep-coach-nick-littlehales/index.html

22 D.S. Black, G.A. O'Reilly, R. Olmstead, et al. (2015) Mindfulness meditation and improvement in sleep quality and daytime impairment among older adults with sleep disturbances: A randomized clinical trial, *JAMA Internal Medicine* 175(4): 494–501.

23 Travis Usinger (2014) Effect of internet administered mindfulness training on anxiety and sleep quality, undergraduate honors thesis, University of Colorado, https://scholar.colorado.edu/honr_theses/727

24 Charles Czeisler (2006) Sleep deficit: The performance killer. A conversation with Harvard Medical School Professor Charles A. Czeisler, *Harvard Business Review* 84(10): 53–9.

25 Suzy Reading (2017) *The Self-Care Revolution: Smart Habits and Simple Practices to Allow You to Flourish*, London: Aster.

26 M. Kodali, T. Megahed, V. Mishra, et al. (2016) Voluntary running exercise-mediated enhanced neurogenesis does not obliterate retrograde spatial memory, *Journal of Neuroscience* 36(31): 8112–22.

27 H. Van Praag, M. Fleshner, M.W. Schwartz, & M.P. Mattson (2014) Exercise, energy intake, glucose homeostasis, and the brain, *Journal of Neuroscience* 34(46): 15139–49.

28 D.E.R. Warburton, C.W. Nicol, & S.S.D. Bredin (2006) Health benefits of physical activity: The evidence, *Canadian Medical Association Journal* 174(6): 801–9.

29 F.J. Penedo & J.R. Dahn (2005) Exercise and well-being: A review of mental and physical health benefits associated with physical activity, *Current Opinion in Psychiatry* 18(2): 189–93. C.B. Taylor, J.F. Sallis, & R. Needle (1985) The relation of physical activity and exercise to mental health, *Public Health Reports* 100(2): 195–202.

30 David Bunce & Fiona Murden (2006) Age, aerobic fitness, executive function, and episodic memory, *European Journal of Cognitive Psychology* 18: 221–33.

31 L.M. Wankel (1993) The importance of enjoyment to adherence and psychological benefits from physical activity, *International Journal of Sport Psychology* 24(2): 151–69.

32 Joseph Ciarrochi, Ann Bailey, & Russ Harris (2014) *The Weight Escape: How to Stop Dieting and Start Living*, Boston, MA: Shambhala.

33 P.G. Nixon (1981) The human function curve: A paradigm for our times, *Activitas Nervosa Superior* 3(1): 130–3.

34 Russ Harris (2012) *The Happiness Trap: Stop Struggling, Start Living*, New York: Little, Brown.

35 Mihaly Csikszentmihalyi (1990) *Flow: The Psychology of Optimal Experience*, New York: Harper & Row.

36 G.X. Mao, X.G. Lan, Y.B. Cao, et al. (2012) Effects of short-term forest bathing on human health in a broad-leaved evergreen forest in Zhejiang Province, China, *Biomedical and Environmental Sciences* 25(3): 317–24.

37 B.C. Feeney & N.L. Collins (2015) A new look at social support: A theoretical perspective on thriving through relationships, *Personality and Social Psychology Review* 19(2): 113–47.

38 L.A. Pawlow & G.E. Jones (2002) The impact of abbreviated progressive muscle relaxation on salivary cortisol, *Biological Psychology* 60(1): 1–16.

39 S.J. Lim & C. Kim (2014) Effects of autogenic training on stress response and heart rate variability in nursing students, *Asian Nursing Research* 8(4): 286–92.

40 E.R. Park, L. Traeger, A.M. Vranceanu, et al. (2013) The development of a patient-centered program based on the relaxation response: The Relaxation Response Resiliency Program (3RP), *Psychosomatics* 54(2): 165–74.

41 P. Lehrer (2013) How does heart rate variability biofeedback work? Resonance, the baroreflex, and other mechanisms, *Biofeedback* 41(1): 26–31.

42 E. Bigham, L. McDannel, I. Luciano, & G. Salgado-Lopez (2014) Effect of a brief guided imagery on stress, *Biofeedback* 42(1): 28–35.

43 X. Ma, Z.Q. Yue, Z.Q. Gong, et al. (2017) The effect of diaphragmatic breathing on attention, negative affect and stress in healthy adults, *Frontiers in Psychology* 8: 874.

44 W.R. Lovallo, T.L. Whitsett, M. al'Absi, et al. (2005) Caffeine stimulation of cortisol secretion across the waking hours in relation to caffeine intake levels, *Psychosomatic Medicine* 67(5): 734–9.

45 J.O.C.P. Delarue, O. Matzinger, C. Binnert, et al. (2003) Fish oil prevents the adrenal activation elicited by mental stress in healthy men, *Diabetes and Metabolism* 29(3): 289–95. F.P.J. Martin, S. Rezzi, E. Peré-Trepat, et al. (2009) Metabolic effects of dark chocolate consumption on energy, gut microbiota, and stress-related metabolism in free-living subjects, *Journal of Proteome Research* 8(12): 5568–79. A. Baublis, A. Spomer, & M.D. Berber-Jiménez (1994) Anthocyanin pigments: Comparison of extract stability, *Journal of Food Science* 59: 1219–21. Y. Oi, T. Kawada, C. Shishido, et al. (1999) Allyl-containing

sulfides in garlic increase uncoupling protein content in brown adipose tissue, and noradrenaline and adrenaline secretion in rats, *Journal of Nutrition* 129(2): 336–42. Y. Oi-Kano, T. Kawada, T. Watanabe, et al. (2008) Oleuropein, a phenolic compound in extra virgin olive oil, increases uncoupling protein 1 content in brown adipose tissue and enhances noradrenaline and adrenaline secretions in rats, *Journal of Nutritional Science and Vitaminology* 54(5): 363–70. S. Prasad & B.B. Aggarwal (2011) Turmeric, the golden spice: From traditional medicine to modern medicine, in I.F.F. Benzie & S. Wachtel-Galor (eds.), *Herbal Medicine: Biomolecular and Clinical Aspects*, 2nd edn, Boca Raton, FL: CRC Press/Taylor & Francis, ch. 13. D.J. White, S. de Klerk, W. Woods, et al. (2016) Anti-stress, behavioural and magnetoencephalography effects of an l-theanine-based nutrient drink: A randomised, double-blind, placebo-controlled, crossover trial, *Nutrients* 8(1): 53. J.K. Srivastava, E. Shankar, & S. Gupta (2010) Chamomile: A herbal medicine of the past with a bright future, *Molecular Medicine Reports* 3(6): 895–901.

46 K. Schmidt, P.J. Cowen, C.J. Harmer, et al. (2015) Prebiotic intake reduces the waking cortisol response and alters emotional bias in healthy volunteers, *Psychopharmacology* 232(10): 1793–801.

47 Michael Cheary (n.d.) What is networking? https://www.reed.co.uk/career-advice/what-is-networking/

48 H. Wolff & K. Moser (2009) Effects of networking on career success: A longitudinal study, *Journal of Applied Psychology* 94(1): 196–206.

49 B. Uzzi & S. Dunlap (2005) How to build your network, *Harvard Business Review* 83(12): 53–60.

50 T. Casciaro, F. Gino, & M. Kouchaki (2014) The contaminating effects of building instrumental ties: How networking can make us feel dirty, *Administrative Science Quarterly* 59(4): 705–35.

51 David Sole & Belinda Roberts (2015) *21st-Century Networking: How to Become a Natural Networker*, London: Elliott & Thompson.

52 Reid Hoffman & Ben Casnocha (2012) *The Start-Up of You: Adapt to the Future, Invest in Yourself, and Transform Your Career*, New York: Crown Business.

53 W.B. Johnson (2002) The intentional mentor: Strategies and guidelines for the practice of mentoring, *Professional Psychology: Research and Practice* 33(1): 88–96.

54 L.T. Eby, T.D. Allen, S.C. Evans, et al. (2008) Does mentoring matter? A multidisciplinary meta-analysis comparing mentored and non-mentored individuals, *Journal of Vocational Behavior* 72(2): 254–67.

Bibliography

• • •

Cain, S. (2013) *Quiet: The Power of Introverts in a World That Can't Stop Talking*, Harmondsworth: Penguin.

Canfield, J. & Switzer, J. (2005) *The Success Principles: How to Get from Where You Are to Where You Want to Be*, New York: HarperCollins.

Carson, M. (2016) *Introduction to Personal Branding: 10 Steps toward a New Professional You*, Seattle, WA: Delightful Communications.

Chamorro-Premuzic, T. (2013) *Confidence: Overcoming Low Self-Esteem, Insecurity, and Self-Doubt*, New York: Hudson Street Press.

Covey, S.R. (2004) *The 7 Habits of Highly Effective People: Restoring the Character Ethic*, New York: Free Press.

Csikszentmihalyi, M. (1990) *Flow: The Psychology of Optimal Experience*, New York: Harper & Row.

Cuddy, A. (2016) *Presence: Bringing Your Boldest Self to Your Biggest Challenges*, London: Orion.

Doidge, N. (2010) *The Brain That Changes Itself: Stories of Personal Triumph from the Frontiers of Brain Science,* Carlton North, Victoria, Australia: Scribe.

Duckworth, A. (2017) *Grit: Why Passion and Resilience Are the Secrets to Success*, London: Vermillion.

Dweck, C.S. (2008) *Mindset: The New Psychology of Success*, New York: Ballantine Books.

Ekirch, A.R. (2005) *At Day's Close: Night in Times Past,* New York: Norton.

Frankl, V.E. (1984) *Man's Search for Meaning: An Introduction to Logotherapy*, New York: Simon & Schuster.

Gilbert, P. (2009) *The Compassionate Mind: A New Approach to Life's Challenges*, London: Constable-Robinson.

Goleman, D. (1995) *Emotional Intelligence: Why It Can Matter More Than IQ*, New York: Bantam.

Goleman, D. (2013) *Primal Leadership: Unleashing the Power of Emotional Intelligence*, Brighton Watertown, MA: Harvard Business Review Press.

Haidt, J. (2007) *The Happiness Hypothesis: Putting Ancient Wisdom to the Test of Modern Science*, New York: Arrow.

Harris, R. (2008) *The Happiness Trap: How to Stop Struggling and Start Living*, Boston, MA: Trumpeter.

Harris, R. (2011) *The Confidence Gap: From Fear to Freedom*, London: Robinson.

Harris, R. (2012) *The Reality Slap: How to Find Fulfilment When Life Hurts*, London: Robinson.

Hoffman, R. & Casnocha, B. (2012) *The Start-up of You: Adapt to the Future, Invest in Yourself, and Transform Your Career*, New York: Crown Business.

Jay, M. (2013) *The Defining Decade: Why Your Twenties Matter—And How to Make the Most of Them Now*, London: Twelve.

Kahneman, D. (2011) *Thinking, Fast and Slow*, New York: Farrar, Straus and Giroux.

Le Doux, J.E. (1996) *The Emotional Brain*, New York: Simon & Schuster.

Leslie, I. (2014) *Curious: The Desire to Know and Why Your Future Depends on It*, Toronto: Anansi.

Lieberman, M. (2013) *Social: Why Our Brains Are Wired to Connect*, Oxford: Oxford University Press.

Lyubomirsky, S. (2007) *The How of Happiness: A New Approach to Getting the Life You Want*, Harmondsworth: Penguin.

MacLean, P.D. (1990) *The Triune Brain in Evolution: Role in Paleocerebral Functions*, New York: Plenum Press.

Newman, M. (2008) *Emotional Capitalists: The New Leaders*, Chichester: John Wiley.

Peters, S.D. (2012) *The Chimp Paradox: The Mind Management Programme to Help You Achieve Success, Confidence and Happiness*, London: Vermilion.

Pretty, J. (2012) *The Earth Only Endures: On Reconnecting with Nature and Our Place in It*, London: Earthscan.

Reading, S. (2017) *The Self-Care Revolution: Smart Habits and Simple Practices to Allow You to Flourish*, London: Aster.

Ridley, M. (2004) *Nature via Nurture: Genes, Experience and What Makes Us Human*, New York: Harper Perennial.

Sole, D. & Roberts, B. (2015) *21st-Century Networking: How to Become a Natural Networker*, London: Elliott & Thompson.

Ted Talks, https://www.ted.com/talks

Tough, P. (2014) *How Children Succeed: Confidence, Curiosity and the Hidden Power of Character*, London: Arrow.

Wax, R. (2014) *Sane New World: Taming the Mind*, London: Hodder.

Wiener, N. (1948) *Cybernetics: Control and Communication in the Animal and the Machine*, Hoboken, NJ: John Wiley.

Books and Resources for Relaxation Techniques and Mindfulness

Alidina, S. (2011) *Relaxation for Dummies*, Chichester: John Wiley.

Anholt, A. (2013) *The Breathing Exercise Bible: Relaxation and Meditation Techniques for Happiness and Healthy Living*, North Charleston, SC: CreateSpace.

Benson, H. (2000) *The Relaxation Response*, New York: HarperCollins.

Bozier, J. (2016) Mindfulness: Progressive Muscle Relaxation, BUPA, https://www.bupa.co.uk/newsroom/ourviews/progressive-muscle-relaxation-podcast

Collard, P. (2014) *The Little Book of Mindfulness: 10 Minutes a Day to Less Stress, More Peace*, London: Gaia.

Fanning, P., McKay, M. & Landis, J. (2008) *Progressive Relaxation* (audio CD), Oakland, CA: New Harbinger.

Farhi, D. (1996) *The Breathing Book: Vitality and Good Health through Essential Breath Work*, New York: Henry Holt.

Harrold, G. (2002) *Creating Inner Peace and Calm* (audio CD), Borough Green, Tonbrige, UK: Diviniti Press.

Kabat-Zinn, J. (2005) *Guided Mindfulness Meditation* (audio CD), Louisville, CO: Sounds True.

Kermani, K. (1996) *Autogenic Training: The Effective Holistic Way to Better Health*, London: Souvenir Press.

Kornfield, J. (2005) *Meditation for Beginners*, New York: Bantam.

Mantell, S. (2000) *Your Present: A Half-Hour of Peace* (audio CD), Carlsbad, CA: Penton Overseas.

Naparstek, B. (2005) *A Guided Meditation for Relaxation & Wellness* (audio CD), Cleveland, OH: Health Journeys.

Robbins, J. (2008) *A Symphony in the Brain: The Evolution of the New Brain Wave Biofeedback*, New York: Atlantic Monthly Press.

Strom, M. (2016) *There Is No App for Happiness: Finding Joy and Meaning in the Digital Age with Mindfulness, Breathwork, and Yoga*, New York: Skyhorse Publishing.

Wax, R. (2016) *A Mindfulness Guide for the Frazzled*, Harmondsworth: Penguin.

Williams, M. & Penman, M. (2011) *Mindfulness: A Practical Guide to Finding Peace in a Frantic World*, London: Piatkus.

Mindfulness apps

Buddhify: http://buddhify.com

Headspace: www.headspace.com

iMindfulness: https://itunes.apple.com/gb/app/imindfulness/id473747142?mt=8

Mindfulness Daily: www.mindfulnessdailyapp.com

Smiling Mind: www.smilingmind.com.au

About the Author

● ● ●

Fiona Murden is a British psychologist, performance coach, trusted adviser, and author. She is a prominent expert on applied psychology and has spent the past 18 years advising leaders of global organizations, policy makers, and "people of significant influence" on how best to fulfill their own and others' potential. She has authored a number of papers relating to neuroscience and behavioral phenomena impacting leadership, decision making, and everyday life.

Fiona is a recognized authority on leadership assessment, unpicking what makes individuals and groups tick. She has advised corporate and organizational boards across the UK, USA, Europe, and Asia Pacific on the behavioral probabilities associated with leadership hires, how to mitigate any risks, and the best ways to enable success. She is also a highly sought-after coach, working with a broad range of people from CEOs and sports professionals to professors and medics. Her speaking commitments take her into establishments as diverse as schools, universities, the Cabinet Office, the Institute of Directors, and the Royal College of Surgeons.

Fiona passionately believes that we should all be better equipped with the knowledge and tools to live a more fulfilled life. She leverages the latest research about our brain and behavior in a "user friendly" way, and is an outspoken campaigner for dispelling the myths around psychology. She recently launched the charity Dot-to-Dot, which aims to accelerate this understanding across society.

A Chartered Psychologist, Fiona has been awarded Associate Fellow of the British Psychological Society. She has a Bachelor of Science in Psychology from Warwick University and a Masters from Warwick University Business School. She also has a Master of Science in Psychology, gained with distinction, from the University of London. She is known professionally as having sharp insight into human behavior, a quick understanding of situational dynamics, and as someone who is able to rapidly get to the bottom of complex issues. Fiona lives with her husband Chris, two daughters, and dog in the Kent countryside.

The Dot-to-Dot charity aims to address the growing problem of society's disjointed understanding of behaviour. If this is tackled we could improve lives on a global scale. Joining the dots on behaviour would not only empower us as individuals to reach our true potential but ultimately have a positive and significant impact on issues such as obesity, terrorism, climate change and conflict.

JOINING THE DOTS ON BEHAVIOUR

...to raise awareness
Talking about behavioural issues, not just mental health but everyday behaviour and what it really means will dramatically improve lives and allow people to fully realise their potential.

...to advance understanding
Bringing experts and innovators together from diverse backgrounds in order to share learning and create profound solutions to growing concerns such as the mismatch between our brain and the world we live in.

...to improve lives
Supporting initiatives proven to have a positive impact on people's lives.

How can you help?
Signing up will instantly join two more dots making the bigger picture clearer. Sharing your support really will make a difference because every single person counts when it comes to changing society for the better.

fionamurden.com/dot-to-dot/

Dot-to-Dot Behaviour Ltd is awaiting charitable status (as of February 2018).

Would you like your people to read this book?

If you would like to discuss how you could bring these ideas to your team, we would love to hear from you. Our titles are available at competitive discounts when purchased in bulk. Bespoke editions featuring corporate logos, customized covers, or letters from company directors in the front matter can also be created in line with your special requirements.

We work closely with leading experts and organizations to bring forward-thinking ideas to a global audience. Our books are designed to help you be more successful in work and life.

For further information, or to request a catalogue, please contact:
business@johnmurrays.co.uk
sales-US@nicholasbrealey.com (North America only)

Nicholas Brealey Publishing is an imprint of
John Murray Press.